DATE DUE

NOV - 2 2004

DEMCO, INC. 38-2931

Educational
Testing for
the Millions

EDUCATIONAL TESTING FOR THE MILLIONS

What Tests Really Mean for Your Child

By Gene R. Hawes

author of *The New American Guide to Colleges* and former editor of the College Entrance Examination Board

with a foreword by
David B. Truman
Dean of Columbia College

McGraw-Hill Book Company
New York   Toronto   London

71,014

Contents

Acknowledgments

This book could not have been written without the help of a great many people. I am especially indebted to the following individuals, almost all of whom I interviewed, and each of whom gave important information and suggestions. They are named essentially in alphabetical order and grouped by their organizations: Robert H. Bauernfeind of the National College of Education; George K. Bennett, president, Harold G. Seashore and Alexander G. Wesman of The Psychological Corporation; B. E. Bergesen, Jr., president, and R. N. Walker of Personnel Press, Inc.; John D. Black, president of Consulting Psychologists Press; Lee D. Brown, president of Learning Materials, Inc.; Oscar K. Buros of Rutgers, The State University of New Jersey; Henry Chauncey, president, Henry S. Dyer, S. Donald Melville and Theodore McNulty of Educational Testing Service; Lee J. Cronbach of Stanford University; Ethel M. Clark, president, Willis W. Clark and Allen A. Arthur of California Test Bureau; Henry S. Coleman of Columbia College; David A. Goslin of the Russell Sage Foundation; S. Donald Karl and S. A. Kendrick of the College Entrance Examination Board; Roger T. Lennon, director, Festus W. Smith and Peter C. Scribner of the test department of Harcourt, Brace & World, Inc.; E. F. Lindquist, cofounder, Paul L. Trump, president, and Donald P. Hoyt of the American College Testing Program; Lyle M. Spencer, president, Robert L. French, John O'Keefe, Donald Bouchard, Esther E. Diamond and

Frank S. Johnson, Jr., of Science Research Associates, Inc.; John M. Stalnaker, president, and William R. Young of National Merit Scholarship Corporation; John Sommer, chief editor of the test department, Houghton Mifflin Company; Donald E. Super of Teachers College, Columbia University; Robert L. Thorndike of Teachers College, Columbia University; James W. Torrence, Jr., of Stanford University Press; Sherman N. Tinkelman and Norman D. Kurland of the New York State Education Department; Arthur E. Traxler, executive director, and Robert D. North of the Educational Records Bureau; Forrest L. Vance of the American Psychological Association; Mary Alice White of Teachers College, Columbia University; Ben D. Wood, professor emeritus of Columbia College; and Paul Woodring of the *Saturday Review Education Supplement*.

Many of these persons also read parts of the book in manuscript and suggested valuable corrections and improvements. A very great service to the reader, as well as to myself, was performed by Dr. Bennett of The Psychological Corporation and Dr. Lennon of Harcourt, Brace & World, each of whom read and commented on the whole manuscript. David B. Truman of Columbia College was particularly generous in writing his fine and forthright Foreword while pressed by heavy demands on his time.

To very many other good friends and acquaintances who were equally liberal in giving help, my most sincere thanks.

The virtues of this book are largely due to all these people; its opinions and failings, solely to myself.

G.R.H.

Foreword

One does not need to be professionally engaged in education to be aware of the intense heat that today can be generated by the subject of educational testing. Almost any gathering of two or more parents with children in secondary school, when the college prospects of these offspring enter the conversation, quickly develops into an animated and frequently anguished discussion of S.A.T. scores, achievement tests, advanced placement examinations, and the whole array of testing devices to which their children are subjected. If these parents are also graduates of one of the country's 300 or so "selective" colleges, to which they are bound by ties of sentiment and from which they frequently expect special indulgence, the intensity of the debate increases.

Educational testing, as Mr. Hawes carefully demonstrates, has implications more extensive and applications much broader than college admissions. Yet it is chiefly anxiety over the obstacles to college entrance and fear of the results of selective admissions procedures that have precipitated current debates.

The near panic proportions of some of these discussions are traceable, however, to a fact more fundamental than the practice of testing. The shortage of places in the nation's colleges, especially those whose reputations are most impressive, would have produced at least as much resentful criticism if objective tests for admission had never been developed. Probably more, for the strong allegiance within American society to a code of essential fairness in deciding among competing individuals would, in the circumstances of the present shortage, have produced bitter and perhaps unanswerable charges of privilege, prejudice, and personal caprice if some sort of objective instrument had not been available. Whatever their shortcomings, the standard national tests now in use at least are free of the personal bias of the examiner.

Educational testing, especially for admission to college, is thus something of a scapegoat. Like others of its kind, it has been cast in this role by a combination of anxiety, ignorance, misunderstanding, and deliberate manipulation. Many intelligent people, including some in the educational world itself, do not understand the meaning, the proper uses, and the limitations of educational tests. Too frequently, moreover, their ignorance has been exploited and their fears excited by popular writers who themselves are acting from a lack of knowledge or of scruple.

Even some colleges have encouraged this scapegoating. In any responsible admissions procedure test scores are only a single element, albeit an indispensable one, in the process of choice. To rely exclusively upon them is not only to ignore their inherent limits but also to transmit to applicants, to their parents, and to guidance counselors in the schools a false impression of the degree of validity that competent admissions officers attach to test results. Correctly suspecting that the tests cannot be expected to measure all the factors that are relevant to the admissions choice, many parents and schoolmen understandably, if unwisely, attack the tests. Much the same effect is produced when colleges, in careless pursuit of the trappings of excellence, advertise the rising average scores of successive entering classes on college entrance examinations. The layman too easily forgets that averages say nothing about the full range of scores and he wisely resents pressure to accept the implication that test scores can answer all the questions he is warranted in asking.

Scapegoating, however, at least in the long run, solves no problems. It merely obscures them, and this is the enemy of appropriate actions and realistic solutions. Gene Hawes is therefore contributing to the cause of understanding and responsible discussion by his careful examination of the forms, the proper uses, and the necessary limitations of educational testing.

It is peculiarly appropriate that this task should be undertaken by a Columbia graduate, for in a very real sense educational testing in general and the College Entrance Examination Board and related organizations in particular were initiated and developed under Columbia leadership. It was Nicholas Murray Butler, professor of education, President of Teachers College, and soon to be President of Columbia University, who in 1899 persuaded the Middle States Association of Colleges and Secondary Schools to establish what developed into the College Board. Butler was the first of a succession of Columbia men to serve over the years as chief administrative officer of the Board and he retained an interest in its affairs throughout his Presidency of the University.

Columbia was probably the first college in the country to require an objective test for admission. In 1918–19, following the creation of tests of general mental abilities for use by the Army in World War I, the College introduced such a requirement. Devised by Professor Edward L. Thorndike of Teachers College, the test anticipated by several years the College Board's independent development of the now familiar Scholastic Aptitude Test, which did not replace the Thorndike test in the College until the late 1930's.

Under the leadership of Herbert E. Hawkes, Dean of Columbia College from 1918 to 1943, and Ben D. Wood, Professor of Collegiate Educational Research, the College took a step that foreshadowed the Advanced Placement Program of the College Board. In 1929 it introduced an "achievement test" procedure, by which a student who felt qualified to do more advanced work could, by test, "achieve" a course required for the degree. Columbia has maintained this "achievement" procedure ever since, and of course has participated in the Advanced Placement Program of more recent date. Under the leadership of Hawkes, who helped to organize the Educational Records Bureau and participated actively in the Cooperative Test Service of the Educational Testing Service, Wood also developed the tests that were to become the subject-matter Achievement Tests of the College Board. He pioneered, in addition, the tests that today form the basis for the Graduate Record Examinations.

It may help to put the current controversies over educational testing in perspective to note that Columbia did not introduce objective tests for admission in order to deal more efficiently with masses of applicants. Rather, in a day when many colleges gauged their quality in part by their high rate of failures, Dean Hawkes sought to avoid the waste and frustration that subjective procedures involved. He wanted, as he wrote in his 1919 report to President Butler, "a more transparent medium through which the mind of the boy can be observed."

Mr. Hawes might well have received the inspiration for his informative book from the words Hawkes's biographer chose to describe his views: "While . . . on his guard against accepting any purely quantitative measurement of the individual student's ability, he became convinced that objective tests when rightly constructed, properly administered, and correctly evaluated could be and were of very great help to educators." As Mr. Hawes effectively indicates, properly understood they can also be of very great help to parents.

David B. Truman
Dean of Columbia College

Morningside Heights
New York City

"As William James warned, psychology can establish general expectations, but cannot hope to give biographies in advance."—*Lee J. Cronbach*

"If a thing exists, it exists in some amount. . . . If it exists in some amount, it can be measured."—*Edward L. Thorndike*

"If you are to live significant lives in the modern world you must learn science; you must learn of its intellectual constructs, of its successes, of its power. You must also learn of its limitations. . . . But you must do more than this; you cannot expect science to do your thinking for you, to make your decisions for you, to make your life for you."—*Polykarp Kusch*

"Wisdom begins with the ability to make valid distinctions."—*Norman Cousins*

Chapter 1

How Testing
Shapes the Lives
of Your Children

We parents have three strikes against us in trying to be realistic about our children. No wonder we find it hard!

In the first place, we boss and bluff and cajole our kids from their earliest days in changing them from helpless savages into more or less civilized beings. After we've seen them master such miracles as language and two-legged locomotion under our tutelage, it's only natural for us to feel that they can become anything—anything we want them to become, particularly if we keep after them about it long enough.

Second, within us burns a fierce parental pride of the elemental kind that sets the fox raging at the wolf that threatens his young. The very quickest way to start a fight with someone is to insult his children. This fiery pride works to blind us to things about our children that counter our fondest hopes for them.

As if these were not enough, we live in a society which almost worships individuals who have the most of any desired personal quality—the fastest, strongest, richest, loveliest, smartest—and which often runs official competitions to pick them out. The Miss America contest, the world's heavyweight boxing championship, the Little League World Series and even the spelling bee are all American inventions. We strain "to make something of ourselves" because others expect it. The variegated though unambitious common man commands far less attention than the successful racketeer, and the spectacle of failure, for whatever cause, gives us the shudders. Too often we scorn our children when they fail at something we'd like them to do.

1

For all these reasons, one of the most difficult arts demanded of parents is to see children as they really are, and to love and help them with a whole heart all the same. Even when doing this may be hard, it is the only way that anyone can be a good parent. And it is certainly the only way to be a happy parent. Surely you remember households poisoned by useless conflicts over what a son or a daughter should be like.

Into this whole explosively delicate area of how you feel and act toward your children, a strange new force now intrudes: objective, standardized testing, which has grown so large that it affects most American families even though they may not know it.

Many *do* know it, only too well. Families have sold their homes and moved to other towns with special schools on discovering that their child has a high IQ. Other families have bitterly resented a child's placement, in part on the basis of tests, in classes for slower pupils. Some families have been alarmed to learn that their eldest child was two years below grade level in, say, reading or arithmetic, according to tests. And many families suffer acute suspense as their children approach college entrance tests.

Testing has revolutionary effects on the lives of us all because, on a massive scale, it reveals certain kinds of rough truths about American children. Often, these truths could not be discovered in any other way. Testing is still a young and crude science in what it can determine, but it is undeniably a science. Anyone who takes the trouble can verify many of its findings, just as objectively as with physics. And among all the sciences and arts which deal with human behavior, it stands almost alone in the rigor with which it specifies what its findings mean and do not mean.

For American families, however, testing poses two serious problems. First, not all varieties of testing reveal the truth about our children, or anybody's children. Some kinds of testing are experimental, and their results may well be totally misleading. Second, the kind of truth that testing reveals can be easily and badly misunderstood. Some meanings popularly attached to IQs, for instance, have no basis whatever.

Over the years, the American public has been seriously misinformed about standardized testing—almost as much by its over-zealous exponents as by its critics. Critics hawking sensational half-truths about it have grown especially numerous in recent years, as testing has spread rapidly in schooling, college admission and hiring.

Yet because testing does reveal some fundamental scientific truths about your children, and about human nature everywhere, you should understand the primary facts about it: what it is, how and why it is used, what it can and cannot prove. This book attempts to explain the crucial, basic facts about testing, all together and in plain English. Knowing these facts, you should be able to insure that testing helps rather than harms your children.

Tests will play special roles in shaping the lives of your children, you may be virtually certain. In one recent year, three-fourths of all high school boys and girls took standardized tests given by their schools, according to a United States Office of Education survey. No one has yet similarly surveyed the elementary schools, but one knowledgeable authority estimates that from one-half to two-thirds of all elementary school pupils take tests of some kind every year.

Many states test all pupils in certain grades annually—among them Texas, California, New York, Iowa, Florida, Minnesota and Virginia. Moreover, almost all big-city and suburban school systems give tests to every pupil at two- or three-year intervals.

Thirty million or more boys and girls take tests in American schools every year, with your own children very probably among them. Their annual total dwarfs the number of people, perhaps ten million, tested each year for jobs in business and industry, civil service posts, professional certification and armed forces assignments. Some 143 million test booklets and answer sheets were sold in 1962, according to the American Textbook Publishers Institute—a total several times the total number of persons tested, because people are most often given a combination of several tests at a time.

Tests bear on pivotal points in children's lives precisely because they are pivotal. The decisions to be made at these points are too important to be reached without test evidence, most educators believe today. For example, a recent joint report by three national organizations of principals and superintendents declared that "to teach without testing is unthinkable"—even though the report was highly critical of certain aspects of testing, which we'll later examine.

The pivotal points at which tests are most likely to shape the direction of your own child's life are as follows:

In the first three or four grades your child's intelligence is likely to be measured with an IQ test—and the test might well be the "Otis Quick-Scoring Mental Ability Tests" from which five sample questions are shown above. These questions are from the series' "Alpha" test, the one for children from the middle of first grade into fourth. Your child's teacher would probably give the Alpha Short-Form both as a test of verbal ability and of nonverbal ability.

In giving it as a nonverbal test, his spoken directions for the questions above would be (after practice by the children on several questions): "In each row you are to find the three things that are alike and draw a line through the one that is *not* like those three."

In giving the Alpha instead as a verbal test, the teacher would voice separate directions for each row of pictures. The directions he would read aloud for each row above (starting from top) would be: "Next mark the girl who is jumping." "Next mark the animal that has the longest tail." "Next mark the thing a man wears on his foot." "Next mark the thing that grows in the ground." "Next mark the thing we use in sawing a board."

Later questions of this kind become more complicated, as their spoken directions suggest: "Next mark the set of four little drawings in which the circle is second." "Next mark the one of the two middle drawings in which three lines cross at one point." (From *Otis Quick-Scoring Mental Ability Tests: New Edition, Alpha Test: Short-Form A-s*, © 1936, 1952, and accompanying *Manual of Directions*, © 1936, 1938, 1939, 1954 by Harcourt, Brace & World, Inc., New York. Reproduced by permission.)

1. At some time in the first three years of school, your child will probably take an IQ test, or a similar test of general mental abilities, to give the school an independent estimate of his or her potential abilities to learn school subjects. Most schools today keep IQ ratings of your child strictly secret—from you, your youngster and all other parents and pupils. But the IQ tends to determine how teachers mark and handle your child all through schooling. The more hard-pressed the school through under-staffing (and, basically, under-financing) the more likely it is that an early IQ will be acted upon as absolute final truth. IQ tests are repeated every few years in many schools for fresh estimates and possibly more accurate ones than were obtained earlier. Successive IQs for a child can vary considerably, as we shall see.

2. Starting in the third or fourth grade, your child will also probably take standardized achievement tests that give independent estimates of how far he or she has advanced in basic school subjects. These will be repeated every two or three years, or even every year. How well or poorly your child does on these tests can irresistibly affect the marks he brings home on his report card. Achievement test scores will also often be used in placing the child in classes for fast or slow-moving pupils which can eventually see the youngster prepared for widely differing future prospects by the end of school years.

3. Because different high school programs lead to markedly different career areas, your child will probably be given an occupational interest inventory—often wrongly viewed as a "test"—in junior or senior high. As with other psychological devices, such standardized questionnaires can be used for benefit or harm. Your child will be shown a plot of his pattern of interests, or the careers they indicate he or she would be happy in, and will then talk career planning over with a counselor. In the process, your child can take steps of far-reaching consequence.

NAME *Larry Hill*　　　　　　　　　　　GRADE *5*

IOWA TESTS OF BASIC SKILLS

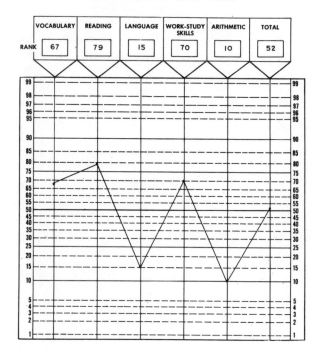

RANK	VOCABULARY	READING	LANGUAGE	WORK-STUDY SKILLS	ARITHMETIC	TOTAL
	67	79	15	70	10	52

Every two or three years from the third or fourth grade on, your child will very probably take standardized achievement tests in school. His scores and standings on the tests will indicate how well he is learning compared with other children—in his class, in his school and in schools all over the country. For example, this "profile chart" shows how a fifth-grade boy, Larry Hill, stands on the widely used Iowa Tests of Basic Skills by a national "percentile rank." As the chart shows, Larry stands at the 67th "percentile" on the battery's vocabulary test—which means that his vocabulary test score placed him ahead of 67 per cent of the fifth-graders in the nation-wide sample of children with whom the test was standardized (by having them take the test so that how those children did on it could be used as the measuring standard for other children). Larry's national percentile ranks on the other ITBS tests are: reading, 79th; language (which tests skill at spelling, punctuation and capitalization), 15th; work-study skills, 70th; arithmetic, 10th; and total, or composite, 52nd.

The charted numbers show that, though Larry has about an average overall standing, he is well above average in vocabulary, reading and work-study skills, but needs to work hardest to improve his capabilities in language and arithmetic skills. Larry's chart is taken from a folder, "How Are Your Skills?," which your child might read and fill out with his own profile of ITBS scores if his school gives him the ITBS. (Reproduced by permission of Houghton Mifflin Company, Boston, and the State University of Iowa.)

4. For college admission, your child will very probably have to take standardized tests required by colleges to which the boy or girl would like to go. Colleges attended by more than four-fifths of all students now have their applicants take tests. Test scores would form part of the evidence by which your child is advised and judged, and the role that scores play in admission or rejection will be more important the more they seem to contradict his or her record in school. If your child is also trying for a college scholarship, which can be worth up to $10,000 or more, test scores may serve an even more decisive function.

5. If your child is enrolled in one of a small number of school systems scattered throughout the country, he or she may be given a "problems check list" that resembles a standardized test to determine possible difficulties in personal adjustment. Further personality "tests" and counseling might follow.

Tests have not generally been recognized as one wide arbiter of destinies in American education because they function in the background. Teachers, counselors and principals properly consider your child's test scores with all the other things they know about the boy or girl. In talking to you and other parents, they often discuss judgments they've made at least in part on the basis of tests without referring to tests. One understandable reason for this is that the testing terminology they use would be unfamiliar to you and difficult to explain. But because test evidence is technical evidence, as well as being expressed in perhaps too easily applied numbers, it tends to be given considerable weight in judging basic qualities of children like your own.

Testing has functioned so much in the background of American education that even educators rarely know one striking fundamental fact about it. That fact is: *Only some twenty-five tests or series of tests account for three-fourths or more of all testing in American education.*

The tests that shape the life of your child are therefore likely to be among these twenty-five tests which are used on a relatively gigantic scale—even though more than 1,000 published tests are now available. These twenty-five include the several tests or test series that will probably be involved in setting the level and direction of your child's whole education; in his first serious choices of possible careers; in deciding whether or not your child gets into college, and into which college; and in deciding whether or not he might win a college scholarship.

So that you might dispel the mystery in which most of America's giant test series have been shrouded, they are identified and described on the following pages. The main purposes for which these tests would be used in shaping the lives of your children are given in the section headings for each type of test.

America's Twenty-Five Giant Test Series

Each of the tests and test series described and illustrated with sample questions here is one that is taken by a half-million or more children annually; some are taken by as many as 8 to 10 million a year. The total number of young people taking each series a year comes to far more than 60 million—more than the country's entire educational enrollment (51 million in 1963) because pupils often take tests from two or more of the series in a single testing or a single year. All together, these giant series account for most of the testing done in America.

Sample questions to show you concretely what these tests are like are included with the descriptions. When your child actually takes one of these test series, you might want to re-read the description and illustrative questions to refresh your memory of what the test measures. An invaluable and fascinating source from which you can get further information about these tests, and about practically any tests your child may be given, is the *Mental Measurements Yearbook* series created and edited by Oscar Krisen Buros. Mr. Buros, professor of education at Rutgers, the State University of New Jersey, commissions and publishes authoritative reviews of tests in his massive *MMY* volumes. Though the reviews in this "consumers' report" for the testing field do go into technicalities, the gist of their judgments can be understood by any teacher or parent. Ask for the book in your local public or school library; in view of the very wide extent of testing, it belongs on the reference shelves of the library in every community in the land. The volumes appear under Professor Buros's imprint of The Gryphon Press in Highland Park, New Jersey; the *Fifth MMY* was issued in 1959, and a *Sixth*, enlarged to some 1,500 pages, is due to appear early in 1965.

It would have been impossible to identify, describe and illustrate America's twenty-five giant test series without the generous co-operation of the publishers of these tests in supplying source information. The test questions given for each series here, though approved by its publisher, can serve only for purposes of illustration. Your child could not significantly increase the score he or she would otherwise earn on one of these tests by memorizing or practicing the sample questions given for it.

Rather than have your child try to "beat the test" in this or some other way, it is far more important for you to obtain and understand the scores he earns on major tests which he takes. The Appendix (p. 272) explains why it could be very important for you to know the scores, and how you might find out what they are.

Tips for Taking the Giant Series—Or Any Tests

About the only important and special thing for your child to remember in working tests in these giant series—or any standardized tests, for that matter—is that they give him many more questions that are very easy and many more that are very hard than do the usual classroom examinations. They do, essentially, because they are made to measure abilities far wider in range than those tested by teachers with the exams they make. In fact, a standardized test on which your child got all the answers right would have failed to measure his abilities, for it would not have indicated their maximum extent. Your child should, therefore, not feel at all upset if he meets quite a few questions he cannot answer on one of these tests; if he is average in ability, for example, he should be able to answer only half or fewer of the questions. The other kinds of advice often given for taking standardized tests apply equally well to classroom exams: answer all the easy questions first; plan about how much time to spend on each question in advance; read and follow the directions and questions very exactly; be alert for short-cuts in logical and mathematical questions; make carefully reasoned guesses if you are not entirely sure of the right answer; and check over the answers in any time which remains. On most of these tests, incidentally, your child will have all the time he needs to answer the questions he can by attentive and steady work; the time limits for most good modern tests are set to make them tests of "power" rather than of "speed."

Tests That Estimate Your Child's IQ or Learning Abilities

Perhaps most mystery has surrounded the kind of standardized tests used to help gauge your child's general ability to think and to learn. These are the ones that have traditionally been called "intelligence tests"—the ones on which your child would make an IQ score. For many years IQs were withheld from parents because the parents so often based excited and mistaken conclusions on their children's IQs. (How you could nevertheless today learn what your child's IQ scores are is explained in the next chapter.) At the same time, newer tests which do not yield IQ scores but which serve much the same purposes in schools as the older IQ tests have been introduced. These newer tests use scores that indicate a pupil's standing in scholastic abilities or specific aptitudes instead of Intelligence Quotient. Current controversy about whether tests really measure intelligence or not will be explored in the next chapter. Despite the controversy, schools use IQ tests and ones similar to them in content to measure the present and future scholastic capacities of many millions of children. Here are the nine giant test series that they use primarily for this purpose:

1. **The "Otis IQ."** More millions of American school children have taken the Otis than any other IQ test series. Versions of it have been used in the schools since 1920, longer than any other paper-and-pencil IQ test still very widely used today. The full name of the most popular current revision of it is the *Otis Quick-Scoring Mental Ability Tests*, a series taken by several million children a year.

On the Otis Quick-Scoring, your child would earn a single IQ score reflecting what experts generally consider as "verbal intelligence" —his ability to understand and analyze word meanings, very largely, and some numerical and pictorial problems. Your child would take one of three "levels" in which the Otis Quick-Scoring is published. He would work the "Alpha" level test booklet in grades 1–4, the "Beta" test booklet in grades 4–9 or the "Gamma" booklet in grades 9 through high school and above. The working time on Beta or Gamma would be thirty minutes. Your child would have twenty-five minutes to do the Alpha Short-Form, which consists entirely of pictures and designs, and for which all directions are spoken aloud by the person giving it.

The Otis is published by Harcourt, Brace & World, Inc., a large publishing firm in New York City, one of the biggest of the "Big Six" in testing—the six publishers or test agencies that issue almost all of the country's twenty-five giant test series. The number of elementary and high school pupils taking Harcourt, Brace & World tests each year is larger than the number of people taking the tests of any other one organization.

In his upper elementary or junior high years, your child might meet questions like these on the Otis Quick-Scoring Beta. As on most standardized tests—though not all, as we shall see—your child would be asked to select the right or best answer from among the several possible ones given below the question. Typical Otis Beta questions might be:

The red candy is sweeter than the green candy but not so sweet as the blue candy. Therefore, the blue candy is (?) the green candy.

1. not so sweet as   2. just as sweet as   3. cannot say which   4. sweeter than
(ANS.: 4)

Which of the five things below is most like a roof, a porch, and a window?

1. a table   2. a chair   3. a bed   4. a door   5. a stove   (ANS.: 4)

One number is wrong in the following series. What should that number be?

1   7   2   8   3   7   4   8   5   7   6   8   7   8   (ANS.: 7)

2. The "Pintner IQ." Another IQ test series issued by Harcourt, Brace & World and taken by about a million children a year is the *Pintner General Ability Tests: Verbal Series.* The Pintner covers all grades through high school in tests on four levels—primary, elementary, intermediate and advanced. Its all-pictorial primary test is one of the earliest of its kind, having been introduced in its original form in 1923.

The "Elementary Test" in the Pintner series is for children in grades ranging from the middle of the second to the middle of the fourth. Questions your child could meet on it in, say, third grade might be like those shown below. Children take the Pintner Elementary of the Verbal Series in two parts—"picture content" and "reading content." A sequence of typical picture-content questions appears first, then another of typical reading-content questions. Practice on sample questions of each type would, of course, come before work on questions that are scored.

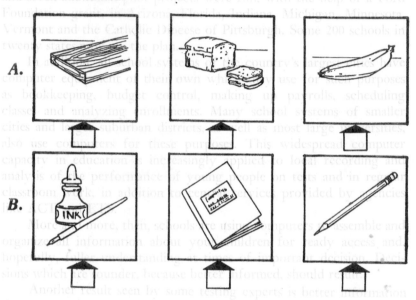

The teacher's spoken directions for the "vocabulary" questions above would be, "For the A row, mark (with an X in the box under the right picture) the picture in that row which means *bread;* for the B row, mark the picture which means *pen.*"

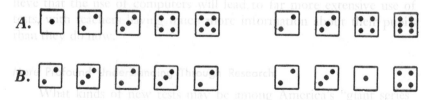

The spoken directions for the "number sequence" questions above would be, "Study each group of boxes at the left and decide how many dots the next box should have. Then find a box with that number of dots at the right, and mark it."

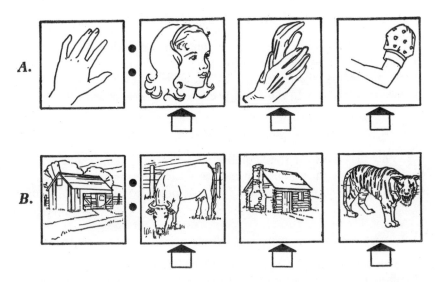

Directions for these "analogies" questions would be, "For row A, I am going to say two words that belong together some way. They are, 'foot-leg.' Now look at the first picture in the row. Find the other picture in the row that goes with the first picture the same way that *foot* goes with *leg*. For row B, the corresponding two words are, '*house-man.*'" (The answers are: for A, the arm; for B, the cow.)

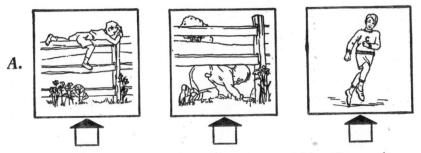

Directions for this "opposites" question would be, "I am going to say a word, and you are to mark the picture that means just the *oppo-*

site. Find a picture that means the *opposite* of '*under.*' " ('The answer is the boy climbing over the fence.)

A. big—	small	large	rig
B. puppy—	happy	cat	dog

For the "vocabulary" questions above in the reading-content part of the test, children are asked, "In each line pick out the word which means the same as the first word." (The right word in each row is to be marked with an X in the circle provided under the word.)

A. 7 8 9 10 11—	14 6 12 11
B. 0 0 1 1 2 2 3—	4 2 1 3

The directions for the "number sequence" questions above would be, "Decide how the numbers in each row have been arranged and what number should come next. Then find that number with a circle under it, and mark it."

A. hat: head — shoe:	foot	socks	boots
B. winter: summer — cold:	warm	frost	ice

For the "analogies" questions above, the directions would be, "Look at the first two words and decide how the second word goes with the first. Then find a word that goes with the third word in the same way."

A. black—	dark	light	white	night
B. down—	below	high	top	up

For these "opposites" reading-content questions above, children would be asked, for each line, to mark the word that means the *opposite* of the first word.

A. child—	teacher	dress	head	toys
B. pail—	iron	water	milk	bottom

The directions for these "logical selection" questions above would be, for each line, to mark the one word that tells what the first word always has.

A. A nickel and a dime—   10 cents   25 cents   15 cents
B. If you have 5 cents and get 3 more cents, then you will have—
                          8 cents   10 cents   7 cents

Directions for these "arithmetic reasoning" questions above would be to work out each problem, and if your answer is correct, you will find it among the three possible answers given. Put a cross in the box below the right answer.

These examples illustrate most of the types of questions on the Pintner Elementary, but do not suggest the test's more difficult questions very well. (The ten questions above are reproduced by permission of Harcourt, Brace & World, Inc., from the *Pintner-Durost Elementary Test*, © 1940—the first four questions above from its *Scale 1, Form A, Picture Content*, and the last six from its *Scale 2, Form A, Reading Content*.)

3. The "California Mental Maturity." Schools in the western states make especially wide use of the *California Test of Mental Maturity*, which is taken by more than five million pupils a year throughout the U.S. in its regular and "short form" editions. One of the longest paper-and-pencil IQ tests published, the regular CTMM has a time limit of ninety-two minutes on its higher levels. Your child would earn language IQ, non-language IQ and total IQ scores on it, and could take one of its six levels at any age from kindergarten into his adult years. Originally developed in the Los Angeles public schools in the mid-1920s, the CTMM was the first work issued by the California Test Bureau. "Cal Test," one of testing's "Big Six," is a company headquartered in Monterey that concentrates almost exclusively on educational test publishing.

Typical questions your child might meet on Level 2 of the California Short-Form Test of Mental Maturity, which is for pupils in grades 4 through 6, would be like these. The instructions for questions of the kind below read, "In each row there is one picture that shows something which is the *opposite* of the first picture. Find it, and mark its number."

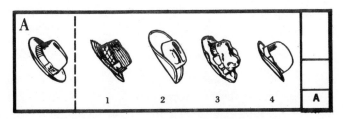

For questions of the type below, the directions say that "the first three pictures in each row are of things which are *alike* in some way. Decide how they are alike and then find the picture to the right of the dotted line that is most like them, and mark its number."

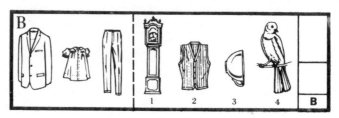

The directions for questions like the one below point out that the first picture in each row is related to the second. "The third picture goes with one of the four pictures to the right of the second dotted line in the same way," the directions continue. "Find the related picture, and mark its number."

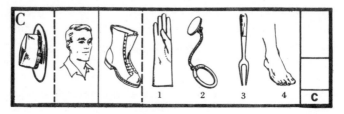

A section of numerical problems on the test asks the pupils simply to "work these problems. Use scratch paper, if necessary. Mark the letter of each correct answer." One of the problems might be:

What number, if multiplied by 4, is equal to 3 times 8?
a. 4   b. 8   c. 6   d. 24

For a series of questions that have the same form as the one below, the directions would be to "mark the number of the word that means the same or about the same as the first word."

blossom   1. tree   2. vine   3. flower   4. garden

In other Level 2 questions on the Short-Form, your child might be asked a question like finding in a list the combination of 5 coins that would make 33 cents, and be asked a number of factual questions about a story that had been read aloud a half hour earlier by the teacher. (The first, second, third and fifth questions given above are reproduced by permission of California Test Bureau from the *California Short-Form Test of Mental Maturity, 1963 S-Form, Level 2.*)

The California Test of Mental Maturity series and its companion Short-Form version were revised and re-standardized in 1963. In the process, the Short-Form series was "scaled" to the Stanford-Binet Intelligence Scale (a famous test discussed in the next chapter), and the California Achievement Tests (discussed later in this chapter) of the same publisher were re-standardized with the Mental Maturity series.

4. **The "Lorge-Thorndike IQ."** The *Lorge-Thorndike Intelligence Tests,* published in 1954, represent the newest of the large IQ test series. Despite its relatively recent introduction, the series is taken by more than a million pupils a year. If your child took either Level 1 in kindergarten or first grade, or Level 2 in second or third grade, he would work the tests without any time limits. In any grade from 4 through high school, he would probably take it in two school periods, for its "verbal" parts have a thirty-four-minute time limit and its "nonverbal" ones a twenty-seven-minute limit.

The series was revised (and "re-standardized") in 1964. The revised "multilevel" edition is one designed to fit the test level more closely to gradations in pupil ability than the original edition, and has somewhat different time limits and other features.

Your child would meet four types of questions in the verbal parts of the test if he were taking Level 3 of the Lorge-Thorndike in, say, fifth grade. A question of the "sentence completion" type might read:

Choose the word that will make the best, the truest, and the most sensible sentence.

There's no man so _____ but something good may be found in him.

A. likable   B. honest   C. upright   D. wicked   E. handsome   (Ans.: D)

A Lorge-Thorndike question of the "verbal classification" type might propound:

Think in what ways the words in dark type go together. Then find the word on the line below that belongs with them.

carrot   **onion**   **potato**

A. stew   B. cook   C. root   D. pea   E. vegetable   (ANS.: D)

In a sequence of "arithmetic reasoning" questions, your child could be asked:

A man has to travel 900 miles by airplane. If his plane flies at 220 miles an hour, how many miles does he have left to go after flying 2½ hours?

A. 450 mi.   B. 550 mi.   C. 300 mi.   D. 50 mi.   E. none of these

(ANS.: E)

And a "vocabulary" question on the Lorge-Thorndike Level 3 might look like this:

Choose the word which has the same meaning, or most nearly the same meaning, as the word in dark type at the beginning of the line.

junket   A. ship   B. coat   C. jargon   D. ticket   E. trip

(ANS.: E)

Look at sample question 0. The first three drawings in the row are alike in a certain way. Find the drawing at the right that goes with the first three.

The first three drawings are alike in that each has four sides and no lines inside it. The drawing at the right that goes with them is at **D**. It has four sides and no lines inside it. Make a heavy black pencil mark in the **D** answer space for question 0.
    Now look at question 00. Find the drawing at the right that goes with the first three.

The first three drawings are alike in that they have three sides and are getting wider. At the right, the only one that is still wider is at **H**. Make a heavy black pencil mark in the **H** answer space for question 00.

Do the others below and on the next two pages in the same way. Try every row.

Two sample questions from the "nonverbal" part of the Lorge-Thorndike Intelligence Tests, a relatively new IQ test series taken by more than a million children a year. These questions are of the "pictorial analogy" type. Nonverbal questions and scores on IQ tests are used mainly to get some indication of the true intelligence or learning ability of children whose vocabulary and reading skill are underdeveloped. (Reproduced by permission of Houghton Mifflin Company, Boston.)

In the nonverbal parts of the Lorge-Thorndike, your child would work three types of questions: "pictorial classification," "pictorial analogy" and "numerical relationship." A pictorial classification question might present your child with three geometrical figures related in certain ways he could discover by analysis and comparison, and would ask him to select from several other figures the one that goes with the first three. In a pictorial analogy question, he could be given two pictures of related things, such as a garage and a car. He would then also be given a picture of a third thing, like an envelope, and asked to pick from several following pictures the thing that goes with the envelope in the same way that the car goes with the garage. In this case, he should, of course, pick the letter from among the several choices shown.

In a numerical relationship type of question on the Lorge-Thorndike nonverbal, your child might be asked:

> The numbers at the left are in a certain order. Find the number at the right that should come next."

1   3   2   4   3–?   A. 2   B. 3   C. 4   D. 5   E. 6   (Ans.: D)

Your child would earn a separate verbal IQ, a separate nonverbal IQ and a composite IQ score after taking both parts of one level of the Lorge-Thorndike. (The directions for the five questions above are reproduced by permission of Houghton Mifflin Company from *The Lorge-Thorndike Intelligence Tests, Level 3, Form A*, © 1954.)

A large and long-established Boston book publisher, the Houghton Mifflin Company, issues the Lorge-Thorndike. Another of testing's "Big Six," Houghton Mifflin introduced IQ testing to the public at large in this country by publishing the first of the Stanford-Binet Intelligence Scales in 1916. This famous test, which is given to only one person at a time by a trained psychologist and in which most answers are spoken rather than written, is still regarded as the most authoritative of all intelligence tests by many experts.

5. The "Henmon-Nelson IQ." More than a million children a year take another Houghton Mifflin IQ test which has been popular for a quarter-century, the *Henmon-Nelson Tests of Mental Ability*. Tests for three levels are offered in the school series, one each for grades 3–6, grades 6–9 and grades 9–12. Each of the three tests presents ninety questions of various types mixed together—sentence-completion, figure anal-

ogies, vocabulary and number series among them—and has a thirty-minute time limit. Houghton Mifflin also publishes a college-level edition of the Henmon-Nelson IQ test.

● The three practice exercises below are given so that you may see how to do the test.

Practice 1. **Boys like to:**

　　　(1) run　(2) hat　(3) lost　(4) red　(5) same............　☒ ② ③ ④ ⑤

Which word tells what boys like to do? Yes, *run* is the right answer. What is the number of the word *run?* The number is *1.* Answer space number 1 has been marked to show that word number 1, *run,* is the right answer. You are to mark your answers in the same way.

Practice 2. **I saw a .... tree.**/ A word for the blank is:

　　　(1) quite　(2) care　(3) big　(4) so　(5) and............　① ② ③ ④ ⑤

Mark the answer space that you think is right. Your mark should be in the answer space numbered 3.

Practice 3.　　☐ is to ☐ as △ is to:

　　(1) ◯　(2) ☐　(3) ◯　(4) ☐　(5) △　... ① ② ③ ④ ⑤

What is the number of the right answer? The answer, of course, is number 5, since a *square* is to a *smaller square* as a *triangle* is to a *smaller triangle.* Mark the answer space numbered 5.

These are the very simple practice questions given on the school levels of the Henmon-Nelson; many of the actual test questions are, of course, much harder. (The three questions above are reproduced by permission of Houghton Mifflin Company from *The Henmon-Nelson Tests of Mental Ability, Grades 3–6, Form A,* © 1957.)

6. **The SRA "PMA."** More than a half-million children a year take the *Primary Mental Abilities* tests, a series published since 1943 by Science Research Associates, Inc., and revised and re-standardized in 1962. On any of the 1962 edition's five levels (for grades kindergarten–1, 2–4, 4–6, 6–9, and 9–12) your child would earn four or five part-scores and a total IQ score. A "Profile Chart" for pupils and parents instead shows the scores as approximate percentile ranges or "stanine" scores. The total testing time for each level is about an hour. Your child's part-scores would reflect his ability in "verbal meaning," "number facility," "reasoning" (omitted in the two lowest levels), "perceptual speed" (omitted in the two highest levels) and "spatial relations." SRA, an educational publishing firm in Chicago, became a subsidiary of International Business Machines Corporation early in 1964. The Midwest

member of testing's "Big Six," it has the largest gross income from testing of any business organization in the field. SRA is perhaps most widely known as the company which makes and gives the National Merit Scholarship Qualifying Test under contract with National Merit Scholarship Corporation. It is also a major publisher of materials for guidance counselors and of new kinds of instructional programs.

Thelma Gwinn Thurstone, professor of education at the University of North Carolina, is the author of the current edition of the PMA. She and her husband, the late L. L. Thurstone, originated the series. Typical questions your child might meet on its level for grades 9 through 12 follow. In the "verbal meaning" test, he would be asked to find the word that means the same as the first word in the row for a question like this:

QUIET   A. blue   B. still   C. tense   D. watery   E. exact

(Ans.: B)

Directions for the "number facility" test would explain that, "in each problem you are to find the answer without using paper and pencil for figuring." One question might pose:

$16 \times 99 =$ A. 154   B. 1,584   C. 1,614   D. 15,084   E. 150,084

Mrs. Thurstone comments on this sample problem that "you should have blackened the space below B for *1,584*. How do you know that 1,584 is the correct answer? Remember, you are to work very quickly and do no figuring with pencil and paper. When you see the problem 16 x 99 you can tell at a glance that if 16 were multiplied by 100 (instead of 99) the answer would be 1,600. If you think about it a second you will see that the correct answer has to be a little less than 1,600."

The "reasoning" test presents three types of questions—"letter series," "word grouping" and "number series." In letter-series questions like the one below, students are asked to find the letter that follows the last letter in the row:

a m b a n b a o b a p b a   1. m   2. o   3. p   4. q   5. t

(Ans.: 4)

In word-grouping questions, students are asked to find the word that does not belong with the other four words in groups like this one:

A. sing B. speak C. whistle D. hear E. hum (ANS.: D)

Finding the number that follows the last number in the row is the problem for number-series questions such as this:

1 4 3 2 5 4 3 6 5   A. 3 B. 4 C. 5 D. 6 E. 7

(ANS.: B)

On the battery's "spatial-relations" test, the directions say that some of the figures in each row of figures are like the first figure, while others are drawn backward. "Find the figures that are the same as the first one in the row," the instructions continue. "As you take this test remember that there may be more than one correct answer and that some of the correct figures may be rotated to various positions." One sample row looks like this:

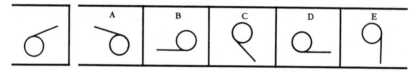

(ANS.: B and E)

A different kind of spatial-relations question is asked on the PMA battery for grades 4 through 6; in one, the first drawing is one part of a square, and the problem is to find the shape that is the other part of the square. Here is a sample:

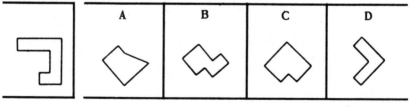

(ANS.: C)

In the "perceptual-speed" test included in the grades 4–6 battery, pupils are to find the two drawings in each row that are exactly alike. Two typical questions look like this:

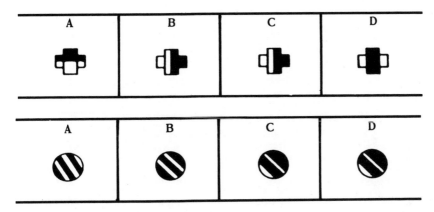

Mrs. Thurstone is also the author of a newer general ability or intelligence test series published by SRA, the Tests of Educational Ability or TEA. (The eight questions above are reprinted by permission of Science Research Associates, Inc., from *The Test of Primary Mental Abilities*, © 1962 by Thelma Gwinn Thurstone.)

7. **The "DAT."** The unusual *Differential Aptitude Tests* are also among those that are taken by at least one million children a year. The DATs are a set of eight aptitude tests designed to be taken together within time limits totaling three hours and ten minutes. Its first two tests, which are thirty-minute tests in "verbal reasoning" and "numerical ability," parallel similar parts of IQ tests; the sum of scores on them, the publisher says, "serves essentially the same purpose as scores derived from standard intelligence tests"—namely, as "an index of scholastic ability." Accordingly, this sum is reported to children as a score in addition to separate scores on each of the eight component tests. Two other DATs also resemble parts found in some IQ tests, ones of "abstract reasoning" (which tests the power to understand and apply ideas expressed in diagrams), and of "space relations" (a test of the power to visualize objects in three-dimensional space). The other four tests assess aptitudes of considerable practical utility—"mechanical reasoning," "clerical speed and accuracy," "spelling" and "sentences" (that is, sensitivity to correct grammar, punctuation and word usage in sentences).

If your child took the DAT, then, he or she would be faced with a variety of questions—including not only ones like those he had probably seen on IQ tests he had taken before, but ones unlike any he had seen on other school tests. As examples, each question of the "verbal-reasoning" type would concern a sentence in which the first word and the last word had been left out. The problem is "to pick out the pair of words which will fill the blanks so that the sentence will be true and sensible," as in the following sample:

_____ is to night as breakfast is to _____.

A. supper ..... corner   B. gentle ..... morning   C. door ..... corner
D. flow ..... enjoy   E. supper ..... morning   (Ans.: E)

The DAT's "numerical-ability" questions pose problems involving such matters as basic computation, fractions, percentages, weights and measures and square root. Its "abstract-reasoning" problems are visual ones, in each of which the four "Problem Figures" make a series, and the student is to find out which one of the "Answer Figures" would be the next, or the fifth one in the series. Two sample questions are:

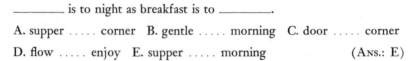

(Ans.: D)

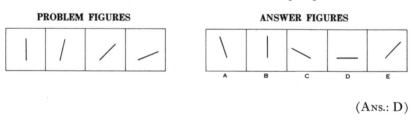

(Ans.: B, since the dot moves clockwise around the square)

"Clerical speed and accuracy" questions are designed "to see how quickly and accurately you can compare letter and number combinations." Each question or item gives five such combinations, one of which is underlined. "You are to look at the one combination which is underlined," according to the directions, "find the same one after that item number on the separate answer sheet, and fill in the space under it." The example below shows a portion of a typical separate answer sheet on which most students taking standardized tests today indicate their answers; the portion shown at the right appears as it would look with these items answered correctly:

TEST ITEMS

V.	<u>AB</u>	AC	AD	AE	AF
W.	aA	aB	BA	Ba	<u>Bb</u>
X.	A7	7A	B7	<u>7B</u>	AB
Y.	Aa	Ba	<u>bA</u>	BA	bB
Z.	3A	3B	<u>33</u>	B3	BB

SAMPLE OF ANSWER SHEET

	AC	AE	AF	AB	AD
V.	⫶	⫶	⫶	▮	⫶
	BA	Ba	Bb	aA	aB
W.	⫶	⫶	▮	⫶	⫶
	7B	B7	AB	7A	A7
X.	▮	⫶	⫶	⫶	⫶
	Aa	bA	bB	Ba	BA
Y.	⫶	▮	⫶	⫶	⫶
	BB	3B	B3	3A	33
Z.	⫶	⫶	⫶	⫶	▮

All of the DAT's "mechanical-reasoning" items ask questions about pictures, as in this sample:

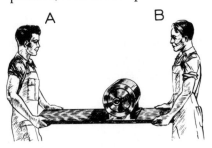

X

Which man has the heavier load?
(If equal, mark C.)

(ANS.: B)

The DAT's "space-relations" questions are also visual, each one presenting a flat pattern which can be folded into a three-dimensional figure. The pattern always shows the outside of the figure. The student decides which one of four figures given after each pattern can be made from the pattern, as in this example:

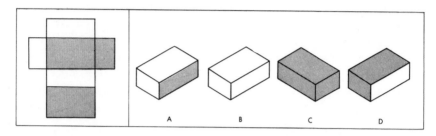

(ANS.: D)

Questions in "spelling" and "grammar," the two remaining types on the Differential Aptitude Tests, involve recognition of errors or correctness in the spelling of individual words and in the grammar of individual sentences. (The six questions above are reproduced by permission. Copyright 1947, © 1961, The Psychological Corporation, New York, N.Y. All rights reserved.)

The school's main purpose in giving your child the DAT would be to help him choose a high school program and career goals that seem realistic in the light of his largely unique pattern of developed aptitudes. It represents another fairly new development in testing, having been introduced in 1947.

The DAT is published by The Psychological Corporation, a business arm of professional psychologists in which only members of the American Psychological Association may own stock. Located in New York City, "Psych Corp" also distributes many tests used with personnel in business and industry, and others for use with the mentally ill. Among testing's "Big Six," it is one of the organizations most widely respected for adherence to the field's demanding technical standards.

8. The ETS "SCAT" Series. Some one million children a year take the *School and College Ability Tests,* a series that measures "developed ability" in "verbal" and "quantitative" skills from grade 4 through college. SCAT scores are reported on a special scale, not as IQs; no claim whatever is made that they parallel intelligence test scores. Five of the

six SCAT levels are numbered downward from the region of college entrance, with Level 1 being for college freshmen and sophomores and superior high school seniors, and Level 5 for children in grades 4–6. A "U" level (for "upper") extends the range through the college senior year. As with an IQ test series, SCAT is intended mainly to serve a predictive function, but a limited one—to help "evaluate the student's capacity to perform academic tasks at the next higher school level." Also as with IQ tests, a total SCAT score is reported—the sum of the separate "verbal" and "quantitative" scores.

Were your child to take one of the SCAT levels, he would receive a single test booklet with four main parts. In the first two parts he would find sentence-completion and numerical-computation questions; in the last two parts, questions in vocabulary and numerical problem-solving. In Level 1, for example, he might be asked a sentence-completion question like this one:

Select the missing word by deciding which one of the five words *best* fits in with the meaning of the sentence.

Motion pictures have an advantage over photographs. They can show movement as well as scenes, thus stirring us with (   ) as well as images.

A. color   B. personalities   C. action   D. beauty   E. sights

(Ans.: C)

Or, as a vocabulary question, he might see:

Pick the word or phrase whose meaning is closest to the word in large letters.

ANTAGONIZE

A. destroy   B. demand   C. expose   D. deprive   E. enrage   (Ans.: E)

A numerical computation question could ask him:

Choose the correct answer, using scratch paper if necessary.

What is 75% of 24%?

A. 1.8%   B. 18%   C. 180%   D. 99%   E. 312.5%   (Ans.: B)

And your child might be asked a question like this in the numerical problem-solving part:

Choose the correct answer, using scratch paper if necessary.

On a certain day, 15 babies were born in a hospital. Of these, 4 babies were twins, 3 were triplets, and the rest were "single" babies. How many different mothers gave birth to babies in the hospital on that day?

A. 9   B. 7   C. 8   D. 11   E. 12   (Ans.: D)

A rather recent development in testing, SCAT was introduced in the 1950s. Tables issued with it in 1962 enable a school to predict, from the SCAT scores of children in grades 8–12, their subsequent scores on the Scholastic Aptitude Test of the College Entrance Examination Board. As we shall see, the SAT is now the main test of the "College Boards"—the college entrance tests about which young people and their parents are unnecessarily yet widely anxious. SCAT closely resembles the SAT in its basic features.

The SCAT series is published by Educational Testing Service, a non-profit organization with main offices housed in five new buildings on a 350-acre rural site outside Princeton, New Jersey. ETS has the largest testing volume by gross income—and in this sense is the biggest—of testing's "Big Six." It is best known as the contract service agency for the College Board tests, which it makes and gives under the direction of the CEEB and its member colleges, universities, secondary schools and educational associations.

9. The "Kuhlmann-Anderson." Close to two million children a year take the *Kuhlmann-Anderson Test* series. Its sequence of test booklets provides for its use with children in all grades from kindergarten through high school. An unusual series introduced almost forty years ago, in 1927, the Kuhlmann-Anderson employs a large variety of subtests—thirty-nine in its successive levels—and many uncommon types of questions. They are not so novel, however, that they would give your child any special trouble were he to work through one of its test booklets. A revised, seventh edition of the series was published in 1963. Your child would be given forty-five minutes to work the Kuhlmann-Anderson test booklet appropriate for his or her grade level. The series measures "substantially the same thing as the Stanford-Binet," one authority believes. Although the seventh edition yields a standard IQ score, the publishers recommend that the test be viewed as a "measure of academic potential" rather than of intelligence. The Kuhlmann-

Anderson is issued by a small company in Princeton, New Jersey, called Personnel Press, Inc., a subsidiary of the large publishing firm, Ginn and Company.

Were your child in junior high school, he might be given Booklet G of the Kuhlmann-Anderson Test's seventh edition, which is for use in grades 7 through 9. He would meet eight kinds of questions in Booklet G if he should take it. For one kind, the instructions are as follows for the word in each question:

If the word contains A, E, and N, blacken the answer space under 1.

If the word contains A and E, but not N, blacken answer space 2.

If the word contains A and N, but not E, blacken answer space 3.

If the word contains E and N, but not A, blacken answer space 4.

Sample words to which to apply these instructions include: NATION; ELATED; PLENTY; and EATEN.

Another kind of question asks pupils to find which number is wrong in each of a number series like this:

A. 9 B. 8 C. 7 D. 6 E. 4   (ANS.: E)

Groups of five words are presented in each question of still another kind. Three of the words in each group are alike in some way; pupils are asked to identify the three, as in this group:

A. sob B. smile C. laugh D. frown E. grin   (ANS.: BCE)

A fourth type of question gives numerical equations and asks the pupils to identify the missing one or two signs (plus, minus, times or division) for questions like this one:

4 ... 2 ... 3 = 11
A   B   (ANS.: A, times; B, plus)

For other questions, the pupils unscramble words so that they "make a good sentence," indicating their solution by identifying what would be the first and last words of each good sentence, as with:

my not is book that
A   B   C   D   E   (ANS.: E, first word; D, last word)

Statements to be completed with correct numbers make up another type of question on the Kuhlmann-Anderson Booklet G of the new edition. A typical question like this would be:

This number is 2 less than ⅓ of 9.   A. 0   B. 1   C. 2   D. 3   E. 5

(ANS.: B)

Rather complicated instructions are given for questions of another kind. Each question gives five items which can be arranged in the order of smallest to largest, least to most or first to last. Pupils are to re-arrange them accordingly, then indicate which item in each question would be the middle one in the re-arranged list. For example:

sprout   bush   blossom   seed   fruit
   A   B   C   D   E   (ANS.: B)

The last type of question consists of simple division problems in which the missing numbers are to be correctly identified, as in this question:

$$\begin{array}{r} 1\ 2\ 7\ 8 \\ 7\overline{\smash{\big)}\,8\ldots4\ 6} \end{array}$$

(ANS.: 9)

(The questions above are reproduced by permission of Personnel Press, Inc., from the *Kuhlmann-Anderson Test, Seventh Edition, Booklet G*.)

Tests That Measure What Your Child Has Learned

The kind of standardized tests used to measure what your child has learned falls least often in the limelight, yet serves one of the most important of all testing functions—and serves it on an enormous scale. These are achievement tests, which are made to appraise how far your child has progressed in his main business of learning in school. What your child does on standardized achievement tests can influence the kind of school program to which he is assigned and hence his eventual life work, as previously observed. When properly used, they can also tell one part of the story—but a vital part—of what your school district is getting for its tax money, though tests should *never* be used alone to judge a school.

For the nation as a whole, the large achievement test series accomplish certain rather remarkable things. On the one hand, they provide the nearest thing we have to national standards of educational accomplishment. With them, any school can determine where it stands on each grade level in cultivating learnings commonly recognized in the United States as fundamental responsibilities of the schools. On the other hand, because achievement tests provide continuous scales of nationally representative accomplishment that a school can decide to match at any point it selects, and because they are completely voluntary, achievement tests leave schools as free as they choose to be in their educational programs. No other country has ever had anything like them in these vital respects, nor has today. They have inherent limitations and can be seriously misused, as we shall see in a later chapter, but they still represent an amazing cultural invention whose significance has been almost completely overlooked.

Basically, your child would be asked on one of the giant achievement test series to show how well he has mastered the old American three Rs—reading and writing and arithmetic. Your boy or girl would probably also find a section on such study skills as using reference works, and reading graphs and maps, with additional sections on science and social studies, in levels for the higher grades. At several points in your child's schooling, he will very likely take one or more of the tests in the achievement series given below. Each one is taken by a million children a year, at the least, and some are taken by several millions a year.

10. "Stanford Achievement." One of the very largest of these comprehensive test series for measuring what your child would ordinarily be expected to learn in school is the *Stanford Achievement Test Series*. Taken in whole or part by as many as ten million children a year, the Stanford Achievement represents both the oldest and the newest of such series. Its first edition, issued in 1923, was the work of several professors, including Lewis M. Terman of Stanford University—the psychologist who also led development of the Stanford-Binet IQ test. The Stanford Achievement series' edition of 1964 is one of the newest full revisions among giant achievement test series.

Five "batteries" or groups of tests make up the full series. Your child would take only one of these batteries in any one grade, but the battery would take quite a long time for him to work. He would have a total time limit of one hour and thirty-five minutes for the "primary" level or battery of tests in second grade—divided, though, into three separate test sessions. In eighth grade he would be allowed a total of three hours and thirty-five minutes to work the complete "advanced" battery, in up to six sittings.

Your child's fundamental skills and knowledge in reading, arithmetic and language usage would be tested on the primary and elementary batteries. Elementary, for example, has six subtests—two in reading (paragraph and word meaning), two in language (spelling, and usage —the latter on capitalization and punctuation, sentence sense and grammar), and two in arithmetic (reasoning and computation). Additional tests in social studies, science and study skills are included, beginning with the intermediate battery for grades 5 and 6.

Harcourt, Brace & World, the large New York book publisher among testing's "Big Six," issues the Stanford Achievement.

11. "Metropolitan Achievement." A second, very popular achievement test series published by Harcourt, Brace & World, the *Metropolitan Achievement Tests,* enjoys almost as wide use as the Stanford. Your child would encounter some differences in emphasis were he or she to take a battery in the Metropolitan series instead of the Stanford. He could take one a little earlier, starting in the middle of first grade, for example, or would find his study skills tested in language or social studies in a Metropolitan battery on one of the higher levels. He might also notice somewhat more stress given to basic ideas and principles in the Metropolitan. But he would similarly find the Metropolitan a long series to take; on its complete high school battery, for instance, he would put in a total of five hours and fifteen minutes of test time in as many as seven separate test sessions.

These illustrative questions are from the "word meaning" test of the six-test battery of Metropolitan Readiness Tests—a series given to several millions of children a year to see how much they have learned of what they must know in order to do early first-grade work. These word meaning questions draw on a child's speaking vocabulary and ability to recognize pictures; the spoken direction for the first row above is to mark the picture of the baby (with a big "X") and, for the second row, to mark the picture of the house. (From *Metropolitan Readiness Tests: Form R*, © 1949, and accompanying *Directions for Administering and Scoring: Form R*, © 1948, 1949 by Harcourt, Brace & World, Inc., New York. Reproduced by permission.)

12. **"Metropolitan Readiness."** As early as the end of kindergarten or the beginning of first grade, your child is likely to take a relative of the Metropolitan Achievement series—the *Metropolitan Readiness Tests*. These picture tests with spoken directions are designed to assess how well your little boy or girl has mastered the various skills and items of knowledge which any child must use in beginning reading and arithmetic. Several millions of children are given the *Metropolitan Readiness Tests* each year. On the six tests, your child would be asked these kinds of questions:

Select from four pictures the one that illustrates the word spoken aloud by the person giving the test (in the test on understanding word meanings).

Similarly select from four pictures the one that illustrates the phrase or sentence spoken by the examiner (in the test on phrase and sentence understanding).

Select from four pictures the one that best fits the description spoken by the examiner (in the information test; for example, one description might say: "Put your finger on the next set of pictures. Mark the one you pack clothes in when you travel.")

Select from four pictures the one that matches a fifth picture which has a line around it (in the test of visual perception involving similarities).

Mark and write numbers under ten, mark the smallest or the middle one of several things pictured in a row, and mark other pictures of series of things to show understanding of simple uses of numbers.

Copy simple shapes, numbers and letters alongside those given in the test booklet.

Your child would have from ten to twenty-four questions to answer on each test. He and his classmates would spend an hour in all on the tests, taking them in at least three separate sittings.

13. "California Achievement." More than five million children a year take the *California Achievement Test Batteries,* a large series extending from first grade through junior college, with batteries on five levels. Your child would find these batteries quite long to work, for he would put in a total of about an hour and a half on the "lower primary" one, or almost three hours on the "advanced" one. On any California Achievement battery, he would work through three subtests—reading, arithmetic (mathematics at the top level) and language. He would also see that each subtest is subdivided again into two parts, with "vocabulary" and "comprehension" in reading, "reasoning" and "fundamentals" in arithmetic and "English mechanics" and "spelling" in language. California Test Bureau, the West Coast member of testing's "Big Six," publishes the series.

14. **The Lee-Clark Reading Readiness.** More than a half-million children a year take the *Lee-Clark Reading Readiness Test* in kindergarten or early in first grade. California Test Bureau first published the test in 1931, and issued a revised edition in 1962. In its four part-tests, your child would be called upon to recognize similarities and differences in printed letters, to mark pictures identified by spoken words and to mark letters and words that match given ones. About twenty minutes in all is required for the test.

15. **The "ITBS" or the "Iowa."** All elementary school children from third graders up in one state, and far more than a million children in all states, take the *Iowa Tests of Basic Skills* every year. Your child might encounter the ITBS or the "Iowa," as the series is familiarly called, in any grade over its range from third through ninth in junior high. Your child would also probably remember it well, for he would spend four hours and thirty-nine minutes of actual testing time on any one of its batteries. However, the ITBS batteries are appropriately much shorter than those of the series' big brother, described below. Schools are advised to give it, though, over a span of four days in sessions of from sixty to eighty-five minutes a day. Your child would be tested in vocabulary, reading comprehension, language skills, work-study skills and arithmetic skills on the ITBS. In the vocabulary test, for example, your child might see a question like this:

Decide which one of the four words has most nearly the same meaning as the word in **heavy** black type above them.

A man's **gait.**

1) fence   2) stride   3) work   4) girth   (Ans.: 2)

A reading comprehension question for third-grade children might say,

Thumper is a big friendly dog. He likes to follow fire trucks.

What does Thumper like to do?

1) Watch fires   2) Bite firemen   3) Run after fire trucks

4) Follow police cars   (Ans.: 3)

By contrast, in eighth grade your child might meet a reading comprehension question like this following a full-page article:

If it were necessary to shorten this article by two paragraphs, which pair of paragraphs could be omitted with *least* harm to the story of the rebellion?

In each of the four language subtests (spelling, capitalization, punctuation and usage) your child would be asked to identify the mistake or lack of mistake in lines like these:

1) aboard   2) hyena   3) versus   4) genorous   5) no mistakes

          (Ans.: 4)

1) Massachusetts was settled

2) by the pilgrims. They sailed

3) on the Mayflower.

4) (No mistakes)

          (Ans.: 2)

1) Mr. White, who lives
2) next door likes to
3) play catch with me.
4) (No mistakes)

          (Ans.: 2)

The work-study skills test of the ITBS gives maps of imaginary state parks, towns, countries and continents, and asks questions about them ("On which corner does the bus line cross the streetcar line?" "Which railroad goes through a mountain pass?" "In which city might the sun be shining at midnight on January 1?" "What is a reasonable estimate of the population in the best agricultural region?") Graphs and tables, sample dictionary listings, an index and encyclopedia volumes identified by letters of the alphabet are also the subjects of series of questions in the work-study skills test.

On the arithmetic skills test of the ITBS, your child would be asked questions about such things as fractions, percentage, Roman numerals, thermometers, map scales, rulers, decimals, angles, time, geometric figures and triangulation. In the arithmetic problem-solving test, your child might encounter questions ranging from:

> Billy had 14 cents. He paid Jack 6 cents for a kite. How much money did Billy have left?

to a question like:

> Mr. Smith bought a 3-year fire insurance policy insuring his house for $9600. If the 3-year rate was 1⅔ times the annual rate of 24¢ per hundred, how much did the insurance cost for the 3 years?

The ITBS are taken each year by every pupil in grades three through eight (and nine in junior high) in the Iowa schools, for which the tests have been made since the 1940s. Houghton Mifflin, the Boston book publisher among testing's "Big Six," publishes the series for use throughout the nation. (The second and third questions above are reproduced by permission of Houghton Mifflin Company from the *Iowa Tests of Basic Skills, Multi-Level Edition for Grades 3–9, Form 1,* © 1955.)

16. The "ITED"—or again, the "Iowa." If your child takes any achievement series in high school, it is quite likely to be the *Iowa Tests of Educational Development.* With more than one and a half million students a year given the ITED or the "Iowa" by their high schools, it outstrips similar comprehensive batteries by some distance. The ITED has long loomed larger than even the giant college admission and scholarship testing programs on which far more public attention has focused. Its full edition is among the longest of any widely used test battery. Your child would customarily take it through two full school days, spending on its nine part-tests 480 minutes in actual testing time— a long eight hours of close concentration.

The ITED has had a very wide influence in testing broad achievement in high school studies. Early in World War II, it was generously offered without charge for use by the U.S. Armed Forces Institute, which gives correspondence courses for servicemen. USAFI issued it with minor changes as the *USAFI Tests of General Educational Development*. Several million men and women in service took this GED. Over a million of them won high school diplomas by qualifying as high school graduates on the test, and several hundred thousand more who were not high school graduates were admitted to college on the basis of their GED scores. Moreover, the ITED's broad base on academic accomplishment in high school has led to its use as the foundation for large college entrance and scholarship tests, as we shall see.

On the ITED, your child would encounter many long reading passages followed by series of probing questions in most of the nine part-tests. The tests would examine your child on the following kinds of accomplishments:

His understanding of basic social concepts, particularly those behind present-day institutions and customs;

His general background in the natural sciences, primarily biology, chemistry and physics;

His sense of correctness and appropriateness of expression in English, concerning mainly the mechanics of good English but also organization;

His mathematical or "quantitative thinking" ability, as reflected in the power to apply mathematical ideas and principles to solving practical problems;

His interpretation of reading materials, such as texts, references and both professional and popular writings, in social studies;

His ability to interpret similar reading materials in the natural sciences;

His ability to interpret literature, in verse as well as prose selections;

His general vocabulary;

And his skill in using source materials like texts, reference works and maps.

As with the ITBS, the ITED was originally developed for the Iowa schools, and is taken by all Iowa high school students. It is published for nation-wide use by the Midwestern member of testing's "Big Six," Science Research Associates in Chicago.

17. **The "SRA Achievement."** More than one-and-a-half million children a year take an elementary and junior high school achievement series which runs as long as the ITED on some levels. This is the *SRA Achievement Series*, introduced by Science Research Associates in 1954 and revised in 1964. Your child would spend from six to seven hours in all taking the 1964 version, depending on his grade in school. If he were in grades 4–9, he might follow a blue, green or red "track." The 1964 multilevel edition for grades 4–9 is designed to provide a testing task that is neither too easy nor too hard for the child, but most appropriate for his present state of educational development. The series stresses ideas and principles as well as factual knowledge, and includes tests in the areas of reading, language arts, arithmetic and, from the fourth-grade level up, work-study skills.

18. **ETS "STEP."** About a million children a year now take the *Sequential Tests of Educational Progress*, an unusual combination of tests that is the newest of the giant achievement test series. Your child would also find it one of the longer tests of his life, taking in all some seven or eight hours in several sittings. Two tests in its seven-test batteries might be particularly surprising to your son or daughter: an essay test in which the student spends thirty-five minutes writing a regular composition, and a seventy-minute, two-part test of his listening comprehension, in which the teacher would read passages and questions aloud while he answers in his test booklet. Your child might also find the seventy-minute writing test rather novel, for it asks him to pick the best of several suggested revisions in actual samples of student writing. The remaining tests—in reading, mathematics, science and social studies—should look more familiar to him. STEP is published by Educational Testing Service, the non-profit agency in Princeton, New Jersey, which is the biggest by income of testing's "Big Six." ETS issues STEP as a companion series to SCAT.

19. **Achievement Tests in Individual Subjects—Notably, the ETS "Co-operative Series."** Many millions of American school children a year also take standardized achievement tests in individual subjects, in addition to the millions who take the major "survey" batteries described above. How many millions of children a year take these one-subject tests is impossible to say with any accuracy, but ten million would be a most conservative guess. Dozens of these tests are published; among the "Big

Six," each organization except "Psych Corp" offers at least eight or ten. In many cases your child would find these one-subject achievement tests similar to the corresponding parts of the comprehensive or survey achievement test batteries. Most often, he would have a single school period in which to work a one-subject test.

Among the most widely taken tests of this kind are the two *Cooperative English Tests* of ETS, Reading Comprehension and English Expression, each of which in turn is available on two levels—high school and junior college. "Nearly three million of these tests are taken by students every year in programs established by their own schools and colleges," ETS observes. A famous old test series originated by the American Council on Education, the Cooperative Tests also include up-to-date examinations in arithmetic, algebra, geometry, general mathematics, general science, biology, chemistry, physics, social studies, American government, American history, ancient history, modern European history, foreign affairs, French, Spanish, Latin, German, Italian and Russian.

More than one million high school students a year also take the achievement tests in individual subjects of the *Evaluation and Adjustment Series*, published by Harcourt, Brace & World. The series, now being revised, consists of some twenty-five achievement tests. EAS tests in mathematics, social studies and science subjects are the most widely used of the series, with some single tests being taken by more than a quarter-million students a year.

Separate standardized reading tests are also given on a very large scale in the nation's schools, especially in the elementary grades. Your child would take one of these in having such accomplishments as his reading rate, comprehension and accuracy tested. Widely used reading test series he would be most likely to encounter include the Iowa Silent Reading series of Harcourt, Brace & World; the SRA Reading Record; the Lee-Clark or Los Angeles Elementary tests of Cal Test; one of the Nelson Reading tests of Houghton Mifflin; or one of the many Gates Reading tests issued by the Bureau of Publications of Teachers College, Columbia University.

20. **The New York State "Regents."** If you live anywhere in New York State, your child will very probably take examinations in the country's oldest program of large-scale achievement testing—the New York State Regents Examinations, which date from 1865. About three-

fourths of all high school sophomores, juniors and seniors in New York —some half-million boys and girls—now take "Regents" each year. They usually take these single-subject examinations, offered in areas ranging from business law to earth science and second-year American history, after finishing the corresponding high school course. Your child would see some similarity between them and the giant achievement test series described above in taking any of the thirty or so Regents now made available. For the Regents are also printed tests made up, in fairly large part, of multiple-choice questions like the many samples previously given. However, your child would notice quite a few questions asking him to write a short composition. Moreover, the Regents exams are not "standardized," as are the large national series— in ways which will be explained in the next chapter—although Regents exam questions are tried out in advance in the state. Also, your child may be acutely aware of a further difference. Regents do have passing and failing levels of performance, while standardized achievement tests do not. Your child would have to pass at least three Regents exams in order to qualify for the Regents High School Diploma, which is highly regarded though not required for graduation.

Were your child vying for one of some 16,000 scholarship awards offered by New York State—the largest number granted in any one college scholarship program—he would take still another Regents test: the Regents Scholarship Examination. It is taken by more than 135,000 students a year.

"Tests" That Help Your Child Choose a Career

In the high school years, as your child must think of choosing a career, the boy or girl will probably take a standardized "vocational interest inventory." This is a psychological measuring device on which your child would earn scores, but it isn't a test. It is designed to see what your child *likes to do*, not what he *can do*. It makes an "inventory" of your child's interests as they bear on occupational fields. Well over half of all high school students take such an inventory at least once. Its effect can be very potent, for its findings seem clear and authoritative to adolescent boys and girls searching for their true identities and future lives.

21. **The "Kuder."** Of the two such inventories that are by far the

most widely used, the *Kuder Preference Record* is the one your child would be more likely to meet. More than two million children a year take the "Kuder." The "Vocational Form C" of the Kuder (or Form E, published in 1964) would provide a comparison between the relative strengths of your child's preferences for activities in ten broad vocational interest areas—outdoor, mechanical, computational, scientific, persuasive, artistic, literary, musical, social service and clerical. In answering it, your child would indicate which one he likes most and which one he likes least among sets of three listed activities, such as:

Visit an art gallery
Browse in a library
Visit a museum

To this, your child might answer "like most" for "browse in a library," with "like least" for "visit an art gallery" and nothing for "visit a museum." A long series of such sets of three alternative activities makes up the Kuder "C." For each set your child would give his greatest and least preferences. The results would show him on a graph just where he stands in such interests compared with typical young men or women among high school students, or college students, or adults. For example, your child's graph might show him that he indicated a preference for outdoor activities more frequently than 88 per cent of high school boys, and for literary activities more frequently than 99 per cent of them, but more frequently than only 3 per cent of them in mechanical interests and only 12 per cent of them in computational interests. A showing like this suggests that the boy should explore the literary field to see if it presents opportunities to his liking, especially if his English grades and aptitude scores agree with his interest pattern.

With another Kuder, "Occupational Form D," your child's pattern of interests could be compared to the typical interests of successful persons in fifty or more different occupations. If the Kuder "D" indicated that your child's interests most closely resembled those of department store salesmen, he too might be happy and successful in that occupation, if otherwise fitted for it.

SRA, the Midwestern firm among testing's "Big Six," publishes the Kuder series. It was with the Kuder, in fact, the SRA entered the testing business in the firm's second year, 1939.

22. **The "Strong," or "SVIB"** Your child might find the other very widely used occupational interest inventory, the *Strong Vocational Interest Blank*, even simpler to answer than the Kuder. Some three-quarters of a million students a year are given the Strong. It would start by presenting him with a list of possible occupations, such as:

Actor (not movie)
Advertiser
Architect
Army officer
Artist
Astronomer
Athletic director
Auctioneer

For each one, your child would be asked to mark one of three choices —like, indifferent, dislike—to indicate how much the prospect of being in each occupation appealed to him or repelled him. Similar lists would inquire about his liking for amusements and activities, and personal abilities and characteristics of other people, and his reaction to personal peculiarities of others. Most of the Strong's 400 items about which your child would be questioned call for a "like–indifferent–dislike" type of response.

Elaborate keys for scoring your child's answers on the SVIB for Men have been developed since it was first issued in 1927. These keys make it possible to compare your child's interest patterns with the typical patterns of interests of men in each of a wide variety of callings, in much the same way as with the Kuder "D." Your child's scores on the Strong would be recorded, most simply, as a list of occupations each followed by A, B, or C—with A indicating close resemblance to the typical interest pattern for that occupation, B less close resemblance and C clear difference between your child's pattern and the occupation's typical one. For example, your child's report might show As for Chemist, Math & Science Teacher and Farmer, and C-minuses for City School Superintendent, Minister and Life Insurance Salesman. An evaluative A, B or C would be given for each of many occupations listed on the report. For your daughter, a separate SVIB for Women could be used. The Strong is rarely given earlier than the junior year in high school, and more of the blanks are given to college students and adults than to younger people.

The Strong blanks are published, not by one of testing's "Big Six," but by a small company, Consulting Psychologists Press in Palo Alto, California.

Professional opinion differs, sometimes sharply, about the meaning of results obtained with the Kuder and the Strong, and how they should be used in advising young people. Both require a highly technical background for sound interpretation of results, for years of some of the most extensive research in the whole testing field stand behind them. Because of this, your child should rely on a well-qualified counselor to interpret his score pattern on either inventory rather than try to determine its significance for him by himself.

Tests That Help Decide Your Child's College Opportunities

Tests have a marked influence on the college opportunities open to your child. If he is very bright and studious, standardized tests will help him go to college almost anywhere he might want, and qualify for much of the financial aid he might need. The less bright your child is, however, and the less well he consequently may do on standardized tests, the fewer the colleges to which he might go and the smaller his chances of getting financial aid.

In order to get into college, your child will very probably have to take either the standardized tests of the College Entrance Examination Board, or the standardized test battery of the American College Testing Program. Most colleges in the country require applicants to take either one or the other. Your child would of course have to take both should he apply to colleges that happen to differ in test requirements. Your son or daughter would also almost certainly have to take tests in order to qualify for a college scholarship.

Both the CEEB and ACT are non-profit organizations composed primarily of college and university participants—more than 550 member colleges in the CEEB, and another 800 or more participating colleges in ACT. These colleges have banded together to sponsor and control the respective tests, which they require or recommend for their applicants. Other colleges interested in using the tests may join, and participation in the two organizations has grown very rapidly over the last ten years. Only 162 colleges were members of the CEEB in 1954, and ACT was founded only in 1959.

However, your child will not be plagued by more admissions testing than he might have been before the massive rise of the CEEB and ACT. Many colleges now in one or the other organization previously used entrance tests of their own. Ten years ago, then, your child might have had to take several different tests for college admission instead of one or perhaps two. Moreover, for many reasons, the large-scale entrance tests can be better ones—ones that are fairer and more useful to your child, as well as to the high schools and colleges—than could entrance tests made by individual colleges or small groups of colleges.

Your child would most probably take the admissions tests of the CEEB or ACT on a Saturday during the school year, working on them for at least three hours of the morning. He would have to register and pay for them by mail several weeks in advance, sending in a test fee of four or five dollars or more. He would take the tests at a high school or college not far from home, under a supervisor paid by the CEEB or ACT, and under strict controls to make sure that no boy or girl sees the actual tests in advance or otherwise has an unfair advantage on them. Through his school, your child would get reports of the scores he had earned on the tests, and a booklet explaining generally what the scores mean. You would very likely examine these and talk them over with your boy or girl, and also with the high school counselor.

Colleges to which your child applies use the scores in complex ways, which we'll look into in another chapter. Essentially, however, very low scores, combined with average or erratic marks in high school courses, could easily keep your child out of some colleges. On the other hand, very high scores, combined with just fairly good marks, could get your child into a college. If your child is a borderline admissions applicant at a college, the scores could tip the balance for or against him. Scores would usually be even more decisive if your child were trying to get a scholarship.

These admissions and scholarship tests that can thus bring happiness or dismay to your child at a turning-point in his life are described below. The tests are made and given under contract with the College Board and ACT by two of the largest members of testing's "Big Six": by ETS for the College Board, and by SRA for ACT.

23. **The CEEB's "SAT."** A million or more children a year now take the *Scholastic Aptitude Test* of the CEEB—most of them high school

seniors applying for admission, but perhaps one-fourth of them high school juniors trying the SAT out a year ahead of time. Among them are seniors applying for admission to the country's most highly selective colleges—ones like Harvard, Princeton and Columbia, Vassar and Wellesley, Rutgers and Michigan, Chicago and Stanford, Caltech and MIT, West Point and Annapolis, Rice and Sewanee. One of the most thoroughly investigated of all standardized tests, the SAT has been refined through constant research since its introduction in 1926 to make it serve one purpose as well as a test possibly can—predicting marks in college courses—while drawing as little as possible on the content of specific high school courses. Every form of the SAT right down through the present has carried an unscored section of experimental questions. If some of these questions improve the SAT's predictive powers, similar ones are later added to the regular sections.

In taking the SAT, your child would be given a total of three hours to work through its five sections. These sections would test two basic abilities of his—"verbal" and "mathematical." Over the years, these abilities "to understand word relationships and to comprehend what you read," and "to understand and reason with mathematical symbols and to use them in solving problems," have proven the best predictors of later academic performance in college among predictors that could be ascertained by testing.

Were your child taking the SAT, he might come upon an "opposites" question like this in a "verbal" section of the test:

Choose the lettered word which is most nearly *opposite* in meaning to the word in capital letters.

REPROACH: (A) commend   (B) requite   (C) reward   (D) excuse
(E) apologize   (Ans.: A)

A verbal "sentence completion" question might ask:

... choose the one word or set of words which, when inserted in the sentence, *best* fits the meaning of the sentence as a whole.

Science is always ————, expecting that modifications of its present theories will sooner or later be found necessary.

(A) final   (B) original   (C) tentative   (D) practical   (E) improving
(Ans.: C)

Your child might be asked another verbal type of question like this one,

> Select the lettered pair of words which best expresses a relationship similar to that expressed in the original pair.
>
> SONG : REPERTOIRE
>
> (A) score : melody
> (B) instrument : artist
> (C) solo : chorus
> (D) benediction : church
> (E) suit : wardrobe
>
> (Ans.: E)

In one of the series of reading comprehension questions, your child might be given several paragraphs that discuss ancient Egyptian and Mesopotamian culture and are followed by several questions about it, including one like this:

> It can be inferred from the passage that the Egyptians and Mesopotamians treated artistic motifs in
>
> (A) an identical way in both the early and the advanced periods of culture
> (B) a basically similar manner, but with small differences of style
> (C) a style that reflects Indo-European origins
> (D) a manner that indicates borrowing on both sides
> (E) a basically unlike manner after the period of borrowing was over
>
> (The answer happens to be: E)

Your child would find that the SAT questions testing his or her mathematical ability call on simple algebra and geometry, and frequent ingenuity. One mathematical question, for instance, could pose a problem like this:

> The houses on the east side of a street are numbered with the consecutive even integers from 256 to 834, inclusive. How many houses are there on the east side of the street?
>
> (A) 287   (B) 288   (C) 289   (D) 290   (E) 291   (Ans.: D)

Your child could also meet a more involved mathematical question, such as:

> Four towns, W, X, Y, and Z, are on a straight road in the order named. The distance from W to Z is ⅘ the distance from W to X, and Y is ⅘ the distance from W to Z. What part of the distance from W to Y is the distance from W to X?

(A) ½ (B) ⅗ (C) ¹⁵⁄₁₆ (D) ¹⁶⁄₁₅ (E) ⅝   (Ans.: C)

On the SAT, your youngster would earn separate verbal and mathematical scores. His two SAT scores would be reported on an intentionally special scale which ranges from a low of 200 to a high of 800.

A number of large scholarship programs require applicants to take the SAT. Among state scholarship programs requiring it are those of California, New Jersey and Rhode Island. Semi-finalists in the National Merit Scholarship Program also take the SAT, as do applicants in the National Presbyterian College Scholarship Program. The colleges which require the SAT for admission have many millions of dollars in scholarships and other financial aid to award, and often use SAT scores in deciding among their financial aid applicants.

(The preceding six sample questions are reprinted with permission from the 1963 edition of *A Description of the College Board Scholastic Aptitude Test*, published by the College Entrance Examination Board. This booklet, which contains many illustrative examples of the different kinds of questions that are used in the Scholastic Aptitude Test, is revised annually and is supplied without cost to high schools for distribution to students before they take the test. The booklet may also be obtained on request by writing to either of the College Entrance Examination Board addresses: Box 592, Princeton, New Jersey 08540, or Box 27896, Berkeley, California 94701.)

—And the "PSAT." Your child might also take a two-hour version of the SAT in the fall of his junior year in high school, the *Preliminary Scholastic Aptitude Test* or PSAT. About one million children a year currently take the PSAT, which the CEEB offers so that high school juniors can become familiar with its big brother and benefit from an early indication of how they are likely to perform on the SAT itself with minimum inconvenience and expense. Your child's school would give the PSAT, if it wishes to do so, and for it your child would be charged a fee of about a dollar. Verbal and mathematical scores on the PSAT range from a low of 20 to a high of 80, corresponding to SAT scores without the last digit.

As with the SAT, your child receives a report of his scores on the PSAT and an explanatory booklet on their meaning generally for college admission. These might be especially useful for you to study and talk over with the boy or girl and his school counselor in order that sound college plans might be made comfortably in advance.

College Board Achievement Tests. About a third of the million or more students a year who take the SAT also take *College Board Achievement Tests.* These are one-hour objective tests in individual subjects. Among the fourteen offered at the regular College Board test sessions are ones in English composition, American history and social studies, chemistry, French, and "level one" or "level two" mathematics. Your child might take from one to three of these tests, as required by colleges in which he were interested, on the afternoon of a Saturday test date following the SAT and lunch. Your child might also do an exercise offered by the College Board along with the Achievement Tests, if it were required by a prospective college of his—the College Board *Writing Sample.* This isn't a test at all, but a one-hour composition of from 300 to 500 words on a topic given at the test session. Your son or daughter would write this with a ballpoint pen, pressing firmly to produce four copies on the carbon-backed paper supplied. The *Writing Sample* would not be marked, but would simply be sent to colleges as requested by your child so they might reach their own conclusions about his or her writing ability.

24. **The "ACT" Test Battery.** If your child wanted to go to college in any of the twenty-eight or more states in which a state-wide college testing program affiliated with the American College Testing Program had been organized, he would very likely have to take the three-hour ACT test battery. More than 800 colleges and universities require or recommend the ACT for their applicants. The ACT is given in all fifty states and is taken by some half-million students a year. Well-known universities using the ACT test include Wisconsin, Illinois, Iowa, Ohio State, Minnesota, Oklahoma, Mississippi, Alabama, Baylor, Maryland and Arizona. Many of the private colleges in each ACT state also have their applicants take the test. Colleges and universities requiring the ACT test would be more likely to use it in guiding your child, placing him in appropriate freshman classes or courses, and considering him as a financial aid applicant, than in deciding whether or not to admit him.

Your child would register and pay for the ACT test in advance, and would take it on the morning of a Saturday test date under the colleges' supervision, in much the same way as with the CEEB's SAT.

He would have three morning hours to work on the four parts of the ACT test, and, through his high school, he would receive a report of his test scores and their composite along with a booklet telling him in a general way what the scores mean. It would be interesting and probably important for you to talk his scores and their meaning over with him and one of his school's counselors.

In taking the ACT battery, your child would come upon a number of reading passages in the first test, "English Usage." Several words or phrases in each passage would be underlined, and for each underlined part he would be asked which one of several changes given, or no change, would be best in the light of the nature and purpose of the whole selection. He might be asked, for example, these questions about the opening part of one passage:

A volcanic eruption is one of the most awesome spectacles in all nature. An explosion or a series of explosions begins
1

1. A. NO CHANGE
   B. beginning
   C. began
   D. begin
   (ANS.: A)

the eruption, sending a great cloud billowing upward from the *crater and in the cloud* are gases from
2

2. A. NO CHANGE
   B. crater. In the cloud
   C. crater while in the cloud
   D. crater in which cloud
   (ANS.: B)

the volcano, water droplets, fragments of solid material from the crater and the upper part of the volcano's orifice, dust and chunks of rock shattered in the earth and hurled upward by the violence of the explosions.

A question in the "Mathematics Usage" test of the battery might ask your child to solve a problem like this:

Two oil wells pump oil continuously. One oil well produces 4000 barrels of oil per day, which is 33⅓ per cent more than the other well produces. How many barrels of oil are produced daily by the two wells?

A. 5333⅓   B. 6666⅔   C. 7000   D. 8333⅓   E. 9000   (ANS.: C)

Your child would again meet a series of reading passages in the ACT battery's third test, "Social Studies Reading." After a paragraph describing one interpretation of the American Revolution, for example, he might be queried:

The internal-revolution interpretation argues that the limited enfranchisement

A. fostered dissension between the North and the South

B. brought about open warfare with England

C. encouraged the formation of a two-party system

D. aided in the development of an elite class

(The answer happens to be: D)

Similarly, your son or daughter would work through a series of passages in the fourth test, "Natural Sciences Reading." One he or she might meet could concern the mineral crystals called "zeolites" and be followed by this question:

X-ray diffraction of zeolites shows

A. numerous interstices   B. water molecules   C. charged atoms

D. the position of the exchangeable ions   (The answer happens to be: A)

The ACT test battery has been developed according to a theory that differs somewhat from the theory underlying the SAT, for it attempts to present a sample of intellectual tasks typical of college studies. As a result, your child's ACT test scores would tend to reflect general ideas and skills he has developed while in high school more than his SAT scores would. It would not, of course, reflect your child's learnings in high school as closely as his scores on the SAT plus several College Board Achievement Tests. Many research studies have shown that, although the ACT test is based on a different theory than the SAT, it can predict your child's average marks in college with about the same degree of probability as the SAT.

(The five preceding sample questions are reproduced by permission from the *1963–1964 Student Information Bulletin* of the American College Testing Program. The Bulletin is revised annually and gives examples of all types of questions asked on the ACT test. It is distributed to students without charge through their high schools, and may be requested by writing to the Program, Box 168, Iowa City, Iowa.)

One distinctive feature of the ACT program is its computation of predicted freshman academic averages of individual students at individual colleges. To any one of several hundred colleges to which your child might have his ACT test scores sent, predictions of the freshman year grades your child is likely to earn in that college would also be sent routinely with his scores. Your child's predicted grade averages would be computed by ACT especially for that college. His predicted grades would be based on his ACT test scores, his grades in high school courses, which he reports just before taking the test, and a research study conducted by ACT for each college using its research service.

If your child had taken the Iowa Tests of Educational Development before the ACT test battery, he would probably notice similarities in the kinds of questions asked in them. The ACT test is patterned after the ITED, and is based on the same underlying theory. The four parts of the three-hour ACT examination are similar to four of the nine tests in the ITED battery. New forms of the ACT test are constructed for each year's administration.

25. **The National Merit Scholarship Qualifying Test, or "NMSQT."** Some 800,000 boys and girls a year currently take the initial test in the National Merit Scholarship Program. This test is known as the National Merit Scholarship Qualifying Test, or NMSQT. Launched in 1955 with a spectacular Ford Foundation grant of $20,000,000, and an additional $500,000 from the Carnegie Corporation, National Merit now awards each year more than 1,600 college scholarships worth more than $6 million for the four college years. Merit scholarships can range in value up to $1,500 or more for each of the four college years.

To compete for a Merit scholarship, your son or daughter would first take the NMSQT. The test is offered to all high schools in the country, and more than 17,000 of them enrolling some 90 per cent of the nation's high school students give it. Your child would take it on one of the two regular test dates in March of his junior year (or, in some cases, the first semester of his senior year), and would pay a test fee of a dollar charged to cover the costs of making and offering the test, and of providing interpretive materials to students and schools.

In September of your child's senior year, Merit would announce the names of some 14,000 semi-finalists selected on the basis of their NMSQT scores alone. The number of semi-finalists in each state would be proportional to the number of the state's high school graduates relative to all U.S. high school graduates. Semi-finalists represent fewer than 1 per cent of the high school seniors in any one state.

Semi-finalists must take a second test, the SAT, be endorsed by their school and complete other routine steps to become finalists. It is from the finalist group that all Merit Scholars are selected. Winners are picked from among the finalists on the basis of factors which include high school record, test scores (both on the NMSQT and the SAT), and high school recommendation. Had your child become a semi-finalist, he would know whether or not he had won a Merit Scholarship early in the spring of his senior year. If he should win, the size of his award would be adjusted according to financial need.

The NMSQT that could open or shut the door to a Merit scholarship for your child is a three-hour test in five parts. Like the ACT test, the NMSQT is similar to the ITED, and its five parts correspond to five of the ITED's nine—English usage, social studies reading, natural sciences reading, mathematics usage and word usage. All students who take the NMSQT receive through their schools reports of their scores and an explanatory booklet, which are helpful in guidance and college planning. As previously noted, the Midwest member of testing's "Big Six," SRA, makes and gives the NMSQT under contract with National Merit Scholarship Corporation.

—*And the "NEDT."* Each year, more than a half-million students in the high school sophomore and freshman years are given the *National Educational Development Tests* by their schools. The NEDT is much like the NMSQT, also being a three-hour test with the same five parts corresponding to five parts of the ITED. The test fee per student is also a dollar, and schools can give it annually only during the week of the two March NMSQT test dates and, starting in 1964, during a week early in November. According to SRA, which makes the test, schools give it for use in counseling students about their choice of high school programs and their college plans, and for assessing their academic progress from year to year.

There are still other tests and test series, each taken by tens or hundreds of thousands of children a year in American schools, but the ones above are the nation's giants. Through his schooling, your child would be likely to take only several of these. For example, he might take the Metropolitan Readiness in kindergarten, the Otis Quick-Scoring in second grade and the California Achievement and California Mental Maturity in grades 5 and 8. In high school, he might take the DAT and the Metropolitan Achievement in ninth grade, the Kuder in tenth, the ITED and the NMSQT in eleventh and the SAT and the Strong in twelfth grade. A pattern like this would be quite typical for a child going through school today.

These or similar tests would bear on your child's future at many points and in many ways. So far, we have seen only something of what these tests are. The vital questions—what they mean and don't mean, how they can help or harm—lie ahead.

Summary of America's 25 Giant Test Series

This listing summarizes the book's identification of almost all of America's most widely used test series. These are the tests taken by the large majority of the country's 50 million schoolchildren; they are also the tests most likely to affect your children's lives. Also summarized are the minimum, or full, estimates of the numbers of children a year who take each series. The estimates were generously provided for this book by the publishers of the tests, and in most cases are being made public for the first time.

Test Series Name (and Nickname or Abbreviation)	Millions of Children a Year Taking the Series *	Publisher

To Estimate Your Child's IQ or Learning Abilities:

1. Otis Quick-Scoring Mental Ability Tests (Otis Quick-Scoring or Otis IQ)	several (full)	Harcourt, Brace & World
2. Pintner General Ability Tests (Pintner IQ)	1 (full)	Harcourt, Brace & World
3. California Test of Mental Maturity (CTMM)	5 (minimum)	California Test Bureau
4. Lorge-Thorndike Intelligence Tests (Lorge-Thorndike IQ)	1 (minimum)	Houghton Mifflin
5. Henmon-Nelson Tests of Mental Ability (Henmon-Nelson IQ)	1 (minimum)	Houghton Mifflin

Test Series Name (and Nickname or Abbreviation)	Millions of Children a Year Taking the Series *	Publisher
6. Primary Mental Abilities (PMA)	½ (minimum)	Science Research Associates
7. Differential Aptitude Tests (DAT)	1 (minimum)	The Psychological Corporation
8. School and College Ability Tests (SCAT)	1 (full)	Educational Testing Service
9. Kuhlmann-Anderson Tests (Kuhlmann-Anderson)	2 (full)	Personnel Press
Approximate minimum total, these tests:	16½	

To Measure What Your Child Has Learned:

10. Stanford Achievement Test	10 (full)	Harcourt, Brace & World
11. Metropolitan Achievement Tests	almost 10 (full)	Harcourt, Brace & World
12. Metropolitan Readiness Tests	several (full)	Harcourt, Brace & World
13. California Achievement Test Batteries	5 (minimum)	California Test Bureau
14. Lee-Clark Reading Readiness Test	½ (minimum)	California Test Bureau
15. Iowa Tests of Basic Skills (ITBS)	1 (minimum)	Houghton Mifflin
16. Iowa Tests of Educational Development (ITED)	1½ (minimum)	Science Research Associates
17. SRA Achievement Series	1½ (minimum)	Science Research Associates
18. Sequential Tests of Educational Progress (STEP)	1 (full)	Educational Testing Service
19. Achievement tests in individual subjects—notably: Cooperative English Tests	3 (full)	Educational Testing Service
Evaluation & Adjustment Series	1 (full)	Harcourt, Brace & World

Test Series Name (and Nickname or Abbreviation)	Millions of Children a Year Taking the Series *	Publisher
20. New York State Regents Examinations ("Regents")	½ (full)	New York State Education Department
Approximate minimum total, these tests:	37	

To Help Your Child Choose a Career:

21. Kuder Preference Record (the "Kuder")	2 (minimum)	Science Research Associates
22. Strong Vocational Interest Blank (the Strong or SVIB)	¾ (full)	Consulting Psychologists Press
Approximate minimum total, these inventories:	2¾	

To Help Decide Your Child's College Opportunities:

23. Scholastic Aptitude Test (SAT; popularly, the "College Boards")	1 (full)	Educational Testing Service (for College Entrance Examination Board)
—Preliminary Scholastic Aptitude Test (PSAT)	1 (full)	Educational Testing Service (for CEEB)
24. American College Testing Program Examination (ACT)	½ (full)	Science Research Associates (for American College Testing Program)
25. National Merit Scholarship Qualifying Test (NMSQT)	9/10 (full)	Science Research Associates (for National Merit Scholarship Corporation)
—National Educational Development Tests (NEDT)	½ (minimum)	Science Research Associates
Approximate total, these tests:	4	

Minimum total, all tests and inventories: 60¼

* "(full)" following a number means that this is an estimate of the full or total numbers taking the series a year; "(minimum)" means that this is a minimum estimate, lower than the total number taking the series a year by a small amount or lower by as many as several million.

Chapter 2

How Bright
Is Your
Child?

As much as any other personal quality, the developing power of your child's mind can determine what your son—yes, or your daughter as well—will accomplish in life. Whether we like it or not, success today comes to people who have enough brainpower and training to master highly specialized skills, and to understand the large and highly involved organizations of modern America.

Opportunities for unusually bright young people abound as never before. Ahead of your children in many schools lie special "enriched" or "fast-track" programs in the elementary grades, and sequences of enriched, "honors" or "gifted-pupil" classes through high school. Even after an ordinary schooling, very bright and enterprising boys and girls will be plied with offers of admission and financial aid by the most renowned colleges in the land. In science, a bright son or daughter could qualify for a fellowship grant to pay for studies beyond college. Corporate recruiters vie to hire the brilliant graduate for executive training programs after college, or for executive or research jobs after advanced study. Spokesmen for one field after another beseech bright young people to consider their own business, science or profession because shortages of superior men and women in almost every field leave wide room at the top.

Opportunities of a different order but of equal importance lie before children of lesser degrees of brightness. Any child bright enough to get through school can find many ways to a useful, economically secure and satisfying adult life. But a child only moderately bright must have appropriate education and training in order to be sure of getting a job and being able to pursue a career.

For the uneducated and untrained, however bright, it has become harder and harder to find a place in the highly specialized working world. And the more wisely your child's education and training are planned in the light of his level of brightness, as well as of his likes and dislikes, the more rewarding a life your child will have.

As a result, you carry a double responsibility for finding out how bright your children may be, and for helping them realize what opportunities their brightness opens to them: first, for the sake of your children themselves, and second, for the rest of us, all of whose lives benefit the more that each person can apply his abilities to the full.

Gauging Your Child's Brightness Without Tests

"How bright is my child?"—that inevitable, age-old question in parents' minds—hits home with special force today. You have unavoidably tried to answer it in many ways. And so have others for whom the brightness of your child becomes increasingly important as he or she grows.

Personal impressions come earliest and stay longest. We depend on our own impressions and those of our friends to tell us how bright our children may be through their tenderest years. We watch for the times when they first learn to smile, to follow things with their eyes, to sit up, to stand, to take the first step, to say the first word. Later, we watch them to see when they first tie their shoes, throw a ball straight, count, read, bat, sew, skip rope, ride bikes, cross the street safely. We notice how fast they seem to catch on when we explain, how quickly they blurt out ideas in playing with other children. Through these youngest days, generally, we compare them with what they've been able to do before—most often, impatiently.

Their school work makes us begin thinking of how bright they are compared with other children. By ingrained custom, teachers usually adjust their evaluations so that a few pupils in the class get the highest marks and a few just squeak through. Report cards and conferences with their teachers tell us—and tell the children themselves—how bright they may seem to a local officialdom if school work engages their interest.

But the reactions of teachers and children vary. Some teachers may have taken a liking to your child; some teachers or subjects may have captured his imagination. Other teachers may have disliked your child, or have been annoyed with his indifference to their subjects. Besides, teachers give marks to sum up what your child has done and not to judge impartially how bright he may be. It is rare, then, that we think that our children's marks truly reveal their potential—especially when the marks are failing or just average, and even when they may be superior.

Hobbies and interests our children develop make up another whole area in which we seek clues to their brightness. Your son may become absorbed in chemistry, collecting rocks, or photography. He might catch fire about Sherlock Holmes or baseball heroes, and read every last word about them on which he can lay his hands. Your daughter might give most of her time to ambitious Girl Scout projects, raise prize sheep in her 4-H club, read about birds or about movie stars or design and make her own clothes. More likely, you find the boy or the girl turning quickly from interest to interest, getting enthusiastic about one for a while, then going on to something else. "Just playing with the other kids" might take up much of a child's spare time, in games, talk, expeditions. So might watching TV.

Would these kinds of things—personal impressions, hobbies and pastimes, even marks in school—leave you feeling at all sure of your child's brightness? They probably would not—and should not. You would have seen too much change in your children to have any fixed ideas of how bright they are. At times you'd have seen your child suddenly outdo himself by far. In occasional slumps or sulks you might have seen him turn terribly listless and dull. Teachers' opinions of the boy or the girl would have varied widely as well, as we saw. If you had long been disappointed, you might always be looking ahead to some great change to take place when he finally grows up.

It is only against this background of doubt that intelligence tests (and all such ones of general mental ability) take on what limited but specific importance they have.

Tests Gauge Brightness Scientifically—But Within Stated Limits

Standardized tests provide the only scientific way for seeing how bright your children are. They qualify as the usual authority on the question in practical life, not because they are infallible, though, nor because they reveal all that needs to be known about your child's brightness. Far from it. They qualify as an authority because they are the most informative and impartial tools for measuring brightness that have so far been developed. With millions of people, IQ tests have proven to be an invaluable check on personal impressions and judgments. How much they do reveal amazed people when they were first introduced—and would amaze us still if we did not take their powers largely for granted and did not hear mostly about their misuse, as we do today. In fact, it is because IQ tests seem to be so good but are actually not perfect that they pose dangers to your children. These dangers make it advisable for you to know as much about the limitations of IQ tests as about their powers.

One of the first things to realize about the limitations of IQ tests is this: Their limitations are defined with a degree of precision and detail seldom if ever found in other ways of judging people—for example, in school marking systems or business hiring decisions. Moreover, the limitations of IQ tests stem from the extraordinary difficulty of measuring the powers of the mind. These powers have fascinated and perplexed many of the wisest men who have ever lived; in "reason" or "intellect" they have seen the difference between human beings and all other creatures, and even one of the deepest mysteries of the universe. The simple question, then, of the powers of a human mind echoes off into infinity, like a cheer in some great desert canyon.

How Your Child's Brightness Would Most Authoritatively Be Measured

Your child's brightness would be measured with most authority, many experts believe, by an "individual" intelligence test which descended directly from the first intelligence test ever invented—the Binet-Simon "Scale" of 1905. For example, Paul Woodring, the psychologist who is editor of the *Saturday Review Education Supplement*, thinks that an individually given intelligence test of this kind produces more satisfactory results than the kind taken by large groups of people at a time. Your child's IQ score on an individual test would not necessarily differ from his IQ score on a group test, but his score on an individual test would be accompanied by qualifying observations made by an expert in giving the test.

Two such individual intelligence tests are widely used in the U.S. today, each being given to well over a million persons a year. Many millions of people throughout the world have taken both. These are the Stanford-Binet Intelligence Scale, the closest lineal descendant of the Binet of 1905; and the Wechsler Intelligence Scales, which differ in certain important details from the Stanford-Binet, but are based on much the same underlying principles.

Your child would be given the Stanford-Binet by a specially trained psychologist, often one who has earned a doctor's degree in psychology. The man or woman might be the school psychologist, or a staff member of the child testing bureau or child guidance clinic in a school system or college to which you had turned for advice; he might be a clinical psychologist in private practice, or a psychiatrist. Even for psychiatrists, the Stanford-Binet and the Wechsler are among the most authoritative instruments for seeing in general how bright a person may be.

Your child would probably enjoy the experience of being tested with the Stanford-Binet, and should certainly not find it disagreeable. Psychologists have to make sure that children taking it are reasonably at ease in order to obtain scores that can be accepted as approximately accurate. Also, the blocks, cards and pictures used in the test are simple and colorful, having been developed to interest children. The test could well seem like a game to your boy or girl.

If your child were given the Stanford-Binet before he was seven or eight years old, the testing might be completed in thirty or forty minutes. Were your child older, the testing might last as long as an hour and a half, including a recess or two. The questions would be put to your child by the psychologist; each series of questions would present an interesting variety of puzzles or tasks that, by and large, can be worked by most children of a particular age according to actual try-outs with several thousand children. Ordinarily, the psychologist would begin with a series or level that is the one for children about a year younger than your child at the time. Your child would work through all the types of questions or exercises for one age level of the Stanford-Binet before going on to questions of the next level.

If your child had not yet started school, the psychologist might begin with the earliest level, that for the two-year-olds. In this level,

Should your child's intelligence be measured with the Stanford-Binet Intelligence Scale, which many authorities regard as the most authoritative intelligence test, the expert giving it to your child would use a standard kit of testing materials like these. There are no multiple-choice questions on the Stanford-Binet. In fact, your child would speak or act out rather than mark or write most of his answers on it. (Reproduced by permission of Houghton Mifflin Company, Boston.)

your child would be asked to take three simple geometric shapes out of the holes in which they fit in a board and put them back again after having seen the psychologist do it. He would also be asked to remember after a short interval under which one of three boxes he had seen the psychologist hide a toy, to point to the main parts of a doll as the psychologist names them, to stack several wooden blocks into a tower after the psychologist had done so and to name or point to pictures of such common objects as a tree, articles of clothing and toys. In higher levels he would be asked to do such things as string beads in certain ways, draw straight lines or circles, repeat series of numbers forward or backward, do several simple things in succession, say what certain words mean, remember things about stories the psychologist reads, explain what to do in simple situations in his everyday life, find the funny or foolish detail in absurd pictures and recognize basic similarities or differences between such things as apples and oranges, or fishes and stones.

All answers on the Stanford-Binet would be spoken or acted out by your child. He would not write down any of his answers, nor would he answer by marking one among several possible choices given to him. The person giving him the test would take full notes on his answers as they went along. A variety of answers or responses to any question could be right, with the examiner using judgment developed in long, supervised training to decide. The examiner would question your child further if any answer were unclear, or would encourage your child if he hesitates over a problem.

The score your child would earn on the test would be calculated as a "mental age" of so many years and months. His mental age score would consist of the age of the highest level of the test on which he answered all questions correctly, plus a specified number of additional months' credit for each question he could answer in the higher levels. The psychologist would have continued giving your child higher and higher levels of the test until your child reached a level on which he could not give the right answers to any of the questions.

Your child's "mental age" would of course indicate by how much he was ahead of or behind presumably representative children of his own age—of course, according to the test. For example, suppose he were ten and a half years old and had earned a mental age score of twelve years and eight months. He would then be two years and two months ahead of average children his age in general mental powers or "intelligence" as measured by the Stanford-Binet.

For the sake of simplicity, a single number would be used to sum up the relation between your child's real age and his measured mental age—the famous and familiar Intelligence Quotient, or IQ. Originally, the IQ was an actual quotient—mental age divided by real age—multiplied by 100. In this scheme, a child of five with a measured mental age of five would therefore earn an IQ of 100 (5 divided by 5 equals 1, times 100 equals 100); a five-year-old with a mental age of seven would similarly earn an IQ of 140, while a five-year-old with a mental age of four would earn an IQ of 80. However, such simple division led to a child's having different IQs at different ages in some cases, even though his test performance with respect to the average performance of children of his age had not changed. Partly because of this, IQs are now calculated so that, if your child performs equally far ahead of or behind the average performance of children at ages corresponding to his, he will get the same IQ at those ages. For example, the current Stanford-Binet IQ for your child if he were ten and a half and scored a mental age of twelve years and eight months, as we assumed above, would be 117—and not the 120½ that simple division would give. As small a difference as 3½ points has little or no practical significance, however, as we shall see.

The old-fashioned IQ score of mental age divided by chronological age is called a "ratio" IQ. The widely used modern IQ score, which is calculated so that a child whose test performance remained equally far above or below average at different ages would get the same IQ scores at those ages, is called a "deviation" IQ. Your child would have earned a ratio IQ on early editions of the Stanford-Binet, but he would earn a deviation IQ on the current edition.

Your child's performance on the Stanford-Binet would carry substantial authority as an index of his brightness for several basic reasons. Most of these reasons stem directly from Alfred Binet's original conception of the "scale" he introduced in collaboration with Theophile Simon in the Paris of 1905. First, Binet thought of "intelligence" as a scientific abstraction, like electricity or energy, that could be detected only by its effects as observed in experiments. To measure its effects, he picked brief tasks or problems that required different kinds of intelligence to work. His major discovery was that such tasks could be used to test intelligence when arranged in ascending order of the ages at which most normal children could do them. Work on these tasks does not require all the kinds of intelligent behavior you could think of. Instead, the tasks *sample* the kinds of intelligent behavior that can be seen objectively by any informed observer. This idea of a test as something that presents a sample of tasks requiring your child to display the abilities to be measured has inspired all standardized testing. On an intelligence test, then, your child is simply asked to do a limited number of things—but typical and significant things, so far as possible—that require various kinds of intelligence.

Second, Binet used what people generally did on the test as the standard of measurement—the standard against which your child's performance, for example, should be compared. In Binet's view, just as the test performance provided an objective example of intelligent behavior, the extensive try-out of the test with large numbers of children provided an objective standard of intelligent behavior. Such try-outs to determine the typical or standard performance on a test remain fundamental in testing today. They are called "standardization." Through the standardization of a test, your child can be compared with typical children of his age and background.

It is mainly these two basic features of standardized testing that make it a quantitative, experimental branch of science. Each testing of an individual child is an experiment in which he earns a certain number of points for his objectively observed behavior in working the test. And the meaning of numerical scores on the test is in turn objectively defined by the large-scale experiment of standardization. Binet based the test, standards of performance on it and the test-taking itself all on experiments that could be analyzed numerically. Doing this made it possible for testing to develop in the same self-correcting way as sciences like physics and chemistry.

However, it was to meet a poignant human problem rather than merely to make a scientific advance that Alfred Binet invented the archetype of all intelligence tests. In fact, the main concern of this lawyer-turned-psychologist, this reserved scholar who wore pince-nez and at one time fashionably sported a waxed mustache and goatee, was the feelings of children and their families.

The immediate problem he solved was posed by the French Minister of Public Instruction. This official decreed in 1904 that retarded children were to be separated from their regular schoolmates and put into special classes and schools to be set up for them. Binet was then head of the experimental psychology laboratory at the Sorbonne. He was asked to advise the commission on the new plan about appropriate examinations for identifying retarded children.

In later explaining his first thoughts about such examinations, he made a statement that could be a credo for standardized testing, even today:

It must be made impossible for those who belong to the Commission to fall into the habit of making haphazard decisions according to impressions which are subjective, and consequently uncontrolled. Such impressions are sometimes good, sometimes bad, and have at all times too much the nature of the arbitrary, of caprice, of indifference.

His concern for the children involved, and the means he proposed to protect them, appeared as he went on to say:

...the interests of the child demand a more careful method. To be a member of a special class can never be a mark of distinction, and such as do not merit it, must be spared the record.... Furthermore, in principle, we are convinced, and we shall not cease to repeat, that the precision and exactness of science should be introduced into our practice whenever possible, and in the great majority of cases it is possible.

Behind Binet's confidence in scientific methods stood much experimentation by psychologists in the late 1800s. These men had measured such characteristics of people as reaction time and sensitivity of hearing and sight. They even looked into separate mental faculties like memory and word association. However, none had discovered through experiments like these an even partially successful way of measuring general mental powers.

Binet again reflected his concern for the interests of parents, children and teachers in explaining the 1908 revision of his scale. He mused, ". . . a father and mother who raise a child themselves, who watch over him and study him fondly, would have great satisfaction in knowing that the intelligence of a child can be measured, and would willingly make the necessary effort to find out if their own child is intelligent."

Of teachers, he declared:

We think especially of teachers who love their profession, who interest themselves in their pupils, and who understand that the first condition of instructing them well, is to know them. All such teachers seek, more or less successfully, to make an estimate of the intelligence of their pupils; but they have no method.... Primary school inspectors have often told us of zealous teachers who have had the ingenious idea of composing psychological portraits of their pupils, and we have looked over these collections of portraits with interest. We have congratulated and encouraged the authors without telling them frankly what we thought, which was that they were working without method, like a very intelligent but unscientific man who would try experiments in bacteriology with unclean tools.

Such teachers analyzed only the individual pupil, in isolation, he noted. The method they lacked was one with which they could compare the individual pupil with his peers generally.

Binet was well aware of the subtleties and complexities involved in appraising intelligence, particularly in the case of young children. He believed that a competent examiner—or "a good experimenter," as he phrased it—should really learn to use the Binet-Simon scale by watching how he and his associates gave it. He warned against one major kind of error in giving the test in words that still epitomize the major advantage of an individual intelligence test: "recording the gross results without making psychological observations, without noticing such little facts as permit one to give to the gross results their true value." (The other major kind of error against which he warned, incidentally, was to give unfair hints in encouraging a child to attempt a problem or clarify an answer.)

Psychologists in many countries translated and experimented with the early Binet scales—among them, Henry H. Goddard, an American pioneer in education for the feeble-minded—and Binet incorporated a number of their ideas as well as his own in still another revision which was issued in 1911, the year of Binet's death at the early age of fifty-four. Before he died, though, he realized through the wide interest that had already been shown in his work something of its eventual significance. ". . . Methods of measuring individual intelligence have not a speculative interest alone," he wrote; "by the direction, by the organization of all the investigations, psychology has furnished the proof (we do not say for the first time but in a more positive manner than ever before), that it is in a fair way to become a science of great social utility."

Both of the widely used individual intelligence tests which your child might be given today are adaptations and improvements of Binet's scales. Of these, the Stanford-Binet Intelligence Scale resulted chiefly from the work of Lewis M. Terman, a psychologist interested in "the great problems of genius" rather than retardation. Terman and his colleagues at Stanford University developed the first Stanford Revision of the Binet. They standardized it on normal and bright children, and had it published in 1916 (by Houghton Mifflin, as we saw earlier). Subsequent revisions appeared in 1937 and 1960. On the 1960 revision there are twenty levels (one each at half-year intervals for mental ages of two through five, and at one-year intervals for mental ages of six through fourteen, with four adult levels named "average" and "superior I, II and III").

The other individual IQ test which your child would be most likely to take, the Wechsler, was developed by David Wechsler, a clinical psychologist, and his colleagues at Bellevue Hospital in New York City. It was published in 1939 (by The Psychological Corporation). Wechsler developed the original version of his scale especially for adolescents and adults, and designed its questions to interest them rather than small children. Its two current versions are the Wechsler Intelligence Scale for Children, issued in 1949, and the Wechsler Adult Intelligence Scale, issued in 1955.

A trained psychologist would use a standard kit of materials related to these in measuring your child's IQ with an individual test that is about as widely used and respected as the Stanford-Binet—the Wechsler Intelligence Scale for Children, or "WISC" (pronounced like "whisk"). A companion individual test, the Wechsler Adult Intelligence Scale or "WAIS" (shown above being taken by the young woman at left), is most commonly used for appraising the brightness of mature men and women. (Reproduced courtesy of The Psychological Corporation.)

Were your child to take the "WISC," which is for children from five to fifteen, he would be given sequences of questions that are all of the same kind in succession. Types of questions would not be mixed in together according to age level, as in the Stanford-Binet. Your child might first go as far as he could on the "General Information" test, then the "General Comprehension" test, and so on through Arithmetic, Similarities, Vocabulary and Digit Span. These are the six "verbal" tests of the Wechsler. The WISC's "performance" tests are these:

Picture Completion, in which your child would be shown pictures of common objects with a part missing and be asked to point out the missing part;

Picture Arrangement, in which he would put the pictures of each set of three into their correct time sequence;

Block Design, in which he would arrange colored blocks into designs like samples shown him;

Object Assembly, a jigsaw-puzzle kind of test using only several large pieces of simple shape;

Coding, in which he would first be shown pictures of things like a star, a ball and a triangle, each with an associated mark (cross, dot, etc.), then be asked to write the associated mark after each pictured thing in a long series of them;

Mazes, in which he would trace the way through given labyrinths.

As with the Stanford-Binet, the Wechsler would be given to your child by a highly trained individual examiner. Your child would meet many questions on the Wechsler's verbal sections which are of much the same types as questions on the Stanford-Binet, though the performance sections would be quite different. He would, accordingly, be given separate "verbal" and "performance" IQ scores, as well as an overall IQ score. Also, as with the Stanford-Binet, your child would earn an overall IQ on the Wechsler based on the extent to which his work on the full test had differed—or "deviated"—from the average given for his age, rather than on the quotient of his mental age divided by his chronological age. Such a "deviation IQ," in fact, was used with the first Wechsler—the Wechsler-Bellevue Intelligence Scale of 1939—which proved to be of "great value" in World War II military hospitals, according to one observer. This Wechsler-Bellevue has since been superseded by the Wechsler Children and Wechsler Adult scales.

How Your Child's Brightness Would Most Probably Be Measured

Your child is far more likely to have his or her brightness measured with a "group" test than with an individual one like the Stanford-Binet or the Wechsler. These group tests are the intelligence or general ability tests described in the first chapter—the Otis Quick-Scoring, the Lorge-Thorndike, the California Mental Maturity, the TEA, DAT, SCAT and so on. Many millions of children a year take these group tests as a matter of course in the schools. By contrast, the special, individual administrations of the Stanford-Binet and the Wechsler in the schools number only in the hundreds of thousands a year at most. Much of their use is in mental health clinics and agencies instead. Group tests, incidentally, are simply those that can be taken by groups of people at once, rather than by only one person at a time.

Group IQ tests burst suddenly and massively on the American scene in World War I. When the U.S. entered the war in 1917, the American Psychological Association appointed a committee of five eminent psychologists to recommend ways of applying psychology in the war effort. Among the five was Lewis Terman, whose Stanford-Binet revision of 1916 had already generated wide interest among psychologists. The five saw great advantages in using Terman's test to classify draftees for assignment to different kinds of training and duties. At first, they considered the enormous problem of giving it individually to hundreds of thousands of men. However, a few psychologists had begun to experiment with group test adaptations of the new Stanford-Binet. Among them was one of Terman's graduate students, Arthur S. Otis, who had just finished successfully developing a group IQ test as his doctor's degree dissertation. Otis was invited to join the five. Together, they led one hundred or more hastily recruited psychologists in writing, trying out and making final selections of questions for group tests essentially like the ones Otis had devised. These early group IQ tests were evaluated by seeing if large numbers of people earned much the same scores on the group tests as they did on the Stanford-Binet test. This is still one of the main ways of seeing how well or poorly a group IQ test works today.

The psychologists then won permission to try the test out on a large cross-section of men in the Army. They found that the average score of corporals was higher than that of enlisted men generally, the average score of sergeants was higher than that of corporals and the average score of officers was much higher than that of sergeants. As Otis later remarked, the results "sold the Army completely," as you can imagine they might.

The "Army Alpha," as the test was called, and a parallel, pictorial "Army Beta" for illiterates, were used to test and classify more than 1,700,000 men in the short nineteen months of America's part in the war. The test questions were quite similar to the ones on the verbal and pictorial IQ tests which your child takes today. No one now doubts that the tests were fairer and more effective than any other techniques that would have been practical to use at the time. Standardized group testing had made its first substantial contribution to American life.

In the 1920s the country entered on a fad of indiscriminate intelligence probing with group tests. The Army Alpha and Army Beta were released for civilian use. The original "committee of five" introduced a National Intelligence Test. Otis developed the Otis Group Intelligence Scale for publication by the World Book Company. Many other psychologists less experienced in the new technique followed suit, and tests. were made for persons of all kinds and ages. School systems and employers began testing on a large scale. "IQ" joined the "Boop-Boop-a-Doo" of the new jazz in the popular lingo.

Like the great bull market in stocks of the 1920s, IQ testing first boomed on a crest of unwise speculation. And like the stock market, the over-inflated crest of careless trading in IQs finally collapsed. More and more people found that IQ tests did not perform infallibly, did not reveal each individual's complete, fixed and innate intelligence. Walter Lippmann, who was then at the beginning of his fame as a journalist, was especially influential in attacking psychologists for what he claimed was their pretense to test what they could not define. Hostility toward IQ tests became widespread. Only the tests from unusually responsible sources, such as the Stanford-Binet and the Otis, continued in fairly substantial use.

By 1930 the reaction against testing had gone so far that one psychologist—a man who had a profound effect on the tests that shape the life of your child today—struck down his major scholarly work up to that time. Carl Campbell Brigham had analyzed the Army test scores of 12,000 foreign-born Americans for his book, *A Study of American Intelligence*, which appeared in 1923. On the basis of test scores, he showed in the book, immigrants from Northern European nations appeared more "intelligent" than those from Southern European nations. He concluded that the Nordic strains had greater *native* intelligence—reflecting a widespread fallacy of the day that IQ tests actually measured native intelligence. The book undoubtedly had an effect on the immigration law adopted by the U.S. in 1924, for the restrictive new law favored Northern Europeans over Southern Europeans.

Brigham demolished his book in an article he wrote for the *Psychological Review* in 1930. In the article he bitterly declared, "Psychologists have been attacked because of their use of the term 'intelligence,' and have been forced to retreat to a more restricted notion of *test score*. Their definition of intelligence must now be, 'score in a test which we consider to measure intelligence.' " Near the end, he said that, "For purposes of comparing individuals or groups, it is apparent that tests in the vernacular [that is, in the language of one country] must be used only with individuals having equal opportunities to acquire the vernacular of the test." And he wiped out his major work in the article's very last sentence: ". . . recent test findings . . . show that comparative studies of various national and racial groups may not be made with existing tests, and . . . show, in particular, that one of the most pretentious of these comparative racial studies—the writer's own—was without foundation."

At the time, Brigham and his colleagues of the College Entrance Examination Board were perfecting a test of what they might have called intelligence some years before. Instead, they called it the Scholastic Aptitude Test. This is the SAT, which is the country's most widely used college admissions test today, as we saw in the first chapter. To this day the CEEB and its contract service agency—Educational Testing Service, one of the biggest of testing's "Big Six"—use "scholastic aptitude" or "school and college ability" rather than "intelligence" to describe their influential tests of general mental abilities.

The Great IQ Controversies: Do Tests Really Measure Your Child's Intelligence?

Carl Brigham's salvo of 1930 was only one of many cannonades fired in battles which have long raged over intelligence testing. At issue is whether or not IQ tests really do measure your child's intelligence. Some authorities think that they do. "For many clinicians, educators, and others concerned with evaluation of general ability level," writes Professor Anne Anastasi of Fordham University, "the Stanford-Binet IQ has become almost synonymous with intelligence." David Wechsler flatly asserts, "The view that we do not know what we are talking about when we speak of intelligence is . . . not true by any comparative standards." He adds, emphatically: "actually we now know more about intelligence than we do about any other mental function."

By contrast, two eminent authorities in testing would not call your child's IQ a measurement of his "intelligence" in the ordinary full sense of the word. Professor Robert L. Thorndike of Teachers College, Columbia University, observes that "perhaps scholastic aptitude" would have been a better name for his own Lorge-Thorndike Intelligence Tests. Although other names, like scholastic aptitude or mental ability, "are to some extent circumlocutions," he comments, " 'intelligence' perhaps claims more than tests can deliver. It is important to temper our expectations of an intelligence test, to realize that it gets at abilities to handle certain abstract symbols that are part of intellectual functioning."

Professor Thorndike's caution about measuring your child's "intelligence" with tests is shared by Professor Lee J. Cronbach of Stanford University. All through his work on the *Essentials of Psychological Testing*, Cronbach scrupulously refers to intelligence tests as "general mental ability tests." At one point he notes with approval that "the term *intelligence test* is being replaced by such terms as *test of general mental ability* or *test of general scholastic ability*." The trouble with "intelligence" as a test name, he says, is that it "often connotes some sort of inborn mental superiority. Performance on the test is influenced by many things not included in this concept of 'intelligence.' The test calls for knowledge, skills and attitudes developed in Western culture, and perhaps better developed in some environments than in others. An 'intelligent' person will do badly if he lacks the background the test requires."

Some professors are even more vehement about IQ tests, denouncing even any attempt to measure general intellectual abilities. In attacking the whole idea, psychologist Calvin W. Taylor of the University of Utah has said that, "The mind is far too subtle and complex to be represented by a single score or by only a handful of scores in a test. It is an insult to the human mind to allow this over-simplified point to stand." Joel H. Hildebrand, a famed chemist of the University of California, has assailed IQ tests not only for allegedly making the child responsible for failure in school and serving as an excuse for poor teaching, but for doing "a great disservice to creativity in education." Criticizing further, he said that "the best person able to appraise promise as a mathematician is a gifted teacher, and not a professional tester."

Looking back, though, you can easily see why the early intelligence testers thought that they really were measuring intelligence. For centuries before them, genius and imbecility had been regarded with the purest superstition. Genius just happened as a gift of the gods—or, as Plato thought, through divine inspiration of otherwise quite ordinary mortals. On the other hand, idiocy blended into insanity, and was long thought to be caused by supernatural forces from the opposite quarter —possession by demons or the devil. Mental abilities between these flamboyant extremes were explained by two theories. Conservatives believed that the rich and the noble were naturally smart, and the common people were naturally stupid, except for those few cases in which God or the Devil had apparently stepped in. Revolutionaries, philosophers and scientists of recent centuries thought instead that all men—all normal men, anyway—had exactly the same mental potential as part of a uniform human nature. In fact, the experimental psychologists who laid the groundwork for Binet's startling achievement insisted that there were no significant psychological differences from one individual to another. Among these leaders was Wilhelm Wündt, who opened the world's first laboratory of experimental psychology at the University of Leipzig in 1879. Wündt and his students measured things like sensitivity of hearing or color vision and reaction time to determine what the uniform human capabilities were. They ignored questions raised by differences they recorded in individual performances.

The first bright light to be cast on the question of how your child's mental capacities differ from those of other individuals radiated from an English scientist, Sir Francis Galton. He in turn had been fired by the theory of evolution introduced in 1859 by his cousin, Charles Darwin. Men of genius fascinated Galton. Their abilities differed so enormously from those of most men that he could not ignore questions about the reasons behind individual differences.

As one example of the tremendous extent to which intellectual performance could vary, he described the results of the mathematics honors examinations at Cambridge University of his day. Students spent forty-four hours taking these marathon examinations—five and a half hours a day for eight days. Among 200 men who scored highest in two successive years, Galton reported, almost half—98, to be exact—earned 1,000 or fewer "marks" or points out of a possible 17,000. But one man earned about 6,000 points, three some 7,000 and the top man some 8,000. In another year the top man or "senior wrangler" had earned *thirty-two times* as many points as the year's lowest man who still won math honors!

We have Galton to thank for first applying the now-famous "normal distribution curve"—the bell-shaped curve according to which your child's teachers probably mark their classes today—to human abilities. Galton had been amazed and delighted to see how Alphonse Quetelet, astronomer-royal of Belgium, had proven that all kinds of physical qualities of people described the normal curve when plotted on a graph—among them, the chest measurements of 5,738 Scottish soldiers, and the height of 100,000 Frenchmen called up in the draft. Then, in an historic demonstration, Galton showed that the marks made by the seventy-two men who took the admissions examination for Sandhurst, the British West Point, in December 1868, followed the normal curve almost perfectly (except at the lower end, where Galton assumed the men either "did not venture to compete or were plucked.") Since then, hundreds of similar graphs have confirmed his insight: in any group large enough to be representative, intellectual powers and accomplishments are distributed in close accordance with the normal curve.

At the same time, to account for the rise of geniuses, Galton seized on Darwin's idea of evolution. Genius was inherited, he believed, and to prove it he played the old British parlor game of tracing genealogies through a whole great book, *Hereditary Genius; An Inquiry into Its Laws and Consequences,* which was published in 1869.

However, you should not jump to the conclusion that your children simply inherit the same mental equipment as yours. There is more to the story than that. Binet's scales of intelligence make up the next chapter. As we saw a few pages ago, they accomplished two things, both of which amazed the psychological world. Where Galton had considered genius, Binet studied idiocy. Accordingly, Binet's scales first of all provided a far more illuminating and reliable way than any then available for telling the difference between children who were normal, retarded, morons, idiots and imbeciles. And second, Binet's whole idea of mental age and tests to measure it provided a means with which the mental powers of *any* child could be measured.

School and College Ability Tests

Sequential Tests of Educational Progress

SCAT-STEP

Score Distribution Sheet

Name of Test: SCAT Verbal   Time of Testing: Fall (Fall or Spring)
School, College, or Group: Midtown City Schools   Grade or Class: 12
Other Characteristics of Local Norms Group: 141 boys and 159 girls

(1) Score Group	(2) Tally	(3) Frequency	(4) Cumulative Frequency	(5) Percentile Rank	(6) Percentile Band
304 - 305	/	1	300	99*	99 - 100
302 - 303		0	299	99*	99 - 100
300 - 301	/	1	299	99*	98 - 100
298 - 299	//	2	298	99	97 - 99
296 - 297	///	3	296	98	95 - 99
294 - 295	/////	5	293	97	91 - 99
292 - 293	//// ///	8	288	95	86 - 98
290 - 291	//// //// ///	13	280	91	81 - 97
288 - 289	//// //// //// /	16	267	86	74 - 95
286 - 287	//// //// //// ////	19	251	81	67 - 91
284 - 285	//// //// //// //// /	21	232	74	59 - 86
282 - 283	//// //// //// //// //	22	211	67	52 - 81
280 - 281	//// //// //// //// ///	23	189	59	44 - 74
278 - 279	//// //// //// //// ///	23	166	52	37 - 67
276 - 277	//// //// //// //// //	22	143	44	30 - 59
274 - 275	//// //// //// //// /	21	121	37	24 - 52
272 - 273	//// //// //// ////	19	100	30	18 - 44
270 - 271	//// //// //// ///	18	81	24	9 - 44
268 - 269	//// //// //// /	16	63	18	5 - 37
266 - 267	//// //// ////	14	47	13	3 - 30
264 - 265	//// //// //	12	33*	9	1 - 24
262 - 263	//// ////	10	21	5	1 - 18
260 - 261	//// //	7	11	3	0 - 13
258 - 259	///	3	4	1*	0 - 9
256 - 257	/	1	1	1*	0 - 5

*Ranks higher than 99 and lower than 1 may be recorded as 99 and 1, respectively.

Total Number of Students 300

This form is a worksheet for preparing local norms. Directions for recording information and computations are given in the SCAT or STEP MANUAL FOR INTERPRETING SCORES for the test used.

For any fairly large group of individuals, scores on tests of general mental ability usually follow the familiar bell-shaped "normal curve of distribution" when plotted on a graph. The fact that scores often do follow the pattern of the normal curve helped convince developers of early intelligence tests that they were measuring a trait of people as physiological as height or weight, which also describe normal curves when graphed for large groups. However, far more than physiology has since been found to be involved in tested intelligence.

The usual normal curve pattern found for mental ability test scores reflects the fact that most people score around the average on these tests, and fewer and fewer people earn scores which are increasingly high and increasingly low. As an example, this tally sheet of the scores on the School and College Ability Test of ETS earned by a few hundred pupils (with the highest-scoring children tallied at the top and the lowest-scoring at the bottom) shows the ends of the tally marks outlining an approximate normal curve—a normal curve which is tipped up on end and a bit fat on the above-average half. (Reproduced by permission of Educational Testing Service.)

Binet's scales struck his contemporaries as a dazzling revelation about human intelligence because of the darkness in which the question of mental powers had been shrouded for centuries. When early experiments with the Binet and the Stanford-Binet showed that scores closely followed the normal curve, the conclusion that indeed they did measure intelligence seemed inescapable. The conclusion became still more solidly fixed as more and more evidence came in to show that, in general, the IQs of children remained just about the same year after year.

But in the shadow of Galton's work on inherited genius, psychologists of the 1920s began one of their first great battles over the meaning of IQ scores. This one hinged on the question raised a moment ago: Do your children simply inherit minds like your own? As more and more men of renown joined the controversy, it became famous as the one fought over "nature or nurture." Early contenders were handicapped in waging it by not knowing even such now commonplace facts of human heredity as the difference between identical and fraternal twins. It nevertheless raged on for many years because of the educational and social issues at stake. If intelligence was·merely inherited, for example, the whole country might eventually freeze into rigid social classes according to heredity—and a child's whole schooling could be completely mapped out even before he were born!

To this day the question has not been answered in favor of either "nature" or "nurture" as the prime source of intelligence. The best answer seems to be, "both," in unknown proportions which do not appear important enough to investigate further. Robert S. Woodworth of Columbia University, a member of the old committee of five on the Army Alpha, and one of the leading psychologists of his time, gave an answer which stands essentially as a final one in 1941. In it he summarized a decade or more of "twin studies"—ones made, at long last, with identical twins.

"Two conclusions seem probable," Woodworth said, "even though the sample is still far too small to make either conclusion sure." His first conclusion concerned "nurture," or environment. "Radical differences in education can create substantial differences in intelligence," he said, "so far as intelligence is measured by our tests." Nevertheless, the effect of "nature" or heredity is still very strong. As he pointed out, "the difference [in measured intelligence] between identical twins reared apart are remarkably small except in those cases where the contrast of educational advantages was very great. For the majority of separated identicals the IQ difference was no greater than for identicals reared together." Woodworth heavily emphasized the importance of heredity, stressing that "the differences [in IQ] found among the children of an ordinary community are not accounted for, except in small measure, by differences in homes and schooling."

You can be fairly confident, then, that your child is not at first a complete blank which only his experiences will shape. As with his physical form, at least part of his mental capacities come from you and your ancestors.

The Burning Question of Negro Intelligence

But the large extent to which your child's experiences could affect his test scores can be judged from a second great controversy which raged over the meaning of IQs and intelligence. This is the campaign in which Carl Brigham repudiated his own major study. It centered around the burning issue of racial differences in intelligence—and especially in Negro intelligence. The resolution of this controversy about the "cultural bias" of IQ tests provides what is probably the strongest reason for not considering IQ tests as measures of pure intelligence.

Army testing in World War I supplied masses of evidence for the great public debate over Negro intelligence. It had shown that Southern Negro recruits on the average earned lower IQs than Southern whites, and that Northern Negroes had similarly averaged lower in tested "intelligence" than Northern whites. Subsequent IQ studies of Negroes and whites living in the same general areas showed much the same thing. A number of leading psychologists concluded that inferior intelligence was thus an inherent racial trait of the Negroes. As one of them put it at the time:

> In the case of the Negro and perhaps in the case of the Indian, we have a race of inferior intelligence as measured by our present intelligence tests when compared with American whites. The greater the amount of white blood entering the various mixtures of the two races, the greater is the intelligence of the resulting progeny, and this takes place because of the inheritance of mental ability.

However, other psychologists refused to believe that inherently inferior intelligence led to the lower average test scores of Negroes.

They attacked colleagues who upheld the theory of racial inferiority in several ways. Otto Klineberg, who came to prominence as one of the attackers, first gave new analyses of the old World War I testing data. The average IQ for Negroes from selected Northern states, he pointed out, had been higher than the IQs of whites from selected Southern states. Later, in the 1940s, when two anthropologists used his figures in a troop information booklet on *The Races of Mankind*, the Military Affairs Committee of the House of Representatives ordered the booklet withdrawn from Army distribution as "unfit for U.S. soldiers." Klineberg also discovered that the IQs of Southern Negroes increased after they had moved north to New York—a finding that was confirmed for Philadelphia as well in a study showing that Southern-born Negro children tended to have higher IQs the longer they lived in Philadelphia.

Another investigator had tested the IQs of more than a thousand Negroes classified by skin color as black, brown or yellow, and had found that, the lighter the skin color, the higher the IQ. The psychologist concluded that the higher the portion of white blood in Negroes, the higher the IQ. Two Chicago psychologists attacked his conclusion by analyzing the mixture of white and Negro blood lines in 103 Negro children in the city's public schools who had Stanford-Binet IQs of 120 or more. Two-thirds of these superior Negro children were of pure Negro or predominantly Negro ancestry; as a group, they had less white ancestry than the American Negro population as a whole. Moreover, the brightest child among them—a girl with the staggering IQ of 200—had no white forebears at all!

Evidence indicating that IQ scores are not determined by color of skin still mounts today. As recently as the summer of 1963 a University of Wisconsin scientist reported on a study of 941 school children on Jamaica in the British West Indies. In Jamaica, skin color does not limit a family's social standing. The investigator found that the tested intelligence of the Jamaican children varied according to their educational and economic advantages, not according to the color of their skin.

As a result of such studies, the theory of inherent racial differences in intelligence has been largely abandoned. Psychologists agree that tests can appraise intelligence only as it is developed in particular cultural surroundings. Some psychologists have tried to make tests that would work as well for the Chinese coolie, the Australian aborigine, the African pigmy, the Bedouin and the Eskimo as it would for the children of Minnesota wheat farmers, New York bankers, Alabama sharecroppers and Texas oilmen. These attempts have all failed. Most psychologists now think it impossible to build an intelligence test that would be entirely "culture-free," as they call it. One authority, for example, notes that a test battery developed to be culture-free over a twenty-year period did succeed in showing no significant differences in group performance when tried out in the U.S., France, Britain and Australia. However, group performances on it were "significantly lower" when it was taken by people in "other and dissimilar cultures." This suggests, he concludes, that "not only is it highly improbable that culture-*free* tests can be developed, but that tests should be labeled 'culture-*fair*' only when used in countries whose cultures are essentially similar."

In other words, all standardized tests yield results which are likely to vary from people of one culture to another. Any test favors people native to the culture in which the test was built and standardized. This holds true even for the all-pictorial "non-language" or "non-verbal" tests, and for such "performance" tests of the Wechsler Intelligence Scale as the picture arrangement or mazes tests. The cultural basis of any test is reflected not only in the kind of things asked about on it, but in the attitudes that its authors assume on the part of the people who take it. With respect to attitudes, for example, co-operation is the soul of the life of the Zuñi Indians in the American Southwest. The Zuñi automatically hold back from outdoing each other. As a result, IQ test scores of Zuñi children usually contradict everything else that is known of their brightness. With respect to the kind of things asked about on a test, an odd illustration of incidental effects occurred in an experiment once made by Egyptian psychologists. These scientists gave a mosaic design test much like the "block design" test on the Wechsler Scale to the children of a primitive desert band. Apparently because the mosaic test resembled some of their favorite games, these children of the desert wilds averaged higher on it than the children of industrial Europe.

Negroes have often averaged lower than American whites in scores on IQ tests, then, because of limitations in their background rather than in their inherent potential. The tests have necessarily reflected the Negroes' cultural handicaps in America—so well, it seems, that we could probably take an increasing average level of Negro IQs as one index of their progress toward equality with American whites.

Your own child could, of course, be similarly handicapped by cultural disadvantage on intelligence tests, or could enjoy a cultural advantage on them. IQ tests do not measure your child's pure intelligence. They measure it only as it acts within a particular cultural setting. As we saw from the sample questions given before, this setting for the most popular IQ tests is often that of American middle class, with its pets, toys, stories, furniture, houses, names, conversation, reading matter, sports, foods, clothes, shops, cars and coins.

Whether or not good IQ tests *really* measure your child's intelligence depends, then, on what you mean by intelligence. After long controversy, research ruled out two parts of a possible meaning—a capacity of your child that is either exclusively inherited or exclusively developed, or a capacity that would be the same whether you were living as a Hottentot or a Malay, on Park Avenue or in Harlem. But if you mean brightness in handling basic language and ideas of our modern industrial world, in solo performance given on demand, then IQ tests do measure your child's intelligence.

This was called "abstract" intelligence some years ago by Edward L. Thorndike, one of testing's eminent pioneers (and the father of the Robert L. Thorndike we have met in these pages). The other two kinds of practical import, Edward Thorndike suggested, were concrete intelligence and social intelligence. Concrete intelligence is ability to work with material things. Social intelligence is ability to work with people. Neither is examined very well by conventional group IQ tests.

The abstract qualities involved in IQs were stressed in a talk a few years ago by Emery R. Walker, Jr., dean of admission at Claremont Men's, Harvey Mudd and Pitzer colleges in Claremont, California, when he said that "our opinion of these tests suffers a little every time we press our noses to the window during a rainstorm and see some of our high IQ colleagues out there talking." He also spoke in the old tradition of Carl Brigham at that College Board meeting when he remarked, "The only definition of intelligence I can get out of the psychologists is, 'that quality which is measured by intelligence tests.' "

However, a modern definition of intelligence is offered by David Wechsler. "Intelligence, operationally defined," he says, "is the aggregate or global capacity of the individual to act purposefully, to think rationally, and to deal effectively with his environment." He agrees with Dean Walker, though, more than one might expect of an IQ test author. "It would seem that, so far as general intelligence is concerned, intellectual ability, *per se*, merely enters as a necessary minimum," he observes of the ability that IQ tests mainly measure. And he adds that "possession of this ability is no guarantee that behavior as a whole will be very intelligent in the sense defined above." Everyone, he says, can recall "persons of high intellectual ability in some particular field whom they would unhesitatingly characterize as below average in general intelligence."

You Can Raise Your Child's IQ—If

As you can probably now guess, you could raise your child's IQ scores under certain circumstances. If he had never seen an IQ test before, he might gain up to three or four points by trying one out; after that, practice alone would probably have no further effect. However, if he were culturally starved, you might raise his IQ scores by as much as forty points with several years of exposure to reading, magazines, museums, plays, art galleries and intensive, heavily financed schooling and guidance. Precisely this has been accomplished in a series of magnificent experiments financed with the help of the Ford Foundation in a dozen large cities. In the well-known "Higher Horizons" program with which this movement began in 1956 at P.S. 43, a public junior high in New York, "more than half the students raised their IQs, some an astonishing 40 points," one writer reports. If your child has been growing up in a typical upper-middle-class American home, though, he almost certainly could not raise his IQ scores by any amount of poring over vocabulary lists, working numerical and picture puzzles and otherwise practicing with material like that on the tests. It would be far more effective for him to spend his time on school work and enthused pursuit of his cultural interests.

What Your Child's IQ Means for His Future

What IQ scores signify in practical consequences matters most for your child, rather than what they stand for in some ultimate sense. And enough research has been done with them to show that they can signify quite a lot.

IQs reveal certain things for your child in relation to everyone else in the country. About what they indicate for the prospects of American children generally, according to a summary of research compiled by Professor Cronbach, appears in the accompanying table on "IQ Expectancies." The table is based on Stanford-Binet IQs. Your child would normally earn about the same IQ score on most up-to-date group IQ tests as he would on the Stanford-Binet. On some IQ tests, or under certain conditions, though, an IQ score of your child could differ rather widely from his Stanford-Binet IQ.

IQ Expectancies (for Stanford-Binet IQ Scores or
Ones Comparable to Them) *

IQ Level	What you can expect of people at this level
130	Average IQ of persons getting the Ph.D. degree.
120	Average IQ of college graduates.
115	Average IQ of freshmen in a typical four-year college.
110	Average IQ of high school graduates. Children with about 110 IQ have a 50-50 chance of graduating from college.
105	Children with an IQ of about 105 have a 50-50 chance of passing in a college preparatory high school program.
100	Average IQ for total population.
90	Average IQ of children from low-income city homes or rural homes. An adult with about this IQ can perform jobs requiring some judgment (operate sewing machine, assemble parts).
75	A child in school with an IQ of around 75 has about a 50-50 chance of reaching high school. An adult with an IQ of around 75 can keep a small store, or perform in an orchestra.
60	An adult of about 60 IQ can repair furniture, harvest vegetables, assist an electrician.
50	An adult of about 50 IQ can do simple carpentry or domestic work.
40	An adult of around 40 IQ can mow lawns, do simple laundry.

* Adapted by permission from Lee J. Cronbach, *Essentials of Psychological Testing* (Second Edition, © 1960, Harper & Row, Inc., New York).

An IQ of 100, you will recall, stood for normal development in which actual age and mental age were the same. A 100 IQ accordingly is used to represent the average of the whole population. In the population, you would not find the same numbers of people in each equal interval over the whole span of IQ scores. Instead, as we saw before, you would find the numbers of them indicated by the normal curve of distribution. Two-thirds or more of all Americans would bunch near the middle, with IQs of about 85 to 115—the levels, roughly, for getting into high school and getting into college. Very few would be out at the extremes above 130 IQ or below 75 IQ. On the average, we would expect to come across only 1 American in 500 with an IQ higher than 145 or 150, or lower than 50 or 55.

Only very approximate and slight indications of the qualities typical of different IQs appear in the table, as you see. Do not take either these indications or the IQ levels too literally. All too often, parents see figures like these and jump to the conclusion that a child of theirs would *have* to have an IQ of 120 in order to graduate from college. You would be foolish to react like this. Young people with IQs far lower than 120, as well as far higher, do graduate from college; 120 is only an average. However, not many with IQs around 90, and very few with IQs of 75 or lower, become college graduates.

Above all, you should realize that IQs give far from complete or decisive clues to the kind of adult life to expect for your child. In citing these general levels of IQs, for example, Professor Cronbach denounces making categorical decisions about "genius" or "feeble-minded" levels on the basis of fixed IQ brackets.

He tells one incredible story about an American mental home which, some years ago, used to lock up as defective anyone who failed to make a certain minimum Stanford-Binet score. Jan Masaryk, the Czechoslovak who later became his country's foreign minister and died fighting its seizure by the Communists, fell into the clutches of this mental home during a boyhood visit to the U.S. For a short time the home held young Masaryk because his English had been too poor for him to make the minimum score!

In condemning the folly of using IQs categorically, Cronbach notes further: "Some persons of IQ 110 make significant original contributions, and some of IQ 160 lead undistinguished adult lives. Some adults of IQ 80 are incapable of adjustment to the world, and some of IQ 60 support themselves and make an adequate home."

Your child's IQ, then, cannot possibly foretell whether he will be celebrated or just self-supporting as an adult. However, if it is accurate, it can suggest something about careers he should head for—or should forget. In World War II, the Army gave an examination much like an IQ test to more than eight million men and women. This was the Army General Classification Test, one of "general learning ability" on which the average score was set at 100, as with IQ tests. Score ranges for various occupations (with the top and bottom tenths of the ranges chopped off) looked like this:

Occupations	AGCT Score Ranges (Less Top and Bottom Tenths)
Acountant, teacher, stenographer, lawyer	about 110 to 140—average about 125
Draftsman, salesman, office clerk, artist	about 100 to 135—average about 120
Stock clerk, machinist, policeman, electrician	about 85 to 125—average about 110
Butcher, auto mechanic, machine operator	about 75 or 80 to 125—average about 105
Carpenter, baker, cook, truck driver	about 70 to 120—average about 100
Farm worker, lumberjack	about 60 to 115—average about 85

From this, you can see two things. One is that the IQ range in each occupation is very wide; on the basis of mental ability, some people in each of the lower-IQ occupations could work in the highest occupations. That is, some farm workers could have been accountants or lawyers instead.

But the second and more important thing for your child that these score ranges suggest is this. *People in the bottom half of some occupational groups by IQ would find it difficult or impossible to succeed in the higher-IQ occupations.* For instance, half the people who were presumably getting along fine as carpenters, bakers, cooks and truck drivers probably could not have become accountants, lawyers or stenographers. You certainly would not be wise to push your child toward an occupation calling for an above-average IQ, then, unless your child really had an IQ above average. Nor would you want to let a child with an above-average IQ go through life as an ordinary auto mechanic or baker, both for his own satisfaction in work as well as his earning power.

But how early, and how dependably, can your child's IQ be determined? There would be no point in your basing prospects and plans on false indications. In the next section, we will see the exact probabilities of what to expect. But to answer the immediate question, here are the main conclusions of practical importance:

1. Pre-school IQs of a tot usually vary so much from one testing to another that you cannot put much faith in them, even though there are IQ tests (as we saw with the Stanford-Binet) for children below five.

2. IQs of children around eight or ten years old usually agree rather well with their IQs at the end of high school, for normal children in normal homes. Even so, schools which use IQ or other general mental ability tests customarily give them to all children every three or four years. Psychologists and guidance counselors would rather not base professional opinions on a child's IQ more than two or three years old because they have seen children's IQ scores change in too many cases within a few years.

In considering your own child's intelligence, you would do well to remember a few of the dramatic accounts of wide changes in the IQs of individual children which psychologists have to tell. One boy named Danny started kindergarten when he was five, but seemed so immature that he was given the Stanford-Binet. He got an IQ of 82, and his parents were told he would have to drop out and start kindergarten again a year later. Entering another school district in the next year, he was given the Stanford-Binet again and scored 98, about normal. But in school his teachers found him absent-minded, awkward and worried, and his mother was called in. She then told Danny's whole story. Her husband had gotten encephalitis while Danny had still been a baby and, in order for her to work, they had moved in with the grandparents. But the grandfather had not been able to stand the child's noise and had been so violent in telling him to keep quiet that little Danny had at times become almost petrified with fear. The young family had finally left the grandparents' home when Danny was dropped from kindergarten. Over the years Danny continued to improve in schoolwork, sociability and intelligence, with the help of treatment by a psychiatrist for his anxieties. At eight and a half his IQ had risen to 111, at twelve to 138.

A little girl, the child of immigrant parents, had IQs as high as 140 or more when tested around the age of three. Her IQ dropped drastically, however, through the divorce of her mismatched parents when she was seven, and reached a low of 87 when she was nine and her mother remarried. But her IQ climbed back up through the 90s as she matured to eighteen.

Though your own child's IQ might vary as much as in these examples, it would not be likely to—especially if your family life has been reasonably happy and stable. It could be perfectly natural for your child's mental capacities to differ from yours. Accordingly, certain courses of action based on your child's IQ or mental ability test scores after he is eight or ten would be reasonable ones for you to take. This is mainly what your child's IQ means for his future.

If your child has a high IQ, one above about 120 or more, you may be fairly certain that you have a youngster of unusual mental endowment on your hands. If the child is a boy, encourage and stimulate his ambition for a career that will use these fairly rare talents. This may be hard for you to do, for it may mean cutting him off, very largely, from your own way of life. In the case of a girl, you should do the same thing. She can have a career if she chooses, and can get an education to befit both her own talents and those of a husband of above-average intelligence and education.

Rather brilliant prospects lie ahead of children with very high IQs, if they can be realized. Lewis Terman was interested in genius, as we saw before, and followed a group of 800 boys with IQs of 140 or more through adulthood. By the age of forty, the 800 had written 67 books, more than 1,400 scientific and professional articles and more than 200 short stories and plays. Among them they also held over 150 patents for inventions. All together, they earned from ten to thirty times as many distinctions and honors as could be expected for 800 men picked at random from the general population. At the same time, however, some individuals among these men of 140-plus IQ had flunked out of college or had led undistinguished lives.

If your child has a low IQ, perhaps one below 80 or 85, you cannot be at all sure it is conclusive in and of itself. Children can make low scores on IQ tests for many reasons—among them, poor reading ability, a bilingual home, a special or barren cultural background, minor defects in hearing or eyesight, emotional conflict, indifference to tests or underlying insecurity. If the low IQ concerned you, you could have a psychologist give the child an individual IQ test in order to see if something that might be corrected is hindering the child's development. By no means should you feel resentful of the child, even if investigation shows nothing apparently troubling him. The low-IQ child needs to be cherished and helped; rejection by you can only add to a natural handicap. But with affection and respect, as well as completion of high school and thoughtfully planned special training for work, the child with a somewhat low IQ can lead as happy and self-confident a life as any genius—and perhaps even a happier one.

You are most likely, though, to find that your child's IQ lies somewhere in the broad middle range between, say, 85 and 115. What difference within this range may mean for his guidance, especially as the child moves into high school, will be looked into later. But do not let an IQ in the middle range bother you one way or the other. Instead, be thankful that you are the parent of a normal yet wonderful and deeply individual human being.

What Your Child's IQ Score Means Right Now

Behind your child's IQ score—indeed, behind any score your child earns on a standardized test—stands a long and precise definition of what it means now. In any one of these definitions you will find only probabilities. There are no certainties in testing. This should not disturb you, and may even reassure you. Some of the medical tests used in diagnoses on which we might stake our lives also establish only probabilities. Many other important things in our lives are also based only on probabilities—safety while out in our cars, life insurance and weather forecasts, for example.

Three key terms are used in defining the probabilities concerning any test score for your child: the test's *reliability*, its *validity* and—odd as it may sound—its *standard error of measurement*. These features can all be precisely measured for any tests. For your child's test scores to have highly probable meanings, the tests that he takes must have high reliability, high validity and low error of measurement.

These terms mean very much what they seem to. The reliability of a test means how consistently it measures. The validity of a test means how valid or effective it is for the purpose at hand. The error of measurement of a test means how accurately it measures—that is, within what limits of accuracy.

The ways of determining these essential features of tests are basically simple, although the complete mathematics for calculating them can be complex. To see how reliable a test would be for your child, the test-makers would proceed as follows: First, they would get a representative group of children who were as similar as possible to your child and other children with whom the test is to be used. This is important because a test can work consistently only with the children for whom it has been designed; second-graders, for example, would not earn consistent scores on a series of sixth-grade reading tests. Then, the test-makers would have the children take equivalent forms of the test twice—actually or in effect. These forms would be either two separate versions of the test that were equivalent in all respects except the detailed content of the questions, or two equivalent halves into which the one test would have been split. Reliability is simply the extent to which the scores made by the children in the two testings would agree. It is given in the form of a numerical "coefficient," as we shall see. A high reliability coefficient indicates that a test would work consistently for your child rather than yield undependably varying scores.

To see how valid a test would be for predicting or expecting what your child can do, test experts would take the scores of representative groups of children on the test and compare them with various criteria. For IQ or mental ability tests, these criteria are very often the average of marks in all courses earned by children in school—in some cases, years after having taken the tests. For achievement tests, the criteria would be the average of their marks in reading, arithmetic, science and so on.

Error of measurement is estimated by a calculation based on probability theory. The calculation converts the test's reliability, plus the extent to which scores earned on it spread out from the average, into the probable accuracy of the score for your child.

Suppose that we put these figures together for, say, an IQ score your child would actually earn in seventh or eighth grade—let's say, 110 IQ. How accurate can you take this to be, according to the reliability of the test and its standard of measurement? A good group IQ test of the kind your child will very likely take in school would typically have a reliability of about .85 and a score spread described as a "standard deviation" of 15 points, which means, roughly, that two-thirds of the children for whom the test is designed would earn scores within

15 points above and 15 points below the average score of 100. With such a reliability and score spread (or standard deviation), the standard error of measurement of your child's score would be some 5.7 points. On any test the odds are about 2 to 1 that your child's theoretical "true" score on the test lies within one standard error of his obtained score. Since he obtained a score of 110 IQ in this case, the odds are 2 to 1 that his "true" IQ score on the test lies somewhere between a high of 115.7 and a low of 104.3. Similarly, the odds are 19 to 1 that his actual IQ score lies within 11.4 points (or two standard errors) either way from his 110 IQ obtained score. This would make it reasonably sure (19 times out of 20) that his true IQ as measured by the test lies between a high of 121.4 and a low of 98.6. This leads to a vital, general conclusion:

Your child's IQ score is not a precise point at all. It is a broad, blurred-edge band 10 to 20 or more points wide, because IQ tests cannot measure any more accurately than that.

You should note that allowing for even a 20-point band would not insure entire accuracy. An accuracy of 19 times out of 20 (corresponding to a probability band some 20 points wide) still means that, on the average, the IQ score obtained by one child out of twenty taking the test will lie outside a 20-point band around his true IQ score.

If a friend brags that his son, then, has an IQ of 116, you should think—or say, as you choose—"It is not 116 IQ, but somewhere between 106 and 126, at perhaps 20-to-1 odds, and possibly higher or lower still in fact."

The reliability and standard error of a test that underlie such probabilities are not established in the abstract. They are established only through the experiment of giving the test to one or more representative groups of children and seeing what they turn out to be. Whether the same values of reliability and standard error can justly be applied to the test scores made by your child when he takes the test depends on how similar he and his classmates are to the children with whom its reliability and standard error were determined in experiment. For example, if certain values of reliability and standard error for a test were obtained only for children living on farms in the South, these values would probably not apply to your child and his schoolmates if they were all children living in middle-class, big-city homes in the North.

For the IQ tests most widely used in the schools, reliabilities, standard errors and other features have usually been established with children comparable to yours. However, someone in your child's school should and probably would look at the test's technical data to make sure before deciding to give the test.

How valid your child's IQ score of 110 would be also cannot be answered in the abstract. You have to ask as well: How valid for what? And in exactly what situation?

You can base some very broad and tentative long-range expectations on an IQ of 110 obtained on the most widely used tests, and so would a psychologist, a counselor or a teacher who had had long experience observing children of various IQ levels and how they may change. However, this would not represent the score's validity, strictly speaking. To have any fairly dependable meaning, the validity of IQ scores must be established in specific validity studies—in your child's own school or school system, for example.

For purposes of illustration, suppose that your child were in one of four small high schools in Queen Anne's County in Maryland. Suppose, too, that a validity study had recently been made for Lorge-Thorndike IQs and the average of course marks of the children two years after taking the test. Such a validity study is reported in the technical manual for the Lorge-Thorndike tests.

If your child were in the ninth grade in one of these schools, his verbal Lorge-Thorndike IQ would have a validity of .59 for predicting the average of his course marks in the eleventh grade. The ".59" number for validity is a "correlation coefficient"—a number indicating the degree of relation between the IQ and the marks average two years later. But what does such a validity of .59 mean for your child?

Very roughly, the .59 validity coefficient means something like this: You should be careful to note that it does not mean simple percentage—that is, it does not mean that the IQ and the marks average two years later agree in 59 per cent of the cases. The degree of agreement is quite different. It's like this: Suppose that you took all the school's eleventh graders and divided them into four groups as follows, according to their measured verbal IQs of two years before and their marks averages now:

Group 1—Children who ranked in the top half among all eleventh graders on the basis of IQs and also on the basis of marks averages;

Group 2—Children who ranked in the top half by IQs, but in the bottom half by marks averages;

Group 3—Children who ranked in the bottom half by IQs, but in the top half by marks averages;

Group 4—Children who ranked in the bottom half by IQs and the bottom half by marks averages.

If there is a validity of .59 between the IQs and the marks averages, you would find just about the following proportions of children in each group:

Group 1—35 per cent;
Group 2—15 per cent;
Group 3—15 per cent;
Group 4—35 per cent;
   Total   100 per cent.

Now, Groups 1 and 2 consist of the children who rank in the top half by IQs; these are the children whom you might expect or predict to rank in the top half by marks averages two years later. Suppose that the 110 IQ that we assumed for your child put him among these children who rank in the top half by IQ, as it probably would. If we predicted that your child would also rank in the top half by marks averages two years later, what are the chances that we would be right? According to the above percentages (based on the .59 validity), your child would be more than twice as likely (35 per cent as against 15 per cent) to earn the top-half standing in marks which we predicted on the basis of his IQ. For every fifty children who also had top-half IQs, our predictions of top-half standing by marks averages two years later would be right for thirty-five of the children and wrong for fifteen of the children, over the long haul. In addition, although this way of explaining a validity of .59 does not show it, if your child did fall into the bottom half by marks in eleventh grade, it is likely that his standing would be near rather than far from the mid-level by marks.

As you can also see from the percentages, we would be right in about the same proportions of cases if we predicted bottom-half standing by marks averages on the basis of bottom-half standing by IQs.

Validities of different amounts would work as follows: Had the validity in this situation been .90, your child would have been more than six times as likely to attain top-half standing by marks in eleventh grade. But had the validity been only .20, your child would have been less than one-and-a-half times as likely to attain top-half standing by marks in eleventh grade.

It is not vitally important for you to remember exactly this explanation of validity. It is important, rather, for you to understand that validities can be established with a rather high degree of precision, but that the predicted outcome for your child will have only a certain degree of probability—and perhaps quite a low probability. IQ tests are indicators, and among the most precise and impartial ones that we have. But their results must be judged in the light of everything else that you and your child's advisors know about him.

Not All IQs for Your Child Would Mean the Same Thing

Your child's advisors, especially, should also regard his IQ or general mental ability test results in the light of what is known about the specific tests on which he earns his scores. Most often, your child would score at about the same broad level on an IQ or general mental ability test regardless of the test which he takes—that is, he would score consistently at the high levels, the middle levels or the low levels on all tests of this kind. However, his scores or standings on such tests could differ somewhat only because of differences in the tests themselves and in the ways in which data showing what the test scores mean has been obtained. In an extreme example, a *Test Service Bulletin* of Harcourt, Brace & World points out, different standard deviations of IQ tests alone could result in your child getting an IQ of 130 on one test and of 178 on another. A result like this could occur because tests have different kinds of questions and are standardized on different national samples of children.

Your child's IQ score on a test says, basically, where he stands compared with the particular sample of children of whom the test was standardized. If your child actually should get an IQ of 130 on one test and an IQ of 178 on another only because of differences in their standard deviations, it would mean that he stands among children scoring in the top 0.2 per cent on each of the tests; that is, it would rank him at the same very high range on both of the tests.

But whether or not your child ranks in that range nationally among all children with whom he is being compared would depend on how nationally representative the standardizing sample of each test is. From the difference in standard deviations of the two tests for their standardizing samples, you would know one thing. You would know that the standard deviation of the test on which he got 130 IQ is 10, and the standard deviation of the test on which he got 178 IQ is 26. This would mean that about two-thirds of all children on whom the first test was standardized got scores within 10 points of 100 IQ—that is, between 90 IQ and 110 IQ. It would also mean that about two-thirds of all children on whom the second test had been standardized got scores within 26 points of 100 IQ—that is, between 74 IQ and 126 IQ. You could not tell from this difference (which is a difference in the extent to which the two tests had spread out the scores of children in their standardizing groups) whether it was due to differences in the kinds of test questions or differences in the standardizing groups. It could be either. To tell which, someone in your child's school system who is trained in testing would have to examine the tests, the publishers' descriptions of the standardizing groups and studies made with the tests.

It would be most unusual, however, for your child's school to give him tests on which his IQ scores could vary from 130 to 178 only because of technical differences. The generally accepted IQ scale is that of the Stanford-Binet, as indicated in what was said before about the general significance of IQ levels. The Stanford-Binet scale has an average or mean of 100 IQ and a standard deviation of about 16. Most of the group tests widely used today have been made so that they also have an average of 100 IQ and a standard deviation of around 16. As a result, your child's IQ scores on different IQ tests would usually show rather small variations for only technical reasons.

Roger T. Lennon, head of the test department of Harcourt, Brace & World, made a study several years ago to see what these variations might be for Harcourt, Brace & World tests, which included the Otis Quick-Scoring and the Pintner Verbal—two of America's giant IQ series, as we saw. For carefully matched groups of students in the four high school grades, he found, Otis IQs and Pintner IQs around 100 are practically equivalent. But Otis IQs become about 4 points lower than equivalent Pintner IQs through the 130s, and about 10 points higher than Pintner IQs through the 70s and 60s. These results are like those we would expect from the standard deviations of the two tests for nationally representative groups—about 16½ for the Pintner and 13 for the Otis. How Dr. Lennon has proposed to end such small but still possibly misleading variations with an "anchor test" will be explained in a later chapter.

In the meantime, would errors like 4 IQ points in the 130s or 10 IQ points in the 60s and 70s lead to different decisions being made about your child in practical situations? Absolutely not—not if the person making the decisions was aware of standard errors and other limitations of IQ scores we have reviewed, as he should be.

"Aptitude" Scores Reveal Factors in Your Child's Mental Ability

While we are looking at IQ tests and their technical features, we should glance at the elegant science of factor analysis and how it has led to changes in the kinds of mental ability tests taken by your child. The decimal numbers that state a test's reliability and validity—correlation coefficients like .90 and .59—have also been used to investigate different parts of IQ and other tests themselves. Correlations can indicate the extent to which various parts of tests are related to each other—"intercorrelated," as it is called—and, hence, to what extent the test parts measure essentially the same kind of ability. Test parts which yield rather small intercorrelations therefore measure different aspects or "factors" of mental ability.

Single-score IQ tests are now considered to measure many of these factors together. But for some kinds of newer tests these factors of ability, or clusters of them, are measured separately and called "aptitudes." This is very approximately the idea on which such tests as the Scholastic Aptitude Test (measuring developed "verbal" and "mathematical" aptitudes separately) and the Differential Aptitude Tests (measuring developed aptitudes of eight kinds separately) are based. As we shall see in a later chapter, factor analysis stands at the confused forefront of attempts to understand intelligence or mental abilities more profoundly. Factor analysis has indicated that intelligence or mental ability is general to some substantial degree, but also that special mental abilities (like memory for numbers or reasoning about abstract figures) can vary markedly between individuals of about the same general brightness.

You Could Find Out What Your Child's IQ Score Is

After the fad of careless IQ testing in the 1920s, most schools refused to let parents know their children's IQs. Too often parents wrongly took an IQ score as the final, gospel truth about their children.

Many schools have since changed their views, however, and now give IQ scores to parents who request them. These schools feel it very important at the same time to have a qualified person explain what the IQ scores do and do not mean. All schools in the states of New York and New Jersey, for example, tell and explain IQ scores to parents who request them, as a matter of state-wide policy.

In a special survey made for this book, all states were asked what their policies or prevailing practices are on having the schools give IQ scores to parents on request. The survey also asked whether or not you could learn your child's scores on achievement tests from his school. A full, state-by-state report on the survey—the first survey of its kind to be made—appears in the appendix of this book.

From the appendix, then, you can tell if you might be able to learn your child's IQ and other test scores from his school. You are urged to obtain, understand and keep records of these scores for your child if they are available to you, for the reasons given in the appendix. Forms on which to record the scores and vital notes about them are included in the appendix.

As you will see, your child's school might in some cases give you an approximate idea of his standing on IQ tests instead of his actual scores, using such terms as "very superior," "superior," "above average," "about normal or average" and "low average." Were your child's standing far below average—so far that keeping up with school work was very difficult for him—the school would go into the question carefully and thoroughly with you if it had sufficient time and staff to do so.

On the other hand, many schools would give you the actual scores with a careful explanation. As you can realize from this chapter, though, the actual numbers would not tell you any more about your child's brightness than words like "superior" or "just about normal" would.

Tests of scholastic aptitude or ability often measure much the same things as IQ tests, as we have seen. Your child's overall standing on such aptitude tests as the ETS SCAT series, the College Board's

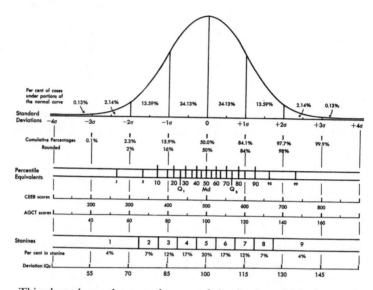

This chart shows the normal curve of distribution which the standardized test scores of large groups of people usually follow when graphed, and the relation of the curve to various widely used scales for reporting test scores: percentile ranks; stanines (a system dividing a score scale into nine parts); the "AGCT" scale (of the Army General Classification Test taken by millions of servicemen in World War II); the "CEEB" scale used with the "College Boards" (the widely taken college admissions tests of the College Entrance Examination Board); and a "deviation IQ" scale frequently used for intelligence tests. From this chart, you can see where any particular IQ score, percentile rank or College Board score for your child places him along the normal curve among persons on whom the test he took was standardized. However, you *cannot* use the chart to find, say, the IQ score that would be equivalent to a given College Board score for your child. You cannot because tests are often standardized on groups of people who differ considerably in levels of ability. For example, the College Board estimates that a verbal score at the 500 mid-point of the Scholastic Aptitude Test score scale would rank a high school senior at about the 85th percentile (among the top 15 per cent of all U.S. high school seniors according to the test). In consequence, a SAT verbal score of 500 is more likely to represent the level of a verbal IQ score at about the 85th percentile for high school seniors—which would be about 115 IQ to 120 IQ. However, equivalent levels like these may also be wrong because even apparently similar tests often measure different kinds of abilities. (Adapted from the *Test Service Bulletin* No. 48 of The Psychological Corporation.)

SAT or PSAT and the verbal and numerical parts of the Differential Aptitude Tests of Psych Corp, for example, would therefore usually correspond to the standing he would have on an IQ test. Where he stands on these tests, that is, would often be about where he would stand on IQ tests—very superior, superior, above average, about normal and the like. However, some IQ tests depend rather heavily on reading ability, and this might cause the standings to differ on occasion. (Other IQ or aptitude tests, though, include non-verbal or non-language parts intended to give some indication of the true mental abilities of children who are backward in reading but not culturally deprived.) Also, as later explained, standings might differ because IQ or aptitude tests are standardized on groups of differing levels of ability; in particular, the College Board's aptitude tests are standardized on young people of unusually high ability, and average standings on these tests are quite a bit higher than the 100 IQ average score on intelligence tests.

You could still find out your child's IQ if his school would not discuss it in any way by having him tested by a psychologist in private practice—usually with the Stanford-Binet or the Wechsler. Psychologists licensed by states to give these individual IQ tests are listed under "Psychologists" in the classified telephone books of most cities; a common fee for giving and reporting on the test is $25.

Tests can tell you very useful and important answers to the question of "How bright is your child?" But it is a test of your own intelligence, and more, to take these answers with the many grains of salt they require.

Chapter 3

How Well
Is Your Child
Learning?

Your child's main business in life now is learning, and it will continue to be for many years. For ten or twelve or sixteen years, or more, your boy or girl will spend the largest part of his time working to learn. We saw how important brightness can be to a child's whole life in the last chapter. But brightness matters so much because bright people can usually learn fast and well. And people who know a great deal and know how to get valuable things done can be paid very well today. Of course, bright children cannot learn if they do not have a chance to, or if some personal or social difficulty gets in their way.

Your child would not be given IQ or other mental ability tests in school, along with millions of other children, to see how bright he is merely as a matter of general interest. Your child would be given an IQ test to see how well he may be able to learn. His intelligence or scholastic ability would be only his capacity. What he actually does learn would be equally if not more important.

Drawbacks to Tests Made and Marked by Your Child's Teachers

What are the various ways in which the school could tell how well your child is getting along in his main business of learning? The time-honored, basic way, of course, is by the experienced judgment of teachers. Because teachers rarely trust their personal impressions alone, they make and mark examinations of their own. Most often, their major examinations consist of broad questions like, "Discuss the causes of the Civil War," or, "How did Walt Whitman's poems reflect the political and social movements of his time?"

Such "essay" examinations have several important drawbacks as tests of your child's knowledge. Perhaps the most serious is that marks on them can vary widely. As long ago as 1912 two investigators named Starch and Elliott stirred up much concern in the schools by showing that there was an "amazing" lack of agreement in the marks teachers gave the same essay exam papers in a variety of high school subjects. In recent years Ernest W. Tiegs gave a current example of such variation. In one experiment, he reported, a teacher re-marked the exam papers of ten children two months after the first marking. Two of the three children who had gotten failing marks on the first marking earned passing marks on the second marking; one shifted from a mark of 60 to a mark of 80! Moreover, the paper marked a top 99 on the first marking dropped to 90 on the second, while another paper jumped up from 90 to the top of 95 on the second marking. And a comfortably above-average 85 paper from the first marking dropped to a failing 70 on the second marking. In not one of the ten cases did a paper get the same mark both times.

Two other prime drawbacks of such conventional essay tests for your child are these: First, they can pose only a few questions and, hence, leave much of the range of his knowledge in a subject unexplored. Second, it is almost impossible to use them to compare his progress with children outside his school or even outside his class.

For reasons like these, schools give standardized achievement tests on a very wide scale. Thanks to their very extensive use by American schools, in fact, they are the world's most widely given type of standardized test.

Swathed in Controversy Despite Wide Acceptance

As you might imagine from their wide acceptance, achievement tests arouse less controversy than any other type. But the calm that surrounds them is merely relative. Some critics—particularly those who have taken least trouble to find out about them—charge that they test only for superficial facts and rote memory. Some school superintendents claim that they freeze the curriculum and stifle attempts to introduce new courses. Some teachers and professors feel that achievement tests are well on their way toward making the ability to write as obsolete as the goosequill. Other teachers fear that principals use the tests as the basis for firing them if their pupils do not show enough progress according to the tests after a year's work. One eminent authority states that a good IQ or mental ability test will generally give you as much information about pupils as an achievement test, so that achievement tests are virtually unnecessary. Another unimpeachable authority states that good achievement tests give you not only essentially the same information about pupils as mental ability tests, but other useful results as well, so that mental ability tests are virtually unnecessary.

Still, at least in part on the basis of your child's performance on achievement tests, he might be put into classes for high-ability or low-ability pupils if your school groups children by ability. From these tests your child's teachers would also learn in what subject areas your child appears to be strongest and weakest, and whether he stands below or above his grade level in mastering each basic subject. Such findings cannot help but influence the marks your child's teachers put down for him on his report cards and his permanent school record. These findings also irresistibly bear on your child's prospects for college.

Knowing about the achievement tests your child would take, then, is important. Moreover, as the controversies swirling around them suggest, you have to pick your way carefully in finding out about them to keep from falling into confusion.

How Achievement Tests Can Protect Your Child From Well-meant Nonsense

Blows in your child's behalf were struck long ago by the men who created our earliest achievement tests with elements of standardization. John M. Rice made the first foray with uniform tests of school learning that were given on a large scale (to some 33,000 boys and girls) and analyzed with statistics to see what the test scores meant. Rice's inquiry of 1895 and 1896 looked into the humble but then bedeviled subject of spelling. Interminable drill was then the regular method for teaching it, and the "traditional standard in spelling is perfection," Rice noted.

Rice found, essentially, that the average achievement of pupils in spelling depended almost entirely on their age or grade level—regardless of how much excessive time was spent on it per day, whether the children were those "of cultured parents" or of "the foreign laboring element," or whether the teaching followed the "most mechanical" or "most progressive" of teaching methods.

A determined investigator, Rice got inconsistent results from the testing of the first 16,000 children "due to the peculiar manner in which the examinations had been conducted" in some classrooms. He accordingly gave the second tests to more than 13,000 under his personal direction in school systems across the country. At the end he concluded:

> Do not these results indicate that, in learning to spell, maturity is the leading factor, while method plays only a subordinate part? And, as the superiority of the old-fashioned spelling grind cannot be demonstrated, is it not our duty to save the child from this grind? Moreover, as the results prove that, beyond a certain minimum, the compensation for time devoted to spelling is scarcely, if at all, appreciable, have we not here discovered an element of waste?

Rice was especially bitter about expecting perfection in spelling. He took it as a natural fact that "in many cases the spelling faculty is weak," and gently derided:

> as some of our most scholarly people are deficient in spelling, and as, in this subject, some of the brightest pupils cannot keep pace with the dullest, our high-pitched sensibilities on the spelling question may be regarded as one of the mysteries of civilization.

His sharp eye also discerned a need for more objective means of judging pupils. He recounts that, once,

> on leaving a classroom in which I had heard a few recitations, I complimented the teacher on the intelligence of her pupils. She replied: "You must not give me credit for that. These pupils are Russians; and one can do anything with Russians." It so happened that on the next day, I visited a classroom, in which the children were exceptionally dull. On this occasion the teacher remarked: "You must not blame me for their stupidity. My pupils are Russians; and one cannot do anything with Russians."

You have largely this pioneer in achievement testing to thank if your own child is taught spelling in a realistic way today. Before Rice, no one knew how to be realistic about the teaching of spelling, and the children were subjected to much misery as well as futile effort in the name of unfounded educational nonsense.

The kind of schooling your child gets today was bettered in many ways by the work of another testing pioneer, Edward L. Thorndike, whose ideas about abstract, concrete and social intelligence were referred to in the last chapter. Edward Thorndike, who long served on the faculty of Teachers College, Columbia University, probably had more influence on the introduction of tests of all kinds in American schools than any other one man.

Edward Thorndike improved your child's education as a prolific experimenter and teacher of other experimenters. Notably, experiments he performed with Robert S. Woodworth in 1901 largely refuted the idea then popular that study of such hard and only remotely practical subjects as Latin and math were good as "mental discipline"—that they somehow developed powers of precision, judgment and reasoning in the mind generally. Skills developed in studying subjects like Latin and math, the experiments indicated, did not "transfer" to other areas. The reason they seemed to develop "good thinkers," Thorndike observed, is because they were taken by people who would be good thinkers anyway. He made related experiments with several thousand high school students in 1924 and concluded: "after positive correlation of gain with initial ability is allowed for, the balance in favor of any study is certainly not large. Disciplinary values may be real and deserve weight in the curriculum, but the weights should be reasonable."

In addition, Thorndike wrote the country's first textbook on educational measurement, *An Introduction to the Theory of Mental and Social Measurement,* which appeared in 1904. He and his students also produced a wide variety of early standardized achievement tests. Among those published by 1915 were tests in handwriting, composition, "arithmetic reasoning," computation and spelling. Still more important, Thorndike and his students led in popularizing the whole idea of conducting experiments in schools and collecting data rather than merely impressions about the results. Educational research bureaus in large school systems opened by the dozens in the years after World War I. Interest in achievement testing had spread sufficiently by 1923 to make possible the successful introduction that year of the first comprehensive achievement test series, the Stanford, as we saw earlier.

Today, achievement tests stand between your child and educational methods which might waste his time and energies. They and the systematic evaluation techniques that have grown out of them now serve as one of the major touchstones for testing educational experiments, as well as long-established practices in schooling.

The Enormous Differences Between Schools—And Between Colleges

Achievement tests first showed beyond dispute that how far your child has progressed in his education—which is the main business of his young life at the moment—might vary enormously according to what schools he went to. His grade level in particular might reflect little of what he or she actually knows.

By how much your child's progress might vary in different schools regardless of his grade level was demonstrated by another influential pioneer in achievement testing, Ben D. Wood. In the late 1920s he and William S. Learned began an inquiry popularly called the Pennsylvania Study. In it they constructed achievement tests to see what high school and college students in Pennsylvania really knew.

What Wood and Learned found seems amazing, even today. In one small part of the study, they gave a 1,222-question, four-hour test of "general culture" to several thousand students throughout the state, who included seniors in high school and sophomores and seniors in college. They assumed at the start that, if calling a student a college sophomore had any generally accepted meaning, college seniors would surely score above the range of college sophomore levels on the test, and high school seniors would surely score below those levels. But what they found would be "wholly mystifying," they declared, "to anyone who thinks that school status, as defined by time spent and courses passed in school or college, has any necessary relation to a definite body of ideas, understood and available as a result of 'education.' "

Almost *10 per cent* of the *college seniors* scored *lower* on the test than the average *high school senior,* they found. And *10 per cent* of the *high school seniors* scored *higher* than the average *college senior!* Wood and Learned concluded that college sophomores "range, as to their command of knowledge appropriate to their status, from a general level of inferior high-school achievement to one attained only by the best ten per cent of senior[-year] college students—indeed, above the average of faculty groups."

Much of this enormous variation, though not all, was due to differences between high schools and between colleges. For example, the average scores of sophomores at thirty-five liberal arts colleges in the study ranged from a low of 185 for one college to a high of 430 for another college. This high average of 430 for sophomores at one college was well above the average score of 314 for seniors at all colleges.

School-to-school differences in learning are as great today as they were then. These differences are so large that, in some cases, there may be no overlap in educational accomplishment between the young people on the same grade level in two schools. For example, the sixth-grade child in one school who knows less than any other sixth-grader in that school may still know more than the top sixth-grader in another school. A College Board publication available to school counselors shows several cases of four-year colleges in which the top few students in one college, according to SAT scores and, presumably, learning, would be on a par with only the bottom few students in another college.

Even children right in the same classroom usually vary widely in educational accomplishment. In a fifth-grade class, for instance, teachers often find pupils ranging in, say, reading ability from the typical third-grade level for the nation to the eighth-grade level. Accomplishment frequently ranges over three or four grade levels even in classes grouped by ability. Moreover, standardized tests have repeatedly shown that children in a class who are far ahead of the typical grade level in one subject, like reading, may be behind grade level in another subject like arithmetic.

As everyone knows, tests made by teachers for classroom use reveal the differences between pupils in an individual class in an approximate way. Though often only spotty in examining pupils for what has been covered in a subject, and marked with quite subjective judgment, teacher-made tests taken by your child fit the course work closely. But marks on these regular classroom tests cannot indicate where your child stands compared with children of the same age or grade level in other schools. Standardized achievement tests do indicate where your child stands with respect to children in other classes and schools, though they probably do not fit your child's courses perfectly. They can also indicate on the average where whole classes, schools and school systems stand with respect to each other and with representative national achievement.

In part to provide tests which could make such cross-country appraisals, the Cooperative Test Service was begun in the late 1920s by the American Council on Education, with Ben Wood as its director. It had produced some sixty different achievement tests for use on the high school and college freshman and sophomore levels by the time of its merger into the new Educational Testing Service formed in 1948. These tests were ones in individual subjects, for the most part. They continue today as the Cooperative Tests of ETS, which are among America's giant series described in the first chapter. Their introduction in the early 1930s was accompanied by the launching of two other giant comprehensive achievement series of today—the Metropolitan in 1931, and the California in 1933.

Do Tests Force a Lock-step Curriculum on Your Child?

Your child's education might be arbitrarily fixed if these standardized achievement tests determined in detail what must be taught in his school. However, just the reverse is true—what is taught in schools determines the content of the tests. Authors of achievement tests today usually pore over textbooks and course outlines from all parts of the country and write questions about the things that schools most often try to teach. Some authors write tests to fit what is taught in only schools or courses of certain kinds. Schools are free to select whatever tests they may want to evaluate your child's work. From among many different kinds of achievement tests now available, a school chooses the series or combination that best fits its program, rather than alters its program to fit the tests.

Only in unusual circumstances may a school feel compelled to "teach to" certain achievement tests of specific subject-matter knowledge. The New York State Regents exams, for example, are deliberately intended to insure that certain things are taught to students receiving the special Regents diploma. But the Regents program permits any school to obtain approval for its own examination if it gives a special course that the regular Regents exam in the subject would not fit. Few schools ever submit such local exams of their own, however.

Dictation of course content by tests was very much the case some years ago in the Iowa high schools because of a test series which was voluntarily but all too enthusiastically "taught to." These tests were subject examinations with titles like Third-Year Latin, Algebra and Botany. They had been introduced by the State University of Iowa in Iowa City as part of an academic contest. The purpose of the contest was to bring recognition to bright young scholars, letting them share in a limelight that had long been occupied by football and track stars and music contest winners. The academic contest proved an enormous success, but schools by the hundreds coached students for the tests all year in order to have a "Latin winner" or a "math winner" in Iowa City at the year's end. What the tests covered thus became the subject matter that the Iowa high schools covered—to a very unhealthy extent, it was felt by Professor E. F. Lindquist at the university.

In the mid-1930s, Lindquist began to plan a new kind of test for the program. When he first broached the idea, however, he met stiff resistance from adherents of the extremely popular contest. Breaking away from the contest's emphasis on subject matter proved "really traumatic" for his fellow Iowans, he says. Lindquist's new tests were not to follow subject-matter lines, but to reflect the "real purpose of education," he says; "not to cram more information into the student, but to measure the important outcomes of education—to improve his abilities to think about problems he would encounter beyond the school," to "make a better problem-solver out of him" as their "main objective." His new tests were accordingly organized around "generalized intellectual skills and abilities," and asked the student to reason about social problems, scientific problems and specimens of writing, to appreciate and understand literature, and to use quantitative ability to solve problems of kinds the student would meet "both in school and beyond."

In "one of the most dramatic changes ever made in an educational system," Lindquist recounts, the old system was scrapped early in World War II and replaced by the new tests and their whole educational philosophy. The action changed an attitude toward schooling which had been completely "subject-oriented," he says, to one that was "pupil-oriented and guidance-oriented along broad subject-matter lines." The new tests, inaugurated in the fall of 1942, were Lindquist's Iowa Tests of Educational Development—the series that, as we saw, is now the country's most widely used high school achievement series, as well as the one from which both the National Merit Scholarship test and the ACT college entrance test have arisen. The elementary school series that was similarly created according to Lindquist's "educational development" theory of achievement testing at about the same time, the Iowa Tests of Basic Skills, was more readily introduced in Iowa because it did not have to replace as deeply entrenched an institution as the old Iowa academic contest. The ITBS series is also very widely used throughout the country today, as we saw.

Your child could take any one of a wide variety of programs of study and still be fairly examined on the Iowa tests, for they present most of the information with which your child would reason in answering the questions. They would test his general development within broad subject-matter disciplines. Precisely because they are designed to do this, they would not examine him closely on what he has learned in particular courses. Other kinds of achievement tests—those in single subjects—would, but they would be fair for your child only if he had taken a course closely paralleling the test content. Today, the Iowas and the other broad, "survey" type of achievement series—the Metropolitan, Stanford, California and SRA Achievement among them—can be widely used because they work about equally well for students who have taken courses differing rather widely in content. This kind of test hence further frees your child's school to teach what it wants while still using achievement tests.

Beware of Nonsense About Your Child as an "Over-achiever" or "Under-achiever"

On the basis of his test scores, your child might be considered an "over-achiever" or an "under-achiever" by his school, and marked, assigned, taught, berated or coddled and guided accordingly. But dubbing him one or the other might be completely wrong.

These odd labels mean that the "over-achieving" child is doing better than children of his ability usually do, while the "under-achieving" child is not doing as well as others of his ability. "Over-achievers" are thought to be "grinds" who put excessive effort into their work; generally, schools are reluctant to put them into classes more heavily demanding than their present ones for fear of critically overloading them. "Under-achievers" are thought to get lower marks than they could because they do not work nor try hard enough; they are considered loafers or problem youngsters.

Your child would seem to be an "under-achiever" to many experts if a mental ability or IQ test score of his were high and his achievement test scores were low. For example, Leo Kanner, professor emeritus of child psychiatry at Johns Hopkins University, declares:

If the youngster has an IQ of 90 you don't expect him to do above-average work in school. But if he has an IQ of 120 and he does below-average work, then you can probably assume that something is the matter, some cause for what the school people call "under-achievement."

What Dr. Kanner says would be true if the youngster does actually have an IQ of, say, 120. However, any one test score like an IQ is accurate only within certain degrees of probability, as we saw. And when scores on two tests are compared, as in looking at the difference between IQ and achievement test scores, their individual "errors of measurement" are in effect compounded.

Your child, for example, might be given a reading test in sixth grade, and his teacher would look at an IQ score for him from fifth grade to get an idea of what his reading ability should be. Professor Robert L. Thorndike has analyzed a situation like this representing quite favorable conditions for drawing valid conclusions. (He assumes, specifically, that these fifth-grade IQ scores in the school have a correlation of .70 with sixth-grade reading scores, and that about two-thirds of all sixth-graders in the school who take the reading test earn scores within the unusually narrow limits of half a grade level either way of average sixth-grade performance.)

But even under these favorable conditions, Thorndike says that you would "occasionally get discrepancies between predicted and actual reading level of as much as a grade and a half" because of "nothing more than measurement error." In other words, simply within the limits of probable accuracy of tests, your child's teacher could not be sure whether your child's reading level ought to be a grade and a half higher or a grade and a half lower than his fifth-grade IQ suggests. But if the teacher were not aware of this, she would certainly think of your child as an "under-achiever" if his tested reading level came out by chance to be a grade and a half lower than his IQ indicated.

You have every reason to be skeptical, then, if one of your child's teachers says that your child has suddenly become an "over-achiever" or an "under-achiever." Only after repeated testings and marking periods through a span of at least many months would you or the teachers be justified in thinking that your child were working below or beyond his capability, compared with other children.

Don't Take Your Child's "Grade-equivalent" Test Scores Too Seriously

On an achievement test battery, your child would earn a fistful of scores which would at first look quite confusing. They would include his scores on the regular score scale of the test—"standard" or "scaled" scores, as they are called. Score scales for achievement tests are deliberately picked to be different from the customary 0- to 100-per cent marking scale of the classroom for a very important reason: standardized tests have no passing or failing levels. On both Iowa test series, for example, the score scale is 0 to 36. Your child would get a standard score for each test in an achievement battery—a score for arithmetic, reading, language usage and so on—and a total or composite score summing them all up. And for each standard score he would probably get one or more additional indications of where his standard scores rank him. In some cases, he might be given such indications of his rank instead of standard scores because they are easier to understand.

These rankings would show rather clearly where he stands according to his scores in one or more representative groups of children —like those on whom the test was standardized or "normed," or all children in his grade in your state, or all children on his grade level in his school or school system.

In some achievement test series, his rankings might be given as "percentiles"—percentage figures showing where he would stand in a group or groups of children. For instance, a percentile rank of 95 would mean that he ranks ahead of 95 per cent of the children in the reference group; a standing at the 25th percentile would similarly mean that, on what the test measures, he stands ahead of 25 per cent of the reference group.

His ranks in achievement test performance might also be shown in "stanines," a system dividing levels of test performance into nine bands that range from a high of stanine 9 through an average of stanine 5 to a low of stanine 1.

Perhaps most often, where your child ranks in achievement test performance might be reported in a set of "grade-equivalent" scores. A grade-equivalent score of seventh grade, for example, would mean that his score was about the same as the average score made by children in the reference group who were starting seventh grade.

You would be wrong if you took these widely used grade-equivalent scores for your child too seriously—even if they showed flatteringly that, though your child was only in fourth grade, he scored at the sixth-grade level in reading and at the seventh-grade level in arithmetic. However welcome to you, these results would be based on a beguiling fiction. They would by no means always indicate that your child was the equal of sixth-grade readers and seventh-grade arithmetic pupils in his school. The grade-equivalent levels are merely national averages which probably do not fit your child's school. Also, children who score at the same grade-equivalent level may have quite different abilities. If your fourth-grade child did get a sixth-grade score on a reading test, his reading abilities would be quite different from those of a child in the twelfth grade who scored at the sixth-grade level.

Moreover, for some spans of grade levels in some subjects, only a slight amount of ability ahead or behind a national average might shift your child's grade-equivalent scores two or three grades up or back. For example, on the Stanford Achievement Tests, the national average scores for grades 9 through 12 on the language test increase very little for the higher grades. But the Stanford's national average scores on the social studies test rise sharply for grades 9 through 12. As a result, if your child were in the ninth grade and made a social studies score at the eleventh grade level, he would be markedly superior. But if he also made an eleventh-grade language score, he would be only slightly above average in the corresponding abilities.

What seems to annoy experts most about grade equivalents, however, is the smugness they encourage. If a school finds that its fifth-graders average at the seventh-grade level in reading, for example, school officials often feel quite self-satisfied. But, as Robert H. Bauernfeind of the National College of Education points out, national averages on achievement tests represent levels which are "really mediocre" compared to the kind of work which should be done in schools with comfortable finances and pupils who come from fairly well-off homes. The reverse holds true as well. Schools which are poorly financed and overcrowded with children from underprivileged slum families may be doing an excellent job and still not attain national averages on achievement tests.

Dr. Bauernfeind points out as well, in his excellent book on *Building A School Testing Program*, that test publishers standardize their achievement series on different national samples of children. As a result, fifth-grade score levels on one publisher's series may represent sixth-grade levels or fourth-grade levels on the series of another publisher.

You can better judge your child's achievement test performance, many authorities hold, by looking at his standing among children at his grade level nationally. They believe that it would make a lot more sense for you to be told that your fourth-grade child stands ahead of, say, 90 per cent of fourth-graders nationally, than for you to be told instead —and on the basis of the same test performance—that your child scored at a national sixth-grade level. Standings reported in this less misleading way are called "percentiles-in-grade" (or "percentiles-for-grade"). Percentiles-in-grade standings are used in some of the country's giant achievement test series.

Are Tests Blocking Your Child's Writing Ability— And Even His Thinking Ability?

Some critics of testing claim that your child may never learn to write good English prose because of standardized tests. The head of the English department at Groton, for instance, has charged:

> Few teachers, administrators and businessmen who employ the product of schools and colleges would deny that written composition is deteriorating. The wholesale substitution of objective tests for essay examinations in all subjects may well be a major cause of the deterioration; for testing influences teaching to a degree little short of control.

Other critics go further still and charge that standardized tests interfere with the development of mature intellectual powers in your child. Professor Banesh Hoffmann of Queens College, for example, has called for formation of a high committee of inquiry to look into the evils of testing. Doing some of the committee's work in advance, Dr. Hoffmann declares that "it would realize how important it is to train students to organize their own thoughts and to put something of themselves into a project, and how damaging it can be to reward them for merely picking wanted answers at rates up to a hundred an hour." The committee, he further presumes, would "be far less willing than the testers to sell our intellectual heritage for a mess of statistical pottage."

Charges like these against achievement tests, if justified, pose serious questions for your child's education. But are they justified?

It is perfectly true that achievement tests do not teach your child to write. No one has yet tried to devise an achievement test that would, nor is anyone likely to try. Rather, your child would learn to write from his teachers, from practice, from study of elements and forms and from much hard work both on his part and the part of his teachers. If he does not learn to write, it seems more the fault of the school for not trying to teach him to than of standardized achievement tests. Tests do bear on writing, though, in two ways important for your child. First, tests of verbal aptitude or ability can give your child's school some idea of how well he may be able to write. This is simply a matter of evidence; verbal aptitude or IQ scores correlate rather closely with average marks in English composition. Tests can thus show the school how easy or hard it should be for your child to learn to write well, and may thereby keep his teachers either from expecting him to be able to write beyond his capability or from under-rating his capability. Second, there are standardized achievement tests of writing ability which work rather well. In fact, for the purposes of predicting average marks in future English composition courses, they work better than written themes themselves.

The leading test of this kind seems to be one in the College Board achievement series, the English Composition Test or ECT. In a recent experiment, scores on the Board's ECT had correlations in the .70s with marks on themes arrived at in an elaborate special system. By contrast, marks on written themes graded in the customary way showed correlations only in the .60s with the specially developed marks.

But does "wholesale substitution" of standardized tests for essay examinations shut out the incentive and practice in writing your child would otherwise enjoy through essay exams? It might, if wholesale substitution has actually been accomplished. However, standardized tests have not supplanted essay exams as midterms, finals and quizzes used in regular schooling. Teachers still use essay exams about as widely as ever because they can closely reflect just what the teacher has covered. Standardized tests tend to be used in addition to essay exams rather than instead of them. In a number of cases the tests simply don't work well enough to serve as course-end or year-end exams instead of conventional classroom finals. As we have seen, some series measure a pupil's broad progress in a subject area rather than what he has been taught in any one term or year.

Some substitution has occurred. "The special merits of standardized achievements tests have prompted many high schools to use them as end-of-course examinations, sometimes in place of and sometimes in addition to their own teacher-built tests," Roger T. Lennon of Harcourt, Brace & World observes. However, this represents modest rather than wholesale substitution for the country's schools as a whole. The teacher's own examination remains by far the predominant kind of final exam for the country.

Is it true, though, that your child's thinking ability will somehow be dulled by achievement tests? They don't seem to have stunted the mental powers of people who took the tests often as children and are now among our Nobel Prize physicists, leading doctors and jurists, Senators, governors and corporation presidents. Moreover, no one would deny that the best schools in the country include such private ones as St. Paul's, Kent, Groton, Milton, Lawrenceville and Hill. These schools would also certainly maintain that they are now doing everything possible to give a better education than ever before in their histories. Yet these and other outstanding schools—some 900 in all, most of them private, but a few public—take part in one of the most extensive testing programs in the country. This is the program of the Educational Records Bureau, in which a large battery of achievement tests is given each fall and spring.

The Bureau's program, which dates from 1927, includes IQ and other aptitude or mental ability tests as well. One of its main advantages is that it provides statistical norms on the test performance of all pupils in the Bureau's private school members. The Bureau selects or makes achievement tests for its members' college preparatory courses. ERB member schools can thus compare the rather detailed subject-matter achievement of their pupils with what pupils of like IQ or aptitudes are achieving in like schools.

There is simply no evidence to indicate that achievement tests dull the thinking abilities of children. Rather, well-adjusted children who think and learn unusually well seem to score high on achievement tests without exception. For all the hostility toward standardized tests in some quarters, no one has yet pointed out a single case of a balanced child who earned superior marks in school subjects but did very poorly on appropriate achievement tests. Brilliant children are sometimes annoyed at the rigidity of achievement tests. They are also occasionally vexed to find test questions pitched at levels of less profound understanding than the ones on which their own minds can work. But they usually take to the tests with zest as intellectual puzzles, and they almost invariably do well on them.

Their zest is quite appropriate, for achievement tests can be exercises of a high order in thinking ability. They can test for far more than memory of facts learned by rote. Jerome Bruner, a Harvard psychologist, notes in his widely admired book on *The Process of Education* that,

> Whether an examination is of the "objective" type involving multiple choices or of the essay type, it can be devised so as to emphasize an understanding of the broad principles of a subject. Indeed, even when one examines detailed knowledge, it can be done in such a way as to require understanding by the student of the connectedness between specific facts.

Illustrative test questions in the first chapter have already indicated how achievement tests can examine your child's broad understanding of a subject. Two more examples here will show this again, for advanced students. They are drawn from a number of unusually searching test questions which Educational Testing Service recently issued. One was this question in modern European history tried out on college students:

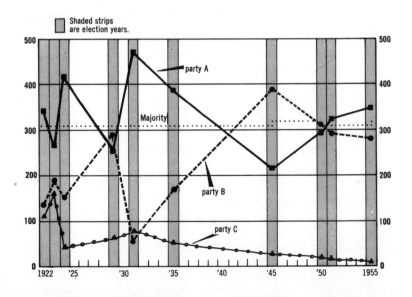

The graph shown in Figure 1 represents the political composition from 1922 to 1955 of which of the following?

(A) German Bundestag
(B) French National Assembly
(C) Italian Chamber of Deputies
(D) British House of Commons

Students could use different ways of working out the answer, ETS points out. One would be to recognize, after having been able to read the graph, that it shows an essentially two-party system. This eliminates the Bundestag because, for one thing, Hitler outlawed all but the Nazi Party in 1933. It eliminates as well the French National Assembly, which had far more than three parties before and after World War II. It also rules out the Italian Chamber, which was superseded by Mussolini's creation of the Chamber of Fasci and Corporations and his suppression of political parties in 1938. More than half of 300 college students with whom the question was tried recognized that the graph shows the composition of the British House of Commons. Party A corresponds to the Conservative Party, which went out of power despite Churchill's leadership right after the war, in 1945. Party B represents the Labor Party, which came to power under Clement Attlee in that year, while Party C depicts the dwindling ranks of the Liberal Party.

Another question, one for students finishing a year of high school physics, presents the diagram shown in Figure 2 and then asks:

Side View

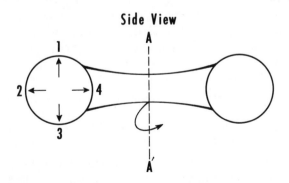

One method of obtaining "artificial gravity" in a space station is to have the station rotating about axis A A′ as it revolves around Earth. The inhabitants of the space station would call which direction "down"?

(A) Direction 1
(B) Direction 2
(C) Direction 3
(D) Direction 4
(E) Any one of the four, depending on the speed of rotation

Solving the problem depends on applying fundamental concepts of mechanics to "a relatively novel situation," the ETS authors comment. The key is to visualize the complex situation and to relate it to something more familiar. Objects free to move in the space station would behave as do particles in a centrifuge and would "fall" to the outer edge. Thus, the "down" direction, the direction in which objects appear to fall, is direction 2, making (B) the right answer. (The two questions are reproduced by permission of Educational Testing Service.)

Will Tests Penalize Your Child If He Takes the "New Math" or "New Science"?

If your child comes home talking of things like "sets" in math or "green" biology, he is taking one of the many new kinds of courses which are bringing revolutionary changes in schooling today. These changes are already far advanced in some subjects. Your child may be one of several millions learning the "SMSG" math program worked out for junior and senior high by the School Mathematics Study Group. He might be one of the million or more taking the "GCMP" modern math published by SRA for kindergarten through sixth grade. Or he might be among many hundreds of thousands taking high school sciences with such inscrutable nicknames as "PSSC" physics, "chemical bond" chemistry, and "blue," "yellow," or "green" biology. Your child may have started learning a foreign language in the elementary grades —and learning to speak it (perhaps with workouts in a "language lab") not just to read it and write it. Changes are stirring in reading, high school English and social studies as well. Almost the entire program of study in the schools is in wholesome ferment.

You might wonder, though, if some injustice would be done your child because the content of new kinds of courses he takes differs from the content reflected in achievement test questions. Several things make it unlikely that your child would be unfairly appraised for this reason. The first would be his school's practice of examining in detail the questions on all achievement tests it gives to make sure that they are good tests of what is generally taught in the school. Second, as we have seen, at least some achievement test series given on the largest scale today tend to demand only general knowledge of basic subjects. These tests thus already fit a variety of courses by testing skills and analytic powers in broad subject areas rather than knowledge in specific courses.

Test publishers and agencies have been doing two more things to keep achievement tests in line with what schools are teaching. Courses of study have evolved in the past; we are in a period of only relatively fast and far-reaching change, rather than a period of sweeping change after years of no change at all. To keep up with course changes in the past, test-makers have periodically revised their tests. Revisions today reflect the much-altered new courses to the extent that they have been adopted in the schools, thus improving the tests for measuring your child's abilities were he taking one of the new courses. Second, new tests in specific course areas like second-year high school math or high-school biology are being made to fit the new content. As we shall see in a later chapter, the building of tests for new courses represents one of the major developments underway in testing today.

Though it may sound strange to you, your child can be fairly examined on a test which includes questions on both traditional and new course content. For several years, for example, the College Board's one-hour physics achievement test was offered in two versions—one for conventional physics and the other for the new, PSSC physics. In 1962, however, the Board made just a single test for all students regardless of which kind of course they have taken. The single test was given experimentally in thirty schools, along with each of the two separate tests. Correlations were then obtained between scores on all three tests and later midterm marks in physics. "All three tests were equally good as predictors of midterm physics grades," it was found. The two separate versions were retired in favor of the new composite physics test. Henry S. Dyer, vice-president in charge of College Board programs at ETS, gives one main reason why specially constructed single tests can serve students taking either new and older programs reasonably well. He says that test-makers can write many achievement questions that "both new and traditional program experts will agree on."

How Achievement Tests Can Be Used to Give Your Child a Better Education

For your child, the real importance of standardized achievement tests is that they can be used to give him a better education than he would otherwise get. Despite what is said against them, achievement tests are one of the prime tools of modern American education. They function to help children and schools on an enormous scale by providing extremely useful bases for comparison that could not be made available in any other way.

Perhaps the most important service these tests might perform for your child would be to show his teachers his "strengths and weaknesses"—the areas in which his work seems to be weak and needs further attention, and those in which his work is strong and may need special tasks to maintain his progress and interest. Your child's strong and weak areas would be indicated by comparisons between his achievement test performance and his age in years and months, his mental ability or IQ and the school grade he is in.

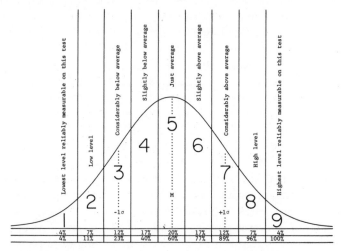

The meaning of stanine scores on standardized tests, both as expressed in words and in relation to the tested abilities of a large group of people whose scores follow a normal curve of distribution. (From *Manual for Interpreting Metropolitan Achievement Tests* [Grades 1–9], © 1962, Harcourt, Brace & World, Inc., New York. Reproduced by permission.)

Revealing critical problem areas for your child would be another important way in which the tests could help your child. For example, a fourth-grade girl, whom we might call Sherry Murphy, was a little younger than her classmates and had the high IQ of 121 on the Pintner-Durost test—in stanine 8, three stanines higher than the average stanine 5 and just one below the high stanine, 9. On the Metropolitan Achievement Tests, Sherry scored in stanine 8 in the tests of word knowledge and word discrimination, in stanine 9 on the reading test, in stanine 7 on the spelling and language usage tests and in stanine 5 on the punctuation-capitalization test and the arithmetic problem-solving test. Because of the errors of measurement in tests which we found out about earlier, only differences of two stanines signify genuine differences in ability. Sherry's cluster of scores in the three highest stanines shows she is doing about equally well in those areas, and also about as well as you would expect from her IQ. She is doing not quite as well in punctuation-capitalization and in arithmetic problem-solving (which involves more reasoning ability than calculation). Why is suggested by her one remaining score: on the arithmetic computation test, she stands only in stanine 2, three below average. Sherry's teacher should take this as a strong indication that the little girl ought to be helped in arithmetic, and that she may be confused about how to carry out such fundamental operations as adding, subtracting and multiplying.

This profile chart shows visually how Sherrell Murphy (a girl whose case is recounted on an accompanying page) scored by stanines on the Metropolitan Achievement Tests. It also shows how her very low score in arithmetic computation suggests the importance of clearing up some special trouble she may be having in arithmetic, in view of her otherwise quite high scores. Sherry's Pintner IQ is also entered on the sheet at lower left. (From *Directions for Completing Individual Profile Chart, Metropolitan Achievement Tests, All Batteries,* © 1960, Harcourt, Brace & World, Inc., New York. Reproduced by permission.)

Similarly, in one average sixth-grade class, it was found that several children scored consistently in the three highest stanines on the Metropolitan even though most pupils scored in the middle three or lower stanines. The teacher of the class should have seriously considered giving these few high-scoring pupils an opportunity to work beyond the general level of the class—as well as giving special help and consideration to the few pupils who scored consistently in only the very low first and second stanines.

1	2	3	4	5	6	7	8	9	10	11	12	13
STA-NINE	TEST 1 Word Knowledge	TEST 2 Reading	TEST 3 Spelling	TEST 4 Language Total (Parts A–C)	TEST 5 Language Study Skills	TEST 6 Arithmetic Computation	TEST 7 Arith. Prob. Solv. & Conc.	TEST 8 Soc. Studies Information	TEST 9 Soc. Studies Study Skills	TEST 10 Science	STA-NINE	Learning Capacity Measure Test used: Pintner Inter.
9	5	22 32		(15) 17	(15) 22	2 22	(14)		(14) 22	(15) 22	20 32	9	(15)
8	12 (15) 32	(15) 29		12	5 29 32	(14)	(15) 20 32	(15) 32		16 29	8	12 (14) 32
7	2 22 24	20 24	2 (15) 32 5 22 11 29	4 (15) 5 22 13 29 (14)	5 24 13 29 (14)	(14) 24	(15) 82 5 16 29	2 27 9 24	3 22 16 17	3 19 27 12	3 (14) 5 24 7 12	7	5 20 24 32 27
6	(14) 29 16 20 3 13 27 8 (4)	2 12 17 9 (4)	8 24 9 14 (4)	2 16 32 4 19 10 21 11 25	16 21 29	1 12 33 3 24 5 25 11 27	3 12 8 16 10 18 11 29	5 8 9 20 27 (4) 29	1 19 2 20 12	4 17 18 22		6	2 21 9 16
5	3 9 18 23 13 19 27 7 17 21	1 9 19 28 4 10 21 7 16 23	3 21 18 23 19 28 20 31	1 20 28 3 23 31 9 27	10 18 11 19 12 20 13 31	9 19 28 13 20 34 17 21 18 26	1 21 28 5 23 33 13 25 19 26	1 2 13	4 13 28 6 23 29 7 24 32 10 26	2 25 6 27 21		5	13 26 17 29 18 19
4	8 25 10 28 11 31	11 18 26	16 6 17 23 10	7 26 8 18	4 8 31	3 27 4 17 34 7 23	4 17 34	11 24 19 25 21 34 23	8 25 9 34	1 25 4 26 11 28 13		4	1 8 31 3 10 4 11
3	1 26 34	25 31 34	26 27	17	26	7 23	7	4 6 8 28	21 31	19 31		3	7 34 23 28
2	(6) 34	(6)	33 34	(6) 25 34	33	(6)	(6) 31	10 26 31	(6) 33	(6)		2	(6) 33
1	(30) 33	(30) 33	(30)	(30)	(6) (30)	(30)	(30)	(30) 33		(30) 33 34		1	25 (30)
Number of Pupils	34	34	34	34	34	34	34	34	34	34		Number of Pupils	34
Median Stanine	5	5	5	5.5	5	5.5	5.5	5	5	5		Median Stanine	5

Above, the graphed stanine scores earned on the Metropolitan Achievement Tests by all the pupils in a sixth-grade class are spread widely throughout the score range, indicating that the class is not one into which the children have been grouped to be homogeneous in ability. The class's teacher can see from the chart that he might consider giving especially challenging work to the high-scoring pupils numbered 14 and 15 on the chart; similarly, he might want to give special help to two low-scoring pupils, indicated by numbers 30 and 33.

Below, the similar stanine score graph for pupils in a second-grade class who also took the Metropolitan Achievements shows the scores clustering more closely together, reflecting the fact that this is a class grouped to be fairly homogeneous in ability. Pupil number 3 has scored generally higher than his classmates, which suggests that he may have been assigned to a class group not as capable as he seems to be. (From *Manual for Interpreting Metropolitan Achievement Tests* [Grades 1–9], © 1962, Harcourt, Brace & World, Inc., New York. Reproduced by permission.)

Sherry's test scores, incidentally, illustrate the utility of having an IQ or general mental ability score in addition to achievement scores alone. Though the IQ score certainly reflects things Sherry has learned rather than just her innate capacity, it reflects comparatively little of what has been taught to her in specific subjects. If you did not have her IQ score and had only her score in arithmetic computation, you would not be able to tell whether this poor showing in arithmetic might be bettered, or if further work would not be likely to bring it up. The IQ or mental ability score provides simply another basis for comparison, besides age and grade level, which you may use to consider what Sherry might be able to do. Doing without IQ or aptitude scores as a basis for comparison, if you have comprehensive achievement scores instead, would not be too serious, as you can see from the general pattern of Sherry's achievement scores. Having IQ or aptitude scores as well, though, could be important in some cases—for example, with a child transferring into a hard-driving school from an educationally unambitious one, or with a child who has some problem which interferes with his learning in almost all subjects.

Your child's teacher can also see from achievement tests if the class as a whole has not spent enough time on certain specific things which may be important, like learning fractions or decimals, or developing skill in understanding the main point of a paragraph. Test-makers provide schools with ways of seeing how classes did on each test question

S R A ITEM ANALYSIS— SRA ACHIEVEMENT SERIES

SCHOOL		GRADE	SEM.	FORM	BATTERY	NO. IN GROUP	PAGE
JONES		8	1	A	6–9	35	10

ITEM NO.	CORRECT RESPONSE	ITEM DESCRIPTION	NUMBER ANSWERING CORRECTLY	GROUP %	NAT'L. %
111	C	FRACTION DIV. BY 1–DIGIT WHOLE NO.	22	63	53
112	B	MIXED NO. (DECIMAL) DIV. BY DECIMAL	6	17	57
113	C	ADDITION (QUART–GALLON UNITS)	18	52	57
114	C	DECIMAL X DECIMAL	15	43	74
115	A	MIXED NO. (DECIMAL) DIV. BY DECIMAL	12	34	50
116	C	WHOLE NO. X DECIMAL (PERCENTAGE)	16	46	64
117	C	SUBTRACT (HOUR–MINUTE UNITS)	21	60	57
118	B	PERCENTAGE–FINDING TOTAL NO.	17	48	77
119	C	FIND AREA OF SQUARE	20	57	45
120	A	FIND AREA OF PARALLELOGRAM	18	52	48
121	B	FIND PERIMETER OF RECTANGLE	15	43	50
122	B	FIND AREA OF TRIANGLE	16	46	25
123	C	SOLVE SIMPLE ALGEBRAIC EQUATION	26	74	58
124	A	WHOLE NO. X DECIMAL (PERCENTAGE)	9	26	40
125	B	SOLVE SIMPLE ALGEBRAIC EQUATION	18	52	30
126	A	FIND PERCENTAGE OF TOTAL	7	20	33
127	C	WHOLE NO. X DEC. DIV. BY 1–DIGIT NO.	8	23	35
128	B	SOLVE SIMPLE ALGEBRAIC EQUATION	25	72	47
129	C	WHOLE NO. X DEC. DIV. BY 1–DIGIT NO.	6	17	33
130	B	ADD POSITIVE AND NEGATIVE QUANT.	14	40	52
131	A	USE FORMULA FOR AREA OF CIRCLE	14	40	18
132	C	USE FORMULA FOR AREA OF TRIANGLE	15	43	24
133	A	MIXED NO. FRACT. DIV. BY SAME	21	60	46
134	C	WHOLE NO. DIV. BY MIXED NO. (FRAC.)	23	66	50
135	C	FIND AVER., NO. DIV. BY 1–DIGIT NO.	19	54	45

Code 7-5811

An "item analysis" of answers on an achievement test battery, like this one for a test in the SRA Achievement Series, can prove helpful to the classroom teacher by showing him (as indicated above) what specific knowledge or skill each test question (or "item," as a test question is called technically) examines, and also by telling him how the class performed on the question compared with a national sample of students in the same grade (by percentages who answered the question correctly, in the class and in the national sample). The teacher can thus find out from an item analysis report, with some precision, in which skills and knowledge the class seems strongest and weakest. Such item-by-item analyses of the test performance of each class, grade, school and school system are provided as an extra service by most of the large achievement test publishers. (Reproduced by permission from the *Item Analysis Workbook for the SRA Achievement Series,* © 1960, Science Research Associates, Inc.)

or item. From these "item analyses" teachers can learn how their own classes compare with others in the school or across the nation generally in specific kinds of knowledge and skill. They can then work further on those that will not get much attention later in the children's schooling. School principals and superintendents can also see from these item analyses what learning objectives they might want to give greater or less stress to in planning and guiding the whole school program.

Parents and teachers should not put any great store in detailed item analyses for individual children, experts generally advise. Even the longest achievement series, like the ones that require a total of eight hours' testing time to take, may have only two or three questions on any one skill, like dividing one fraction by another or the use of the semi-colon. Your child may therefore have missed half the items concerning semi-colon use or dividing fractions because of a momentary fluke rather than genuine lack of knowledge. In such instances, experts say that the items are too few to yield reliable results. Reliability increases for more items or questions answered by an individual child, so that your child's score for many questions asked in arithmetic or punctuation should be quite reliable. Reliability also increases for an individual item as it is answered by more children, so that an entire classroom of children can be said with satisfactory reliability to be comparatively poor in dividing fractions if most of them missed even as few as only three or four questions on this skill in a long test.

You should also note that tests only sample accomplishments rather than examine them exhaustively. As a result, for example, suppose that your child really did not know how to divide one fraction by another. If so, he could not learn how to do it simply by finding out how he should have answered the few test questions about it. Rather, he would have to learn it from a whole textbook section or period of study with his teacher. It is largely because of this that coaching or cramming for achievement tests, which is occasionally done in schools and homes, is a particularly vicious waste of time. Genuine learning, actual educational development, is what equips children to answer achievement test questions. Anxious, mechanical memorization of answers to questions like those on a test does not equip children to answer the questions they will actually encounter. Instead, it takes time which they could spend on the genuine learning that would equip them both for the test and for all future schooling and work.

Your child might get most out of taking an achievement test battery, ETS suggests, if his teacher does have the class discuss the questions and answers missed by most of the boys and girls while the test is still fresh in their minds. Such discussion can be "a fascinating, illuminating, humorous adventure," the teacher's guide for the STEP series observes. "There is often ten times as much fun and profit in learning what led a student to a wrong answer than in learning what led another to the right one." Holding such a post-mortem discussion provides an especially interesting opportunity for a teacher to conduct a quick review of matters which might have been slighted in the pupils' prior schooling.

Your child's teacher would not be judged categorically in the light of the performance of your child and his classmates on standardized tests if the principal followed the recommendations of the test-makers. The administrator's manual for the Iowa Tests of Basic Skills points out, for example, that, "If, then, the pupils under teacher Clara Jones make an average score seriously below the norm on most of the tests in the battery, it does not necessarily follow that Miss Jones has not been doing all that could reasonably be expected of her in instruction."

The reverse also holds true, the manual points out as well: "Similarly, the fact that the pupils under Mabel White made an average score well above the norm does not rule out the possibility that Miss White has been seriously negligent of her instructional duties." Among many questions which would have to be answered before a supervisor could draw conclusions about how well a teacher has been working on the basis of tests, it says, are these: What is the intelligence level of the pupils? Does the teacher get the books and equipment he or she needs? What did the children learn before entering the class? Does the school administration make it easy or hard for the teacher to do good work?

How heavy is the teacher's teaching load? What is the pupils' home background like? Does the whole school take classwork seriously? How well were the pupils taught in their other classes?

Questions somewhat like these also have to be asked about the achievement test scores for your child if you would understand what they really mean. Such questions, however, are neither unending nor unanswerable. And they center around a core of knowledge that is one of the major inventions of our civilization, as was suggested in the first chapter. That core of knowledge has been built in a searching and sustained investigation of one of our country's most valuable and costly assets: what American children learn in becoming the men and women who will inherit all the hazard and promise of our world. The core of knowledge that achievement tests represent can show where your own child stands in his progress toward the role he will play in the world of tomorrow. It can show where he stands without bias, whether you are rich or poor, whether your child's manner is exuberant or quiet, or whether others may happen to think him handsome or ugly. It can show where he stands on flexible and voluntary standards which you and his school may freely select, then choose to meet at any point that you wish. Above all, it can show where he stands for the sake of helping him make the most of all that he might become.

Chapter 4

What Career Areas
Should Your Child
Aim For?

Walter's father desperately wanted the boy to become an engineer. A self-made man, the father had built a flourishing structural steel business, but was not himself an engineer, as were many of the men with whom he worked. Walter liked the business and could eventually run it without having an engineering degree, but this made no difference to the father.

The moment of truth for Walter approached in his high school senior year. He had not met engineering college requirements, for he had dropped Spanish and never taken sciences. Besides, he had gotten Cs and Ds in his academic courses, and averaged only C-plus in taking geometry the second time. It seemed very unlikely that he could do passing work in engineering college studies. In the eighth and tenth grades he had gotten California Mental Maturity IQs of 114 and 102, and his eighth-grade California Achievement scores ranged from grade-equivalents of 5.9 to 7.9, with the single exception of an 8.8 in arithmetic "comprehension."

To assess the boy's college prospects again, Walter's counselor had him take an aptitude test in twelfth grade. Walter stood ahead of only 20 per cent of high school senior boys nationally on the test's verbal and numerical aptitude scores, which are particularly sensitive forecasters of ability at college studies. The counselor suggested a two-year college program which might fit Walter's talents, but the father refused to consider this and instead insisted that the boy still aim for a four-year engineering college.

When last heard from, Walter was trying to enter a private school to make up his requirements. All signs indicated that he was doomed to go through one punishing failure after another until he changed his plans.

Another boy, Robert, was also doing below-average work in high school, despite an unusually good record in early schooling. His mother and dad were college graduates and were prominent in community affairs. They hoped very much that he would go to college, but his steadily worsening high school marks made college less and less likely. He developed a dislike for reading in high school, and avoided doing written assignments whenever possible. On a Cooperative Reading Comprehension Test in ninth grade he had scored a composite percentile rank of only 32—that is, ahead of only 32 per cent of ninth-graders nationally.

A counselor helping Robert with his problems also had him take an aptitude test in his junior year. The results electrified the boy, for he earned scores at the very high percentile ranks of 95 on verbal and numerical aptitudes—in the top 5 per cent of high school seniors across the nation. Apparently, though he had severe handicaps in reading and language abilities to overcome, he was basically very bright. With confidence renewed by his high scores, he buckled down to the problems he had dodged for so many years. His new, responsible attitude much impressed his teachers, and he began to pull his marks up. Late in his junior year he was thinking about possible engineering colleges to which he might go.

Your Child's Career Horizon Hinges Largely on Ability Tests

As the actual experiences of these two boys show, your child's career horizons could be deeply affected by what tests of ability revealed about his academic powers. Education required for higher-income careers today is pitched at a more demanding level academically than the work of the average high school. Your child would have to show his capability for the higher education that is now almost the sole route to higher-income careers in order to be even recommended for it by his school. And the two main ways in which your child would have to show his capability are by his regular schoolwork and his performance on standardized tests of ability. These tests would probably include both tests of academic aptitudes or intelligence, and tests of achievement. Aptitude and achievement tests, then, can bear heavily on the level of career choice open to your child—more heavily than any other kind of psychological measurement.

Moreover, aptitude and achievement tests can bear heavily in either of two ways. They can indicate that your child has more ability than had been believed, and can thus tend to increase his opportunities for getting ahead in life, or they can indicate that your child has less ability than had been hoped, and thus tend to limit his opportunities for getting ahead. In the latter case, ability tests could still benefit your child if they are measuring accurately, for they could be used to fore-warn him of ill-advised efforts—like Walter's in the above story—in which he is likely to fail.

Career "Interests" in Your Child Could Be Probed For With "Inventories"

For almost any level of ability that your child may have, however, he still has a bewildering array of occupations from which he or she might choose. There are more than 40,000 different ways of making a living in the country today, according to the U.S. Bureau of Labor Statistics. How can your child possibly identify and look into all those in which he or she might be interested?

To help answer this pre-eminently American question, psychologists have developed measuring devices which resemble tests but which most emphatically are not tests. As we saw in the first chapter, they are called "occupational interest inventories." These inventories are used with more than half of all young people going through the nation's high schools. The two types of inventories used by the millions with young people are the Kuder Preference Records and the Strong Vocational Interest Blanks, as you will recall. Your child will very probably have his occupational interests appraised by either the Kuder or the Strong at one time or another in his high school years—most probably not before his last two high school years or even his college years, in the case of the Strong.

Psychologists themselves hotly dispute the value of occupational interest inventories. Those on each side cite actual cases to show that the inventories yield useful or useless results. For example, one of the nation's leading authorities on vocational counseling and vocational choice, Donald E. Super of Teachers College, Columbia University, upholds the inventories. The research evidence that has been collected for the Strong in particular, he says, "is so convincing that I don't think anyone can examine it and dismiss it." Many of those who condemn the inventories, he remarks, "just don't look at the evidence and set aside their biases."

One case that Dr. Super describes to illustrate the usefulness of an interest inventory was that of a very good-looking girl to whom he gives the fictitious name of Marjorie Miller. Marjorie started in vocational counseling at sixteen, when she was a high school senior doing well in a college prep program in which she liked chemistry, languages and history best. She also led a Girl Scout troop and painted, acted, did photography and wrote for the school paper. Marjorie was thinking then of going into chemical research or dietetics, and wanted help in deciding between them. On the Strong interest blank, Marjorie showed interests most typical of people successful in scientific careers and, secondarily, people successful in social welfare careers.

On the basis of her Otis IQ of 124 and her consistent course marks in or near the 90s, her counselor asked Marjorie about college. The girl said she had thought of two nearby colleges which her father, an insurance company executive, could afford. The counselor pointed out that these were specialized rather than liberal arts colleges. He suggested instead an academically demanding college that offered a scholarship for girls from their part of the state. She was pleased to learn of the scholarship possibility, and of the fact that she could take a general program to explore her interests in her first two college years, then major in a field to qualify for making a living; she hadn't known she could do this. She tried for the scholarship and won. Marjorie's first college year reflected her science interests, but she later shifted to a child-study major. After college she embarked on a career in administration with the Girl Scouts. The counselor concluded that the secondary interest field revealed on the Strong, social welfare work, thus eventually became dominant.

By contrast, occupational interest inventories are deplored by John W. M. Rothney of the University of Wisconsin, who is one of the nation's leading authorities on school guidance counseling. After summing up his criticisms of them, he states with heated emphasis: "Counselors who need such crutches for their interviews as responses culled from long lists of inventory items ought to consider seriously whether or not they are skilled enough to stay in their profession." Dr. Rothney relates an anecdote told him by a school counselor to illustrate how misleading inventory results can be. His incomplete tale has been given wide currency by popular writers critical of testing.

After an only partially literate country boy had taken an inventory, the story goes, his counselor saw that the boy had scored highest in "literary" interests, at about the 85th percentile. The puzzled counselor asked if he read much and the boy replied, "Naw, I don't read nawthin' much—onct in a whal a detectif magazine." He had filled out the questionnaire, the lad further explained, thinking that it might be nice to lead an easy life writing books. However, the story does not go on to relate the important facts of what the boy actually did in later life.

These are the inventories which will probably be used to explore the occupational interests of your child—and to considerable effect. Henry S. Dyer of Educational Testing Service, who is skeptical about the value of the inventories, tells of one witless counselor who dismayed a bright girl who was all set for college by insisting against all other evidence that she would be happy only in clerical work because that was her highest interest area according to an inventory. A counselor as uninformed as this, though, could misuse any kind of information.

As you can see from such stories, the truth about inventories is that they have both values and dangers, both severe shortcomings and considerable advantages, depending on how they may be used with your child.

Your Child Would Not Be *Tested* on Vocational Interest Devices

The process through which your child would go in answering an occupational interest inventory is basically different from the process through which he would go in taking an ability test. Although ability tests and interest inventories may appear similar on the surface, and though they are often lumped all together as "tests," you should know the fundamental difference between them. Recognizing the difference can help keep you from becoming misled by findings for your own child.

An ability test asks your child to take action in which he directly exhibits the things that are to be measured when he works an aptitude or achievement test. His actions on a test—figuring out the next number in a series, getting the answer to an arithmetic problem, identifying the meaning of a word or a paragraph—are samples of your child's behavior in working the problems posed by the questions. Anyone can look at the result and see that your child must have followed a certain line of thought (or two or three similar lines, possibly) in picking each correct answer. Ability tests, then, ask your child to act in certain ways which can be assessed objectively—that is, in such ways that any informed persons who look over the result can agree on what your child has done in at least reaching his right answers. His getting the right answers provides objective evidence that his mind behaved in certain ways—as a result of its capacity and general cultivation on intelligence tests, and of capacity with general and special cultivation on achievement tests.

"There are many ways in which a child can earn a low score on a test," Paul Woodring says in pointing out the importance of this feature of tests, "but there is only one way in which a child can earn a high score." Dr. Woodring, who is editor of the *Saturday Review Education Supplement,* accordingly advises parents and teachers to place initial confidence only in high scores. They should take low scores only as clues subject to further inquiry into the question of why they are low. When the tests are given properly, high scores can result only if the child actually knows how to work most of the questions, he comments. However, low scores can result from an emotional upset, a complex about school or just looking out the window instead of working the test.

By contrast, an occupational interest inventory asks your child to answer questions about what he thinks he likes and dislikes. It does not ask him to provide samples of the behavior that is being investigated. Instead, it asks him to give his impressions of how he feels about many things. It is a "self-report" device, in technical language.

You can appreciate the fundamental difference between ability tests and interest inventories by taking the question, say, of general mental ability. A test of this ability would ask your child to exhibit samples of it by using it directly on certain problems and questions. But an inventory concerning this ability would ask him about his impressions of it, perhaps with indirect questions such as, "Is it fun for you to work hard arithmetic problems?" and "Do you read many non-fiction books for grown-ups?" You could probably tell something about your child's mental ability by asking him about it in an inventory. As you can imagine, however, the results you would get from a test should have a more direct meaning and should be more dependable.

What the "Kuder" and the "Strong" Would Seem to Reveal for Your Child

Your child would be most likely to take the "Kuder" or the "Strong" inventory in his pivotal high school years. These are the years when children must decide on at least a general future direction in life. The two big questions are either on to college or into work after high school. Many important specific questions—questions like which kind of work or which kind of college, and why, and how—follow rapidly in the wake of the two big ones. Daughters face these questions just as urgently as sons, for they need economic independence and educated talents regardless of their prospects for marriage.

On either the Kuder or the Strong your son or daughter would mark likes and dislikes in long lists of things, as we saw in the first chapter. A minor difference between them is that the Kuder is a "forced-choice" questionnaire while the Strong is not. That is, your child would have to answer "like most" or "like least" for two out of every set of three things on the Kuder. On the Strong, he could indicate "indifferent" instead of only "like" and "dislike" for each item.

It would probably be fun for your child to fill out either the Kuder or the Strong. Doing so takes little effort, and the results could not possibly reflect on his capabilities. On a vocational interest inventory, in a sense, everybody wins. Moreover, your child would probably find it exciting to check off how he feels about things like being an actor or a flyer, or designing engines or buildings or bookkeeping systems.

The results or scores your child would receive would be quite different for the two inventories. As we saw in the first chapter, your child would receive a plotted "profile" of his interests in ten broad vocational areas on the most widely used type of Kuder, the Vocational Form C. These are:

Outdoor	Artistic
Mechanical	Literary
Computational	Musical
Scientific	Social Service
Persuasive	Clerical

For each of these, your child would receive a percentile ranking, showing how he stands in his responses compared with the way in which a standardizing group responded. For your child, this norming population would be "a representative group of 3,418 boys and 4,466 girls in grades 9 through 12 from high schools well distributed over the country," according to the Kuder "C" administrator's manual. A percentile ranking above the 75th percentile in an area indicates "high" interest in it, according to the manual, while a ranking below the 25th percentile indicates "low" interest. An accompanying "job chart" lists occupations which seem appropriate to each interest area and each of various combinations of them. For example, if your child's interests in the "persuasive" area came out above the 75th percentile, he might consider becoming a "public relations worker" or "lawyer" or "sales engineer" on the "professional" level, according to the manual's job chart. Or, on the "clerical and kindred" level, occupations suggested as appropriate for young people high in the "persuasive" area include "adjustment clerk" and "collector of bills and accounts." If your child came out high on both "outdoor" and "persuasive" areas, suggested occupations include "4-H agent," "playground director," "hunting and fishing guide" and "barge captain." Capable counselors, it should be noted, consider such interest area findings and corresponding occupations only as general possibilities to be looked into, rather than as hard-and-fast determinations.

Strong Vocational Interest Blank results for men, by contrast, list forty-five occupations divided into eleven categories, and not broad interest areas. Your son's results on the Strong would consist of a letter grade—either A, B-plus, B, B-minus, C-plus, or C—for each of the forty-five listed occupations. Those listed are quite specific; they include artist, psychologist, physician, engineer, farmer, carpenter, YMCA physical director, salesman and lawyer. Results for your daughter would similarly give a letter grade for each of twenty-seven listed occupations, which are not divided by categories. An A grade for an occupation would indicate a pattern of interests very similar to the pattern found to be typical of the successful people in the occupation who filled out the inventory in a standardization of it. A C grade for the occupation would, in turn, indicate a pattern of interests quite unlike the typical Strong inventory interests pattern of those people.

Though the Strong gives scores for each specific occupation, counselors would generally interpret the results broadly, according to the

Your son's profile of vocational interests, as indicated by the Kuder Preference Record, Vocational CH, might look like this if his interests, according to the inventory, came out highest in the "outdoor" and "persuasive" areas. More than two million children a year take the Kuder vocational in high school and often plot such interest profiles of their own for help in considering possible careers. Interest profiles like these should be viewed with many qualifications, as explained on the accompanying pages. (Kuder Preference Record Profile for Vocational Form C, reprinted by permission of Science Research Associates, Inc. Copyright 1949 by G. Frederic Kuder.)

eleven main categories of "interest clusters" on the Strong Blank for men. That is, a counselor would probably not tell your son that his interests suggest work as a YMCA physical director, but that they suggest a group of social welfare occupations as possibilities.

Results for your child on either the Kuder or the Strong would look like quite potent medicine. Right there in black and white, on the basis of research and in neat letter grades or precise percentile ranks, his occupational interests would seem to be completely mapped out. Low interests or disinterest should have as much force as high interest, for your child would presumably not be happy in occupational fields or areas in which his interests were low, and he ought to stay out of them. High-interest areas, of course, suggest satisfaction and success.

Why Your Child's Measured "Interests" Should Not Be Taken Literally

However authoritative they may look, though, your child would be mistaken to take his results on the Kuder "C" or the Strong as the final, revealed truth about what he ought to do in life. This is not because they are technically casual devices, based on little or no research. The two inventories have been developed and investigated with extensive research for thirty years or more. The Kuder "C" interest areas were established through statistical analysis, and hundreds of people in a number of the occupations listed in the Kuder "C" job chart actually have been found to have interest patterns in general accord with the Kuder scheme. The Strong vocational interest patterns have been investigated for several thousand people in the respective occupations; in fact, the interest patterns presented as typical for the different occupations by the Strong scoring system were the patterns actually found to be more or less typical for people in those occupations.

It is this research itself, though, that suggests why you should not take the inventory results too literally. For one thing, the research has shown that, although interest patterns for some children who reach a firm occupational decision by their early 'teens remain remarkably stable, patterns for many children shift considerably until after the age of seventeen, or even twenty and older. Second, the research has also shown considerable variety of interest patterns within occupational groups as well as typical patterns for them. As the Kuder "C" manual itself observes:

> Thus, there may be a place for individuals with quite different interest patterns within a single occupation. Closeness of correspondence with the typical may be pointed out to the person, but he should not neces- sarily avoid an occupation solely because his interest pattern departs from the typical.

Research has also shown that other factors besides interests assessed on inventories shape occupational decisions. Charles McArthur, a psychologist at Harvard, has found that wealthy prep-school boys generally go into the fields in which they say they are interested rather than those in which the Strong indicates they are interested. For them, the attraction of family advantages outweighs what may be an apparent natural bent in another direction.

Research with interest inventories also often gives values of reliability and validity lower than those considered advisable for tests of ability. Inventories differ from tests in reliability and validity because of their basic difference in nature. As pointed out before, inventories are "self-report" devices which question your child about how he feels, while tests have your child show the qualities being measured in action, in actual behavior.

Because of this difference, the bottomless problem of distortion afflicts inventories. Distortion is a problem from which tests are almost entirely free (because normal Americans try to score high on tests in most situations; however, as an example, soldiers have deliberately scored low on some ability tests to avoid being assigned to, say, truck repairs). To apply interest inventory profiles with confidence, a counselor must be sure that your child reported his true feelings on the questionnaire. But the counselor can never be sure enough that your child did not "fake" consciously or distort unconsciously.

A story is told of one boy's unconscious but human distortion. As a college student, this boy became engaged to the daughter of a wealthy man who offered to set him up in business. At the time he preferred to be independent. When he filled out a vocational interest inventory, he scored high in his intended career field, psychology. But after another year, poor marks led him to think better of his father-in-law's offer. He took the inventory again and, to his pleased surprise, found that his interests this time were high in the business career area.

The Kuder does have a special "verification score" based on rarely chosen responses. The "V" score seems to identify many children who may have faked most deliberately, or ones who may have simply answered carelessly and at random. But the "V" score "by no means detects all types of distortion," Professor Cronbach declares.

It is quite remarkable that interest inventories can yield possibly helpful results for your child in the face of such problems of making effective inventories. But it has been shown with the Strong in particular that people in different career areas do tend to have distinctive patterns of inventoried interests, and that these typical patterns remain stable for years. E. K. Strong, Jr., the originator of the inventories bearing his name, followed up 663 Stanford University students an average of eighteen years after they had first filled out his inventories; this was Strong's celebrated eighteen-year follow-up study. Some 78 per cent of the 663 former students were found to be in occupations for which they had originally gotten A ratings, while only 23 per cent were in careers originally rated C for them.

One last problem is that an interest inventory may not apply to all fields in which your child might be interested. Professor Rothney has said of the Strong that "its range of occupational keys outside the professional fields is so limited that it is not informative for the majority of students who will not go into the professions." Professor Cronbach seconds this motion by noting that many routine jobs, as in factory assembly line work, have little or no intrinsic interest; interest in such jobs stems largely from matters external to the nature of the work itself —from things like pay, working conditions, security, camaraderie and freedom from responsibility.

Use Your Child's Interest Inventory Results Only With These Precautions

For your own child, then, you can take interest inventory results as scientific, all right, but also as scientifically limited in how they should be used. When your child comes to considering careers, you might remember these limitations specifically:

First, your child's interests may well go on changing as he learns more about people, the world and himself in his late 'teens and early twenties. An interest pattern of his at an early age might reflect his current feelings to at least some extent, but these feelings often change in young people as they grow up. In Columbia College, for example, about half the young men change their intended fields of major study while in college. And if your child's interests remain stable, it is probably because he reached a firm career decision in his early 'teens which you could discover just by asking, without giving him an inventory.

Second, your child may have either clear-cut or potential interests in a career not reflected in an interest inventory system. If so, your child's counselor would be wrong to have him give his inventory results more importance than his own preferences.

Third, as the Kuder manual points out, people with a variety of interest patterns can be found in an occupation. Your child's interest pattern need not conform to an occupation's typical pattern in order for him to find a satisfying place in the occupation.

Fourth, other factors besides interests as reflected on an inventory affect career choices—for example, in the case of prep-school sons of the wealthy whose advantages of family position and connections can make their opportunities in fields like banking, law or corporate management more attractive to them than their inventoried areas of interest.

Fifth and last, your child's abilities can exert an even more tyrannical effect in determining outlets for satisfaction of his career interests than family advantages might. We saw at the start of this chapter how a boy named Walter wanted to be an engineer, but that he probably could not become an engineer because his abilities did not lie in that direction. Apparently, the most common mistake which children and sometimes even counselors make with interest inventories is to assume that they appraise abilities as well as interests typical of various occupations. They most emphatically do not. The Kuder manual flatly declares, "In no case is the Kuder intended to substitute for measures of ability."

How Inventory Results Still Might Help Your Child

Even with all these limitations, interest inventories could be used by a school counselor to help your child. Many children go through high school with only a vague idea of what they would like to do in life, and with no idea of how to begin searching through all the thousands of possibilities. Interest inventories are among the few devices which counselors can use to obtain some sort of impression of a child's interests detached from his personal confusions and defenses, if the child is all mixed up about possible careers. Inventories like the Kuder and the Strong enable the counselor to help your child identify career areas which might be likely to interest him, and to start him exploring career areas in relation to himself realistically. This is the proper use of the Kuder and the Strong—to open vistas and provide starting points rather than to close vistas and obtain final answers. It is mainly for these purposes that the inventories are used by the millions with young people today.

Interest inventories might also suggest other promising career lines if your child had started on one without finding satisfaction or success. For example, one college girl was majoring in child psychology and working with nursery school children with only mediocre results. She had gone into the field because, years before, she had read a book about a woman who worked with orphans. The girl had been inspired then and there to decide on orphanages as a wonderful life's work. However, on a Kuder "C" interest profile obtained in college, the girl ranked below the 20th percentiles in the "social service" and "persuasive" areas which would seem to be important in orphanage work. Her standings in "clerical" and "computational" areas, though, had been above the 90th percentiles. These four had been the only markedly high and markedly low standings for her among the ten interest areas. Moreover, she reported having "just loved" a summer job of routine filing, and had obtained quite good marks in typing and shorthand courses. If this girl had become discouraged about her original choice, a counselor could have tactfully suggested that she might consider office and secretarial work instead.

Your Child Might Discover Career Clues in His Aptitudes

Your child might have a somewhat detailed appraisal of his career abilities—or rather, his "aptitudes" as they relate to career fields—made with bona fide tests while in junior or senior high school. These would most likely be the Differential Aptitude Tests of The Psychological Corporation. The tests do have reliabilities and validities as high as those generally thought satisfactory for any ability tests. As we saw in the first chapter, the DAT battery is one of America's giant test series. It was developed to serve in vocational as well as educational counseling in the junior and senior high school grades. Its eight tests apply, generally, to three areas:

Educational (with the first two tests, verbal reasoning and numerical ability, corresponding to conventional IQ or general ability tests, and the third, abstract reasoning, paralleling a "nonverbal" IQ index);

Manual occupations and courses (with tests four and five, space relations and mechanical reasoning); and

Office work occupations and courses (with the last three tests—clerical speed and accuracy, spelling and sentence usage).

Any appropriate combination of the tests besides these three groupings can be examined for the aptness of any specific career possibility—for example, spelling and sentence usage as well as verbal ability in the case of journalism.

Your child's whole pattern of eight aptitude levels on the DAT would hold meaning for him. The aptitudes could be compared directly with each other, for all eight tests were re-standardized together on a national sample of more than 45,000 children in grades 8 through 12 in 1962. Your child's performance on the DAT would usually be shown to him as his percentile rank on each test among those children in the 45,000 who were on his own grade level and of the same sex.

You might wonder what two tests that are clearly ones of achievement—spelling and sentence usage—are doing among tests of aptitude. Many people suppose that tests of aptitude measure inherent capabilities rather than capabilities developed through consistent schoolwork. This is not true. Tests are defined by type according to the purpose for which they are designed to be used, rather than their functional content. As we saw, all IQ and general ability tests reflect educational background, as well as cultural background, to at least some extent— that is, they do reflect some degree of educational achievement. The DAT includes at least these two tests of specific educational achievement because spelling and sentence usage are good indicators of a child's aptitude for office work and editorial work. Your child's verbal ability score on the DAT would indicate how well he might be able to do in using language skills, but his spelling and sentence usage scores would indicate how far he has actually developed in two basically important skills of this kind.

Actual cases illustrate how the DAT might be used in your own child's vocational counseling. Do any of the following children remind you of your own? Their stories are a few of those told in the excellent Psych Corp manual, *Counseling from Profiles; A Casebook for the Differential Aptitude Tests*, by George K. Bennett, Harold G. Seashore and Alexander G. Wesman.

Dorothy, a bright-eyed, poised senior in a large high school, had transferred that year from a small school. She wanted counseling about her idea of preparing for a career either in math and science or in nursing. An otherwise superior student, she was concerned particularly by the C grades she was getting in trig and solid geometry after having previously been an A student in math. Dorothy's numerical ability and abstract reasoning scores on the DAT placed her above the 90th percentiles in those aptitudes. The standings confirmed her capabilities in math, and suggested that her math teacher was marking her far too severely. The scores, plus great satisfaction with later part-time work in an insurance company's statistical department, led her to decide to be a math or statistics major in college, and perhaps go into research in economics or statistics.

Will was a husky farm lad who was doing very well in the freshman year of his high school's four-year program in agriculture. He had gotten an Otis Quick-Scoring IQ of 118, and on the DAT stood very high on most aptitudes—from the 75th to the 95th percentiles. Both Will's test scores and his top rank in the agricultural program suggested to the counselor that the boy might benefit from college. Will said he was not planning on college because he thought his family could not afford to send him. But he did say that he would like to learn more in high school than he was getting in the agriculture program. When the counselor talked to Will's dad about college costs and his son's impressive abilities, the man said that he might be able to pay most of Will's college expenses if going would do the boy good. Will transferred to the college prep program.

Lola, a quiet, purposeful girl in her high school sophomore year, was apparently even more capable than Will. She had gotten an Otis IQ of 127, and on the DAT ranked at the following high percentiles: verbal, 93rd; numerical, 85th; abstract, 95th; space relations, 91st; clerical, 70th; spelling, 85th; and sentence usage, 93rd. It was no surprise to the counselor that Lola was getting straight As in the school's secretarial course. Lola saw the counselor about preparing for college, but said that her father was very much against her going. After she and the counselor had talked over her whole situation, though, Lola decided not to try for college and instead to finish in the secretarial course and go to work. The counselor reassured her by noting that, in a few years, she would probably be earning as much as many girls with college degrees. Also, with good general academic courses on top of secretarial studies, the counselor said, she could be not only an excellent secretary but a useful citizen and interesting person as well.

Charles, who was also a sophomore, looked worried as he entered the counselor's office. He had been working very hard in the high school's college prep program and had just scraped by until this year, when he failed Latin. His parents were determined to have him go to a rigorous four-year college, and he had been trying desperately to please them. Trouble in the academic program had been indicated for him by his Cooperative Reading test results at the 30th and 35th percentiles in ninth and tenth grades. His DAT verbal standing at only about the 35th percentile tended to confirm these other indications of insufficient ability with words to succeed in college prep work; also, in spelling and sentence usage he stood at only about the 15th percentiles. However, in DAT mechanical reasoning he stood at the 91st percentile, and also at the 80th in abstract reasoning, the 76th in space relations and the 60th in numerical reasoning. The counselor suggested that Charles explore mechanical and technical areas, which he apparently liked. Charles transferred to easier sections in English and history, in which he had been having difficulty, and dropped Latin for mechanical drawing. In his junior year, Charles took mostly shop, science and math courses; he easily did passing work in them and had cheered up considerably. He also planned to go to a two-year college or technical institute, an aim in which his mother and dad by then concurred as a wise one for him.

By contrast, Grace was miserable in her junior year because of her failing work in the high school's commercial program she had chosen. The program seemed to fit her interests, for her high areas on the Kuder "C" were computational and clerical, along with social welfare. However, the DAT indicated that commercial studies did not fit her abilities. She ranked at only the 10th percentile in verbal, the 30th in numerical, about the 51st in clerical and about the 21st in spelling. Her space relations and mechanical reasoning ranks were rather high, though—at about the 80th percentiles. After her counselor had talked with her about developing new interests and plans, Grace asked to be transferred to the dressmaking program in a vocational high school. She did good work in her dressmaking courses and average work in the rest of her courses in the new program, and thought she would get her diploma without any trouble at all.

Before high school, while Harry was in the eighth grade, he had deep misgivings about his mother's fond hope of having him go to a Hebrew high school and eventually become a rabbi. He felt sure he could not succeed in these plans, and instead wanted to take the commercial course in a public high school. He had gotten poor marks all through school even though he was a year behind his regular grade. That spring the counselor went over Harry's school record and his DAT results with the boy's mother. He had done only about average on the numerical and space tests, stood only at about the 12th percentile on the verbal and abstract tests; he ranked very far down, at the 1st percentile, on the mechanical test. Clerical was Harry's highest aptitude, in which he stood at the 85th percentile. The mother reluctantly agreed to let him try the high school commercial course, at least for the ninth grade. After Harry had made good progress in ninth-grade commercial studies, she agreed that this had been the right decision for him.

After children like these half-dozen real boys and girls we have been considering are supplied with their DAT scores and percentile rankings, they can plot the rankings themselves. The plots are set up in a way which well illustrates certain basic features of standardized test results. For example, the full DAT plot that the counselor reviewed with Harry's mother in the case just above looks as shown.

Your own child may well take the DAT and plot his differential aptitude findings while in high school. These somewhat odd things about the plot on which he indicates his aptitude results reflect fundamental features of testing, as follows:

1. The base line is the middle—not the top or bottom—and your child would indicate how his aptitude standings differ from the middle,

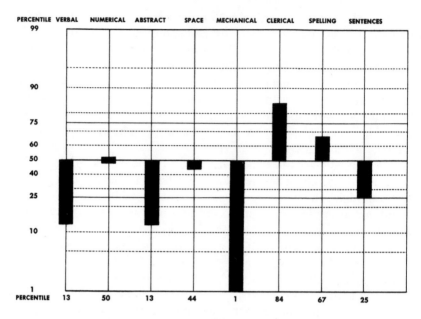

or average. On regular classroom tests, the important base line is the passing level set by the teacher or the school—if not the top or perfect mark for all right answers. But standardized tests have no "passing" levels, and they measure far wider ranges of ability than classroom tests. Accordingly, the importance of your child's standing on a standardized test is how far above or below normal or average he may rank. DAT standings below the average are by no means "negative" in any sense, even though the bars to designate them extend downward rather than upward; a standing at the 25th percentile represents just as positive an aptitude as a standing at the 75th percentile. Also, the base line of average performance carries no moral significance whatever; average or above-average standings are neither good nor desirable in themselves. Instead, standings at various levels mean only that a particular course of action a child has in mind may be advisable or inadvisable in the light of his present aptitudes.

2. Along the left-hand side of the DAT plot form, percentile

rankings bunch together around the middle. This reflects the fact that most children score close to the average on tests, and that fewer and fewer children score in the increasingly high or low extremes.

3. Children are advised that their aptitudes probably differ only if the levels of their rankings on the DAT plot differ by an amount equal to more than ½ inch of vertical distance on a plot the size of Harry's, as shown above. (This distance happens to be 1 inch on the full-size plot your child would actually use.) That is, Harry's abilities as reflected on the DAT's numerical, space and spelling tests probably do not differ from each other, but they probably do differ from his abilities as reflected on the other tests. This feature of the DAT plot form reflects the error of measurement of tests, and especially the compounding of errors of measurement which occurs when results from two tests are compared.

Ability tests, interest inventories and aptitude tests can at least help focus attention on important questions when it comes time for your child to plan for a career. They can help your child in the ways we have seen when he works with a wise and well-informed counselor, and he would be the better for having them used well as he explores his possibilities. However, they cannot provide your child with complete and clear-cut answers to the problems of making sound career decisions. We have seen some of the reasons why not in this chapter. We shall see even more fundamental ones in the next, which looks into persisting mysteries of human personality.

Chapter 5

Does Your Child
Have Personality
Problems?

Your Child's Personality Affects His School Marks and Test Scores

How well or poorly your child does in school and on tests depends in part on his whole personality, and not just on the qualities of his mind. His whole personality will have an even greater effect on his success in a career, as you can appreciate. How personality can influence school-work is shown by the case of one impulsive girl who had a very strict, domineering father. The girl had gotten very good marks and test scores all through the early grades. However, when she was thirteen her growing need for personal independence led her to resist and argue about her teachers' demands, and the quality of her schoolwork started to drop sharply. Another example is that of a boy who had been greatly coddled by his mother. He had seemed quite bright in his early years, getting Stanford-Binet IQs of about 125. But in junior high he began failing in his courses; another Stanford-Binet IQ he got then had slipped to 111, and on the Otis Quick-Scoring he earned an IQ score of only 92. A likable but easily discouraged boy, he had never buckled down to learn fundamental skills—reading, in particular—apparently because of his mother's constant, doting indulgence.

Emotional attitudes in your child which would affect his performance on even an individual intelligence test have been described by David Wechsler, author of the Wechsler intelligence scales. He characterized them as your child's interest in doing the tasks set, his persistence in attacking them and his zest and desire to succeed—items which might more generally be described as temperamental or personality factors, but which nevertheless must be recognized in all actual measures of intelligence. For this reason, one might appropriately refer to them as the ... non-intellective factors in general intelligence.

Such "non-intellective" or personality factors cannot help but influence everything·your child does in using his intelligence. As we saw in the two actual cases above, personality factors can hinder your child's use of potentially good mental powers so much that his schoolwork and hence his whole life could be changed as a result. Because of this, a variety of psychological devices that attempt to detect personality problems are used in American schools. Such test-like devices are used widely in the schools, though not with large numbers of children. None are employed on a scale even approaching that of the nation's twenty-five giant test series. Your child is thus not very likely to encounter them, but the results might be quite important if he did. For if he should, his school would be using them for the purpose of helping him with a personality problem which may be interfering seriously with his learning and whole development.

Should Your Child's School Help Him With Personality Problems?

Vocal minorities of parents in some communities—Oxnard, California; Whitehall, Ohio; and Island Trees, New York, among them—have objected strongly to having devices designed to detect personality problems used with their children. These parents believed that the school had no business questioning their children about how the children felt toward such matters as their parents, dating, sex and religion.

Whether or not the school is justified in making such inquiries in trying to help children depends entirely on the community, according to George K. Bennett, president of The Psychological Corporation. "Some school systems want to restrict their efforts entirely to the traditional concerns of education," he says, "and do not want to be involved with even the question of whether or not the pupils have had a good breakfast." Restricting the school's efforts just to instruction is perfectly legitimate, in his judgment, if that is what the staff, the school board and the parents of the community want. But it is also legitimate and widely prevalent, he points out, for a school to take at least some responsibility for improving personal influences outside the school which affect how the child learns and grows.

Furthermore, Dr. Bennett declares, "If the community expects the school to take responsibility for the 'whole child,' the school has to inquire, by one means or another, into sensitive areas. It seems preferable to do this systematically, by a checklist, rather than informally by a short interview."

Your Child's Personality Could Not Be "Tested"

Your child's personality might be probed in school with three kinds of devices which are often mistakenly referred to as "tests." The kind he is most likely to meet, as it is given most widely, would be one of a number of long questionnaires which ask him to indicate the things that bother him in such areas as his home and family, his school, his future, his self-confidence, his friendships, his health, the opposite sex and his outlook on life. Questionnaires like this are generally called problem checklists or adjustment inventories; most often, they are for junior and senior high school students. Among the most popular ones are the Mooney Problem Check List of The Psychological Corporation; the Youth Inventory and Junior Inventory of SRA; the Billett-Starr Youth Problems Inventory of Harcourt, Brace & World; the Mental Health Analysis of Cal Test; and the Pupil Adjustment Inventory of Houghton Mifflin.

The second kind your child might encounter is the full-blown personality inventory. These are questionnaires which would attempt to identify major traits or features of your child's personality. Personality inventories used fairly widely by the schools include the California Test of Personality of Cal Test; the Allport-Vernon-Lindzey Study of Values of Houghton Mifflin; the Gordon Personal Profile and Personal Inventory of Harcourt, Brace & World; and the Minnesota Counseling Inventory and the Minnesota Multiphasic Personality Inventory distributed by Psych Corp.

Your child might meet the third kind of personality assessment devices only on rare occasions. These are the "projective" devices. Among those known to some extent in the schools are the Thematic Apperception Test and the Blacky Pictures distributed by Psych Corp, and the Rorschach inkblot technique outlined in manuals distributed by Harcourt, Brace & World. Projective instruments like these would have to be given to your child by an individual examiner. But a problem checklist or a personality inventory could be given to your child in a group.

With any or all of these devices your child's personality could not possibly be "tested." Despite the names of some of them, none are tests in the same sense of the word as an academic ability or achievement test. Problem checklists and personality inventories are "self-report" devices in which your child would give answers about his worries, likes and dislikes, in just the same way as on the occupational interest inventories we took up in the last chapter. With projective devices your child would be expected to reveal his inner nature in an indirect way, usually by telling what he sees in pictures or images.

The first two kinds are superficially similar to tests, in that some of them yield numerical scores which can be compared with the range of scores made by a reference group used for standardization. The third kind—projective devices—superficially resemble individual IQ tests in that they would have to be given to your child individually by a trained examiner.

But all three kinds differ from ability tests in a fundamental way. They do not have your child produce samples of his behavior which can unmistakably evidence the qualities of his that are being investigated. Ability tests have your child show what he can do, or demonstrate what problems he can solve, so that anyone can look at the results and decide objectively what your child has actually been able to do in specific testing situations. But personality devices instead investigate your child's emotions by asking him to reveal them through direct or indirect questions.

As a result, the reliability or consistency of findings with these personality devices is almost always lower than the reliability levels acceptable for ability tests used in the schools. Also, personality devices have much lower validity for predicting specific consequences than ability tests. For your own child, then, these personality devices would yield results which could vary too much to be dependable in themselves, as well as results which could not be used with some confidence by themselves to predict important future consequences for your child.

Personality inventories and projective devices are regularly used by clinical psychologists, who find them helpful as sources of clues and indications when their results are interpreted according to what the psychologist knows from long training and experience. But research evidence shows that they have relatively unreliable and invalid results when those results are not interpreted by a highly skilled psychologist.

The principal professional organization in the field, the American Psychological Association, recognizes these limitations of personality assessment devices in two major ways. First, in a body of *Technical Recommendations for Psychological Tests and Diagnostic Techniques* which it officially approved in 1954 and 1955, it advised against having the word "test" used in the titles of personality questionnaires and similar inventory devices. It did so to avoid having the public misled.

Second, according to the APA's official statement on *Ethical Standards for Psychologists,* test publishers are advised to distribute interest inventories and personality screening inventories only to persons who have had an advanced university course in psychological measurement, or its equivalent in training under a professional psychologist. The statement advises still more stringent distribution for personality inventories and projective devices, recommending that they be used only by persons with at least a master's degree in psychology. These restrictions on who may use personality questionnaires are recommended because your child's advisers would need advanced training in order to employ them in constructive ways. Unfortunately, neither the stricture against using "test" in the titles of such devices, nor the recommendation against letting these devices get into the hands of people who may not know how to use them constructively, are closely enforced. Your child could, therefore, not only be misled by the name of some of these devices, but confused by an incorrect interpretation of a summary of his answers on one of them.

How a Personality Problem Checklist Might Help Your Child

Your child could benefit from being given one of the personal problem checklist questionnaires in his school. No harm to your boy or girl could result which would not otherwise be risked anyway, as we shall see. If your child should fill out a problem checklist, his school would be using it for either or both of two purposes—as a survey in the school system aimed at seeing how it might be improved, or in trying to find out which children might want the help of a counselor.

A few school systems across the country, particularly ones in large cities, regularly use checklists to survey the different kinds of problems which seem to be bothering the children in different parts of the system. The school systems do so in order to relieve what problems they can for the children.

The responses of your child and his schoolmates on a problem checklist could also provide their school's counseling staff with somewhat urgent cues for interviews.

However, schools could not rely heavily on the checklists to identify children with serious psychological problems; disturbed children might answer to hide their difficulties, trying to prove even to themselves that they are all right. These children would be "misses"—ones who labor under difficult problems, but miss detection on the questionnaire. Or a child might be a "false positive"—one who seems to need help, but who really doesn't. As we shall see, even the most highly developed of personality inventories have large proportions of "misses" and "false positives."

About the only risk your child would run from being given a checklist is that of possibly being embarrassed or made tense by an unskillful counselor on the basis of checklist results. However, if the counselor is not skilled, your child runs the same risk even if there is no checklist in the picture.

At best, these personal problem inventories help give the school a general idea of the kinds of things which are bothering the children, some of which might be corrected. Also on the plus side, the checklists seem to relieve children by helping them see their problems in some systematic way, and by giving children an opportunity to show what they would like to get in counseling. At worst, the most popular problem checklists could prove futile for your child rather than downright harmful.

Personality and Projective Devices Could Err Seriously for Your Child

If your child's school was to have him answer a personality inventory or projective device, it would do so for much the same reasons as with a problem checklist—that is, in attempting to help him with some problem of his personal situation or psychological adjustment under which he was laboring. However, as mentioned a few pages ago, the school could put far less confidence in the results than it could in the case of genuine tests of your child's abilities. Just what the school might do on the basis of the device's results alone would also be far less clear than with ability tests. For these reasons, schools do not use these personality instruments with any large numbers of children, and your child would not be likely to meet them.

Nevertheless, questions of the whole personality are vital in schooling. We all expect schools to help make our children happy, co-operative, upright and loyal. Children with confident, friendly, industrious, obliging and cheerful dispositions are rewarded in school. On the other hand, schools penalize children with strongly rebellious personalities because a class cannot learn effectively if even one very disruptive child is in the room. Children are expelled from school—cut off from their friends and from the opportunity school offers them to become competent and independent adults—basically because of their personalities.

Your child's teachers and advisers judge his personality practically all of the time by how he acts. He would be given a personality instrument in school in an attempt to see *why* he acts as he does, if he were to take one at all.

The older type of personality inventories your child might take would attempt to measure a number of character traits—attachment to values deemed theoretical, economic, political, esthetic, social and religious on the Study of Values, for instance, or traits like "ascendancy," responsibility, emotional stability and cautiousness on the Gordon Personal Profile. Newer types of personality inventories would yield scores indicating how normal or abnormal your child seemed to be in certain areas. On the Minnesota Counseling Inventory, for example, these areas would be family relations, social relations, emotional stability, moodiness, conformity, adjustment to reality and leadership. On the California Test of Personality the areas would include sense of personal worth, nervous symptoms, family relations, feeling of belonging and antisocial tendencies.

Psychologists today generally reject the notion that traits of character can be measured with any substantial degree of accuracy. They disagree, for example, on what sociability is, as well as on how much of it might be desirable in general. They also doubt that any sensible agreement about traits could be reached. The psychologist who is president of the National Merit Scholarship Corporation, John M. Stalnaker, declares that he, of course, wants National Merit awards to go to young people who are honest. "We don't want to educate someone who will be the best gangster, or the best thief," he says. But he doubts that any definition of a desirable trait can be made that would be "independent of a specific situation." Motivation is another trait which educators deem important today, he observes, but students do not have motivation to achieve in school activities regardless of what the activities may be. His own daughter, Dr. Stalnaker notes, "is motivated for sports but not for studying German." Because of basic complexities like these in the whole idea of traits, your child's traits could not be assessed with any assurance with a personality traits inventory.

How poorly such an inventory might work for your own child is illustrated by one study which was made of eighty-one college girls with the Bernreuter Personality Inventory. The Bernreuter gives scores in self-sufficiency, introversion, dominance and neurotic tendency. Observations of the actions of the eighty-one girls were made continually for a year as part of the study, and competent persons rated the observation records according to the Bernreuter traits. The ratings were then compared with how the girls scored on the inventory itself.

Sixteen of the girls came out within the "maladjusted" extreme on the instrument's neurotic tendency scale. However, only six of the sixteen girls were considered actually maladjusted by the raters. Moreover, two of the girls who came out least maladjusted on the inventory were considered actually maladjusted by the raters. In other words, so far as the important matter of maladjustment was concerned, the inventory was right on only six cases and wrong on twelve—identifying ten "false positives" who were rated not maladjusted and scoring two "misses" for girls who were rated maladjusted. The Bernreuter was therefore apparently wrong in twice as many cases as it was right about adjustment among these eighty-one college girls.

But the difficulty with a device like the Bernreuter goes still deeper. This study concerned itself only with that inventory's definition of "maladjusted." However, as we saw, psychologists by no means closely agree on what "maladjusted" means, or on other inventory trait score terms. One expert notes, "The meaning of 'introvert' is twisted and turned so that it represents for one [inventory] author a brooding neurotic, for another anyone who would rather be a clerk than a carnival barker. 'Ascendance' ranges from spontaneous social responsiveness, in one theory, to inconsiderate and overbearing behavior in another." In consequence, even if your child were found validly "maladjusted" according to the Bernreuter's definition, the boy or girl might well not be considered maladjusted in fact by at least some fully qualified psychologists.

Personality inventories of newer types which your child might take are based on more widely accepted ideas than the notion of traits, but statistical evidence of their validity—the touchstone of all psychological measurement—shows them almost as haphazard as the older inventories. The Minnesota Multiphasic Personality Inventory, familiarly called the MMPI, is the most highly regarded of these newer devices. The MMPI and its shorter derivative, the Minnesota Counseling Inventory, are among the most widely used of the newer types of inventories. The MMPI's reputation stems from the enormous amount of research which has been done with the inventory. More than a thousand published research studies concerning the MMPI have been made since it appeared in 1940. At least five books, including an 844-page *Atlas* of MMPI "profiles," explain how to use it.

At first glance, the MMPI looks alarming—not so much in its questions as in its "scales," or scoring keys. Among its 550 questions, for example, are ones asking if the person believes he is being plotted against, or if he wishes he could be as happy as others, or if he drinks lots of water a day or ever gets muscular twitches. The original nine keys used to score a person's "true-false" or "don't know" answers to the MMPI's questions include ones called "hypochondriasis," "depression," "paranoia," "psychopathic deviate" and "schizophrenia." As these names indicate, the MMPI was developed to help tell the difference between various kinds of insanity—as it happened, in people arriving for diagnosis at the neuropsychiatric division of the University of Minnesota hospitals. The MMPI tries to meet an important need for rapid and fairly sure initial diagnoses by hard-pressed admitting psychiatrists at the country's overloaded mental hospitals. For this purpose it seems to work well enough to help in running mental hospitals. According to the MMPI's originators, clinical psychologist S. R. Hathaway and psychiatrist J. C. McKinley, "a high score on a scale has been found to predict positively the corresponding final clinical diagnosis or estimate in more than 60% of new psychiatric admissions."

You should not be overly impressed by their statement, though, for various reasons. The MMPI scales still failed to agree with the final diagnosis or estimate for four of ten new admissions—a rather important fact for the patients concerned, and their families. And the 60 per cent agreement was presumably found at the University of Minnesota hospitals—yet it is well known that different hospitals reflect different schools of thought for diagnosing the mentally ill, and the diagnoses of other psychiatric hospitals might differ widely from those of the University of Minnesota. Finally, the authors have said of various scales—most creditably—that validity evidence for one is "certainly not conclusive," that a second scale proved only "slightly better" than others they rejected and that attempts to validate a third scale were "always disappointing."

By a somewhat remote chance, your child might be given the MMPI in his school. Experiments have been made with it in schools, not to see if the children were paranoids or schizophrenics, but to explore their personality patterns. One most unusual study investigated all ninth-graders in Minneapolis, some 4,000 children, who were given the MMPI and followed up for the next two years. Some predictive power was found. Of the 21 per cent of these ninth-grade boys who scored high on the inventory's "4" (psychopath) scale, 22 per cent committed acts of juvenile delinquency within the two-year span. Only 5 per cent of all the boys scored high on a verifying "F" scale, but, of those in this 5 per cent, some 48 per cent later became delinquents.

These results indicate that the MMPI should be valuable in estimating the total numbers of future delinquents which might be expected to develop among a large group of children. But it could not tell which ones among the high-scorers on, say, the "4" or the "F" scale would become delinquents—and more than three-fourths of the high-scorers on "4" and half on "F" would not turn delinquent. A counselor working with an individual child could only consider a high "4" or "F" score as an improbable but possible hallmark of a future delinquent.

If your own child were to be given the MMPI by a school counselor who hoped to find and relieve troubled elements in your child's personality, it would be very important for the counselor to be well trained. Counselors with the least training, Paul Woodring points out, are the ones most likely to be careless in jumping to conclusions. It is a counselor like this, Dr. Woodring observes, who would give the MMPI to a child, score it, then tell the child, "You're a schizophrenic!"

An insufficiently trained counselor might not know, for example, that the MMPI does not work at all well in telling the difference between normal people and people who suffer from severe mental illness. As Dr. Hathaway and Dr. McKinley state in their MMPI manual, "It should be continually kept in mind that the great majority of persons having deviant profiles are not, in the usual sense of the word, mentally ill, nor are they in need of psychological treatment." This has been confirmed in various experiments. In general, scores of 50 on the MMPI scales are considered average or normal, while scores of 70 or higher are viewed as indications of mental illness. However, among a group of Northwestern University students picked at random, 39 per cent had scores over 70 on one MMPI scale and 14 per cent had scores over 70 on two scales. Yet the professor making the experiment declared that "no other supporting evidence" indicated that high a degree of abnormality among Northwestern students. Apparently, the MMPI works fairly well in mental hospital admissions because most people brought for admission have already acted in ways which strongly indicate real mental illness. They are decidedly not typical of the general population.

How an inventory derived from the MMPI might nevertheless work to help your child is illustrated in a story told by Ralph F. Berdie. Dr. Berdie, director of the student counseling bureau at the University of Minnesota, is the senior author of the Minnesota Counseling Inventory. It is based substantially on the MMPI. He devised the inventory for use in the state-wide testing program for Minnesota junior and senior high schools.

In the case history he relates, a high school girl named Nancy Kaye was referred to a school counselor for help because she had become increasingly worried in her junior year. Until then, she had been happy and academically successful in school. In her first interview she and the counselor talked over her social life, health, family and activities generally, but nothing showed up which might be causing her trouble.

The counselor then had her fill out the Minnesota Counseling Inventory. All her scores turned out to be in the normal range except for the abnormally high one in family relations. The counselor accordingly started the next interview by having her talk at length about her family. Halfway through the interview Nancy said that her parents were putting more and more pressure on her to continue getting As and Bs in her courses. However, she had only limited academic ability, and was finding it harder and harder to continue getting high marks in the face of increasing competition in the upper high school years.

All that personality inventories can do in the case of your own child, most psychologists agree, is to provide tentative indications or clues. These clues could be verified or discarded only in further talk and examination of other evidence. When inventory findings are verified and do lead to the source of a problem, as in the case of Nancy Kaye, they can prove valuable. But in themselves, inventory findings for your child should not be taken as conclusive or even fairly probable. On the evidence—the statistical evidence which is the warrant of all psychological measurement—no personality inventory device could produce anything more than slightly probable findings about your child's personality. On any one occasion, such findings could be flatly wrong—and there is no simple way of telling on *which* occasions they would be wrong.

Just as uncertain results would be obtained from one of the "projective" devices used by a psychologist to explore your child's personality. As mentioned before, these devices include the famous Rorschach inkblots, the misleadingly named Thematic Apperception Test and the sometimes maligned Blacky Pictures. On these or any projective device, your child would look at an image or a picture and say what he thinks it portrays. The assumption is that your child would necessarily "project" his conflicts, worries, tensions and complexes in his interpretations of what he saw. For example, the Rorschach inkblots are irregular cloudy shapes which actually portray nothing but what your child may see in them. The Thematic Apperception Test consists of pictures of people in undescribed situations. The first card, for example, shows a boy of about ten looking at a violin lying on a flat surface. Your child would be shown this and nineteen other pictures one by one, and asked to tell a story about each one as a "test of his imagination." The Blacky

Pictures are a series of cartoon-style drawings about the family life of a little dog named Blacky; with them, your child would similarly be asked to tell a story about what each picture shows. The very rare use of the Blacky Pictures with school children has once or twice raised storms of parental protest, for they were developed for investigating "psychosexual development." The projective method is also applied in words in the "sentence completion technique," in which your child would be asked to finish sentences like, "My mother is . . . ," and, "When I make a mistake . . ."

Most often, projective devices are used only by psychologists who have had long training and experience, and who interpret projective findings in complex descriptions rather than numbers. Some rudimentary or partial scoring systems have been developed for projective instruments. Whenever projective technique results have been reduced to numbers in this way, though, the values of reliability and validity obtained have been far lower than those considered adequate for genuine tests of ability—and in studies involving so few people that no more than barely suggestive significance can be attached to even these results.

For these reasons, as with personality inventories, projective devices should not be used with your child by a counselor who is not highly trained in psychological analysis nor long experienced in using projective techniques. An untrained counselor could get only meaningless or alarming results for your child in a mechanical, cookbook way. Even if the results should be valid for your child by some chance, the counselor would be likely to misinterpret them in trying to help your child.

If properly used, projective devices would be given to your child only by a fully qualified and experienced psychologist. He would interpret the results, not mechanically, but according to what is called "psychological dynamics"—that is, in the light of all his experience, insight and knowledge of your child's past history and psychological make-up. Under these circumstances, projective devices might play a helpful part in resolving some persistent difficulty from which your child had been suffering.

In fact, for any deep-seated personality problem your child may have, no problem checklist or personality device in the hands of an amateur could begin to help as effectively as a trained and capable school psychologist. We have seen in this section how ineffective printed instruments which resemble tests can be when they are used alone in trying to get at the root of personality problems. In the next section, we shall see by contrast how effective school psychologists can be not only in analyzing personality problems, but in helping clear them up.

How a School Psychologist Might Best Help Your Child With Personality Problems

Stories about actual children clearly show how a capable school psychologist can effectively cope with personality problems. These stories are based on some of the case histories given by Mary Alice White, associate professor of psychology and education at Teachers College, Columbia University, and Myron W. Harris in their very good book on *The School Psychologist* (© 1961 by Mary Alice White and Myron W. Harris; adapted by permission of the authors and Harper & Row, Inc., New York).

The case of the impulsive girl of thirteen who had a domineering father and whose school work had suddenly become very poor was mentioned at the beginning of this chapter. As you will recall, the girl's studies suffered because she started to express her growing need to feel independent by rebelling against her teachers and assignments. But there is more to the story. Since the girl also wanted to keep getting high grades, she went to see the school psychologist. With the psychologist, the girl could let her anger and hostilities burst out in talk. The psychologist understood how this relieved her tensions, and listened sympathetically. She continued to see the psychologist once every few weeks, as events especially annoyed her, through her last three years in the school. She did finish with high marks as a result.

Nightmares so fearful that he remembered them with dread for days were the problem of a ten-year-old boy. He was sent to the school psychologist, who used a technique called play therapy to discover and help the boy understand what his terrors were about. Many of them came from fear of asserting himself. The psychologist also saw the boy's parents every other week to get them to lighten the demands which helped stir up their son's fears. The boy's gym teacher and classroom teacher were seen by the psychologist as well, so that they would help him act with normal initiative and aggression, and not be anxious about it. The bad dreams stopped after some six months of interviews.

Another boy, one fifteen years old, went out of his way consistently to antagonize his classmates. They jeered at him because he would not make friends, while he would answer their taunts by sneering at their lack of culture. However, a teacher he liked got him to go to the school psychologist because he was also doing poorly in his studies. The psychologist discovered that the boy had a neurotic problem of long standing. Because no mental health clinic services were available in the community and the family could not afford private treatment, the psychologist saw the boy twice a week for two years. His problems in getting along with other children, and doing well in his school work, greatly improved.

One sixteen-year-old boy was a conspicuous troublemaker in school, and had often been suspended and otherwise disciplined for defying teachers, cutting classes and not doing assignments. The school psychologist was called in after all else had failed and the boy was about to be expelled. The boy had a very discordant home life, the psychologist found, and he could put up with the feared authority represented by his parents only by determined rebellion against them. His behavior in school was accordingly marked by what psychologists call "acting out"—that is, acting out explosive feelings and resentments generated at home mistakenly in the different situation of school. Such self-defeating acting-out of strong resentments and fears with people whom one has no reason to fear or resent in that way is rather commonly seen in rebellious children in school.

The boy's expulsion from school was cancelled by the principal when the psychologist outlined his difficulty and offered to see him twice a week for perhaps a year. The boy brightened after finding a friend in the school psychologist—especially one who was a school official who did not have to punish or blame him for his hostile behavior, as his classroom teachers did. The boy's whole attitude in school began to change, and he was soon able to benefit from his studies and to stop bedeviling his teachers and classmates with his misbehavior.

One girl of fourteen went to the school psychologist herself for help with three problems she claimed to have—her parents' refusals to let her do what she wanted, her trouble in getting along with the school's most popular boys and girls and her wish to transfer into an

English class given by a good-looking young man who had just started teaching. In her third interview, the girl showed the psychologist razor scratches on her wrists which she said she had made the night before in a suicide attempt. The psychologist said that this would have to be told to her parents. Her mother and dad were not particularly alarmed, however, and described some of the girl's frequent melodramatic antics. Further diagnosis of the girl showed strong resentments and fears, but ones which she lived with by scorning and manipulating other people rather than turning against herself. She was definitely not a suicidal risk. From the girl's teachers, the psychologist learned that she was bright and could write well. The psychologist suggested to her that she write for the school paper in order to win the recognition she needed. At first she hung back, afraid of being turned down. But when encouraged further, she tried and was accepted, and became a feature writer. The psychologist met once more with her parents to explain how they might help their daughter express herself without giving in to her attempts to manipulate them.

On occasion, the most important finding of a school psychologist can be that no therapeutic help is needed. At eleven, one boy had had difficulty ever since starting school. He fell farther and farther behind, grew very restless and acted as the "clown" of his class. His teacher tried very hard to help him, but had no success at all. She concluded that the boy must be emotionally disturbed, and she and the principal asked his parents to have the boy go to the school psychologist.

After very carefully diagnosing the boy, however, the psychologist believed that he was not emotionally disturbed in the ordinary sense. Rather, it seemed that serious difficulty in learning was the source of disturbance in other parts of his personality. His trouble seemed to be centered particularly in reading, and the psychologist had him see a reading specialist. The boy was found to be suffering from a rare and apparently inherent mental defect, one which makes it very hard for children who have it to put letters together into words and remember them clearly. The reading specialist, in fact, thought that the eleven-year-old boy had shown remarkable accomplishment in getting as far as he had despite his handicap. This kind of handicap is sometimes called "reading dyslexia" today, and children with it can develop normal reading ability after long, special instruction. So it was with this boy. In a year's time he made two-and-a-half-years' progress in reading, according to achievement tests, and could keep up with his classmates at last. Personally, he was acting like a different boy altogether, and a happy one.

Skilled school psychologists can help with serious personality problems in the ways these stories show because they have long training and experience for it. They are not always right in their judgments, and a few tend to see a psychosis behind every stomach-ache. But their training acquaints them with the great complexities of personality disorders, and the difficulty of finding causes and cures. Rather than jump to conclusions, the capable ones frame hypotheses about the troubles which beset an unhappy child. Generally, they prefer not to treat children in school because it takes far too much of the time they need to spend serving the needs arising among all the pupils in their schools. But the test of their hypotheses, whether they treat the child, or an outside clinic or doctor does, is always whether the child improves.

School psychologists do use personality inventories and projective devices like those we have considered in this chapter. They, with clinical psychologists and psychiatrists seeing people as patients, are the main users of these strange personality assessment instruments. In fact, specialists like these should probably be the only users of them, for only they know enough about the instruments' vagaries and the aspects of personality the instruments do not take into account. Specialists like these can capitalize on the clues such instruments do provide, and at the same time discount misleading indications. Less highly trained persons who might be tempted to use them—teachers, and many guidance counselors now in the schools—simply do not have the necessary background to recognize possibly valid clues and to discard probably invalid ones. Personality instruments and projective devices should not be used by even partial amateurs because their results are so uncertain in consistency, and even meaning, for the inadequately trained. These are the psychological measuring instruments which are still in an experimental stage of development. Specialists do not take their findings at face value, and you should certainly not.

You might wonder if your child's guidance counselor should be able to help in some way with personality problems. Absolutely yes. Generally, guidance counselors are trained to help the broad range of normal children with the many problems they have—in personal development as well as in educational and career planning. Help in getting over shyness, in making friends, in getting along with the opposite sex, in adjusting to you as a parent or in developing good study habits, is the kind of help with personal problems a guidance counselor should be well qualified to provide your child. Information about his capabilities and school achievement, and about good career possibilities, is the kind of help from the guidance counselor for you to expect ·par excellence. The guidance counselor is also very likely to have a sound and professional idea of what your child is like personally. A counselor could also recognize children with difficulties who do not respond to the normal kinds of help the counselor gives, and who may therefore need full-scale diagnosis and possible therapy. But it would be an extremely rare guidance counselor who had sufficient training and experience to actually diagnose and treat without doing more harm than good. Most often, a counselor would refer a child who seems to have really serious problems to someone better qualified to help.

Not all referrals involve serious problems, however, nor even personality difficulties. School psychologists, particularly those working with elementary school children, help with learning problems that need special attention—and prefer to do so while the problems are still minor ones.

Count yourself fortunate if your child does have a good guidance counselor in his school and a good school psychologist in his school district, for both kinds of specialists are in short supply. Most guidance counselors whom we do have work in high schools. Authorities like James B. Conant recommend about 1 counselor per 300 children in a school. Instead, we have about 1 guidance counselor for every 1,000 children now in high school for the nation as a whole. Similarly, the American Association of School Psychologists recommends that schools have 1 psychologist for each 1,000 to 3,000 children, while the national average is far below 1 for every 10,000 school children. Moreover, the counselors and the psychologists that we have in the schools could well do with more training. Many counselors do not have master's degrees in the field, as they should. Many school psychologists have only master's degrees, while it is desirable—according to Paul Woodring, for example—for them to have doctorates.

Though our ignorance of human personality is enormous, there are still a great many useful things that we do know about it. The limitations in our knowledge of personality and its disorders, as reflected in the quite imperfect state of personality and projective instruments, is bad enough for the welfare of our children. Still worse is the fact that we apply so little of what we do know to helping children by not having enough of these specialists—the guidance counselor and the school psychologist—at work in the schools. Their numbers have risen rapidly in recent years, though, and it is heartening to think that they should continue to outpace our rising numbers of school children.

Pressure to do well in school figures especially often in a child's personality problems today, as we have just seen. Your child may feel this pressure already, even if the boy or girl is only in the second or third grade. Some of this pressure stems from yours and your child's natural desires to see him do well in what he attempts. More, probably, stems from the point of greatest pressure in children's lives today—the point at which they try to get into college. The tests which bear on your child at this point—and all of the concern, criticism and misunderstanding which surround them—are themselves examined in the next chapter.

Chapter 6

Can Your Child Get Into College—
And Win a Scholarship
Worth As Much As $10,000?

For the large majority of young people hoping to go to college today, the question of getting in turns in part on standardized tests. More than four out of every five students entering college now take tests required for college admission in their high school senior year. Your child would almost certainly have to take these admissions tests given by the colleges if he planned to go.

Scores on these tests would definitely affect your child's chances of admission. Among parents and children, this is known all too well in the case of the sixty or seventy most sought-after colleges in the land, ones like Harvard, Vassar, Columbia, Princeton, Carleton, William and Mary, Rice, Stanford and Caltech. At these colleges, as you have probably heard, your child would ordinarily have to earn rather high scores on admissions tests in order to have a fair chance of admission, and even very high scores would not guarantee getting in. But most colleges in the country now require entrance tests, and of course take scores on the tests into account in either deciding or advising on admission.

The admissions tests which your child would most probably be asked to take would be those in one or both of the two nation-wide entrance testing programs described in the first chapter—the program of the College Entrance Examination Board (CEEB), in which the long-respected "College Boards" are given, and the American College Testing Program. The 543 member colleges and universities of the CEEB in 1963–1964 require the Board's three-hour Scholastic Aptitude Test (SAT) for applicants, as do perhaps 100 or more non-member colleges. Several hundred also require from one to three of the one-hour Achievement Tests of the Board. More than 800 other colleges and universities participate in the American College Testing Program by requiring or recommending the three-hour ACT examination for their applicants. As with all standardized tests, your child could neither pass nor fail on any of these CEEB and ACT tests because they have no passing or failing levels.

In the states of Florida, New York and Washington the state universities and other interested colleges use special state-wide admissions tests for their applicants rather than CEEB or ACT tests. A number of similar state-wide testing programs consolidated in 1959 to form the ACT program, which is organized as a federation of college testing programs in individual states. ACT's affiliated state programs numbered twenty-eight in 1963–1964.

Your child would find out about registering for and taking CEEB and ACT tests in his high school, or from the colleges to which he writes to ask how to apply. He would take the tests advised by the colleges when he is a high school senior on one of the several scheduled Saturdays a year they are given—probably on a Saturday in early November for the ACT examination, or the first Saturday in December for the SAT. To take the tests, he would go to a "test center" set up in a nearby high school or college. Your child's testing would be run by men and women serving the CEEB or ACT as "test center supervisors" to insure conditions as uniform as possible and to protect against any form of cheating or other unfair advantage on the tests.

About a month after your child had taken the test, his scores would be reported to the colleges and scholarship programs he had indicated when registering for the tests, and also to his school. His school would then very probably give him a booklet provided by ACT or the CEEB which would have on its cover a report of the scores he had earned and which would explain the meaning of his scores. This report would look much like one or the other of the two facsimiles of student score reports below. The first is for the SAT; the second, for the ACT examination.

It is numbers like these which will almost certainly help decide where your child could go to college, and whether or not he might win a scholarship, in the ways this chapter explains.

```
COLLEGE ENTRANCE EXAMINATION BOARD
                              TEST    SCHOLASTIC APTITUDE TEST
                       GRADE  DATE    VERBAL    MATH
SMITH ROBERT            12  1264  625  585

     AH 615    EN 635    FR 615
          ACHIEVEMENT TEST CODES AND SCORES
```

NAME OF STUDENT	ENG.	MATH	SOC. S.	N. SCI.	ENG.	MATH	SOC. S.	N. SCI.	ENG.	MATH	SOC. STUD.	NAT. SCI.	COMP.
JONES ROBERT F	B	C	B	A	A	C	B	B	20	20	22	23	21
	HIGH SCHOOL GRADES								STANDARD SCORES				

ACT   THE AMERICAN COLLEGE TESTING PROGRAM   PRESSCORE ®

Hundreds of scholarships worth as much as $10,000 for the four college years are available throughout the country—a fact of special importance with families now paying an average of some $7,500 for a child's four-year education at private colleges and a corresponding $5,000 even at public colleges. But standardized tests often play an even more important role in winning a scholarship than in gaining admission, as we shall see.

Shortages of College Places—Not Tests in Themselves— Are the Source of Pressure

Admissions tests alone do not generate the anxiety about getting into college which afflicts many American families today. Rather, the fundamental cause is that college has more and more become the sole route by which a boy or girl can enter the middle or upper strata of American life in income, prestige and responsibility.

Great pressure for admission has been brought to bear on the most sought-after, "prestige" colleges because they seem to provide a surer route upward than other colleges, and also because they spend extra millions of dollars on distinction in education—on famous professors, large faculties and small classes, huge libraries, elaborately equipped laboratories, special courses and programs, big gyms and playing fields and handsome living quarters and grounds. But increased pressure for admission has hit almost all colleges because their strenuous efforts to expand have not received the financial support needed for them to keep up with the faster and faster pace of demand.

That demand has grown with the need for people with advanced academic training in our increasingly technical and highly organized economy. We see this need as very good career prospects for many kinds of college-trained specialists. The prospects continue to improve despite the fact that the numbers of college students, and hence the output of college graduates, has already almost doubled in the last fifteen years—from 2.4 million enrolled students in 1948 to 4.4 million in 1963.

You should realize that, as this has happened, it has been the decisions of the students and not of the colleges which have made some colleges selective in admissions. "It isn't a college that decides to make itself selective," an admissions officer has remarked. "Students decide it. No college can afford to be selective until more students decide to apply than the college has room for." And more students heading for college have steadily forced increasing numbers of our colleges to become selective over the last twenty years.

As a result, among middle-class families of our great urban areas especially, the question of getting into a "good" college exerts heavy pressure. It is with the eventual Judgment Day of applying to college at the back of their minds that parents push their children to start reading early and to get high marks all through school. Schools have responded to the need, and stress mastery of formal subjects on a scale never seen before in America. Big-city and suburban schools vie with each other and with private schools to teach their pupils as much of academic subjects as possible. Suspense about college admission thus puts more pressure on the lives of American children today than any other force acting upon them.

Admissions Pressures Around Your Child Will Increase in the Coming Years

Through the next few years your child may find it even harder to get into college than it has become today as these factors of swelling demand and lagging expansion continue to operate. More and more young people of college age have been entering college; 25 per cent of them in only 1951, some 40 per cent today. The proportion will rise to 66 per cent in the years ahead, according to the wishes of parents of young children tallied in a Ford Foundation survey a few years ago.

Just this increasing percentage sent the nation's college enrollments soaring to successive record highs through the late 1950s and early 1960s, when the numbers of young people reaching college age each year stayed about the same. But the increasing percentage has very recently combined with sharp rises in the numbers reaching college age to start the "tidal wave of college students" long forecast for the 1960s. The tidal wave is due to start breaking on college shores in earnest in 1964, when the numbers reaching 18 will suddenly jump by 20 per cent in the first of a series of similar (though smaller) annual jumps to which no end is in sight. Knowing the part which admissions test scores should play in the case of your own child will therefore be more important for those years than for the present.

Send Your Child to College If He Is Well Above Average in Ability— And Possibly Also If He Is *Below* Average in Ability

Still more important than knowing about college tests for the years ahead is your responsibility to see that your child gets a college education if the boy or girl likes and is really good at academic studies. Too many children who could do unusually well or even brilliantly in college fail to go to college today—as many as 100,000 or more high school graduates a year who stand in the top one-third in ability, some authorities estimate. These are often girls, or Negroes, or slum children, or children in poor families on farms or in remote small towns. They could lead satisfying lives without college, but they should be able to lead richer lives with it. Moreover, giving them a chance to develop their unusual talents should benefit the country in general. There will be places for them in college, and financial help with college costs, even in the years of very heavy college crowding ahead. It could be tragic for you to let the crowding keep your child out of college if the boy or girl could do unusually well at college studies.

On the other hand, it may be extremely vital for your child to go to college if the boy or girl is *below* average in scholastic abilities—odd as this may sound to you, or even to many college educators.

Leading college spokesmen have said for a number of years that only students who represent the top half scholastically among all high school graduates should consider going to college. For example, Frank Bowles, director of the education program of the Ford Foundation, has said in his book on *How to Get Into College* that, "basically, college is for students who are above average in ability and above average as students." Being "above average in ability" usually means "an IQ of 110 or better," he explained, which would place a student "toward the bottom of the group of students in college." Above average as a student means above average in his schoolwork in at least one subject area—as compared with students nationally rather than just with students in his school.

Such above-average ability is usually needed, however, for college education of traditional kinds—four years of study in the regular academic or liberal arts and science subjects. The majority of students now in college still take such traditional programs. Colleges today, though, give many newer kinds of programs. With these programs at least partly in mind, Mr. Bowles more recently noted that increasing numbers of students with IQs of about 90 and over were going to college. These programs prepare students for work in a great variety of occupations—as secretaries and many other kinds of office workers; in the operation and repair of mechanical, electrical and electronic equipment; as laboratory technicians and engineering aides; in many different agricultural specialties; and in such service occupations as auto repair, beauty culture and retail sales. Some of these programs are given by two-year colleges, others by four-year colleges. Many of the programs combine courses preparing students for employment with basic studies in traditional academic subjects.

Programs like these can be vitally important for a son or daughter of yours who is below average in scholastic ability because they can arm the child with employable skills. How important this is was recently pointed out by H. Wilson Eaves, guidance counselor at the Westlake High School in Thornwood, New York. Like many other comprehensive high schools today, Westlake offers not only strong college prep studies, but a broad range of "vocational education" courses—secretarial, auto repair, carpentry and electrical or mechanical "industrial arts" courses among them. These resemble similar programs given particularly by two-year "community colleges" and "technical institutes." When asked why such programs were given both on the high school and college levels, Mr. Eaves explained by saying: "Every student in this school can learn, or he wouldn't be here. However, some students learn faster than others."

Westlake offers vocational education courses for faster learners who decide not to go to college, he went on to say. By graduation, students like these can complete both the academic requirements for a high school diploma, and a vocational sequence which prepares them for immediate employment. But many slower learners seem able to complete only the academic work required for the diploma in their high school years; it is they who continue on to a community college after graduation, or even to a four-year college or university, for specialized preparation for earning a living. Of course, some faster learners also go on to the first two years of demanding four-year liberal arts programs at community colleges and later transfer to a four-year college.

For your own child, getting such preparation for earning a living in college could be very important if he were a slow learner of below-average ability, and had not acquired a good set of employable skills before high school graduation. Young men and women without skills today find it harder and harder to get a job. Slow learners can also complete traditional four-year college programs if they have enough interest to keep at their studies for many long hours year after year—and if they enroll in a program or a college without too fast an academic pace.

You and your child might have to do some searching for a college which offers training in employable skills appropriate for slower learners. In many instances, these colleges are not the famous ones about which you often read in magazines and newspapers. However, their programs of "technical" or "semi-professional" instruction serve a very important function, and one of them could prove vital in preparing your child for a productive life.

It is fortunate that many colleges giving such programs are public and low in cost, for slow learners seem to occur more often in lower-income families, although they do develop in families of all income levels. But whether the income of his family be high or low, every slow-learning child deserves the best of chances to get employable skills plus a good basic education—in high school or, if necessary, beyond.

How Admissions Tests Help Your Child Get Into College

Many popular articles and books on testing of the last few years have suggested that college admissions tests threaten to keep your child *out* of college. *They Shall Not Pass* trumpets the title of one of the latest books, while an earlier work denounces *The Tyranny of Testing* —of admissions testing, very largely. Critics have attacked admissions tests for penalizing creative students, profound students, strongly motivated students, late-blooming students, brilliantly one-sided students, impoverished students, Negro students. With all these onslaughts, you might think that college admissions officers were either dupes or dolts for requiring tests.

Nevertheless, almost the exact opposite of the popular misapprehension about admissions tests happens to be the case. It is far more likely that admissions tests will help your child get into college than keep him or her out. Basically, colleges use these tests to make it easier for your child to get admitted to those for which he is qualified—not to make it harder.

Entrance tests make it easier for your child to get into college by giving him a way of showing any college in the country what kind of marks he would probably earn in that college. His test scores serve as a kind of standard academic currency, good at hundreds of colleges which would have no way of appraising the value of the local coinage of his high school marks.

For example, L. Winchester Jones, admissions director at the California Institute of Technology, may well have no way of knowing what your son's B-plus average at Sunnydale High School at the other end of the country means. That is, he may not know if your son is likely to average A or F at Caltech, in the light of your boy's high school average alone. But if the boy has verbal and mathematical scores of over 750 on the Scholastic Aptitude Test of the CEEB, Mr. Jones would have some idea of how your son might do at his college. For he would know that, say, some 80 per cent of the students at his college with double 750s on the SAT get freshman-year averages there of B or better.

Entrance tests can also make it easier for your child to get into college by enabling him to show what he can do in academic work more or less aside from the kind of courses he took in high school. The SAT and the ACT tests give students from weak high schools a fairer chance in being considered for admission along with students from expensive schools. These tests show up general academic ability that poor schooling may have left undeveloped. Even in the College Board Achievement Tests in individual subjects, every effort is made to prepare the tests so that students will have an equally fair chance on them regardless of the kinds of courses in the various subjects they may have taken.

Without such tests as these, your child would probably have to take a rigidly prescribed program of studies preparing for specific colleges. He would probably also have to take essay examinations made up by those colleges to cover their rigid requirements in minute detail. If he could not attend a school giving the fixed preparatory program, he could not consider going to those colleges.

A situation like this is not just imaginary. It was the actual situation in America before the CEEB introduced standardized entrance tests in the 1920s and 1930s—the days when the Board's detailed "Definitions of Requirements" controlled college prep studies with a grip of iron. It is the actual situation today in most other countries of the world. For example, in France and Japan, in Egypt and Chile, a child must get into one of the right secondary schools and must be examined on great masses of rigidly fixed rote learning for admission to a university. To get into a university in some countries your child would have to go to an expensive commercial cram school for a year *after* his secondary education—and he still might not have memorized enough in the extra year to qualify on the entrance exams!

America's present entrance tests do have their limitations. But in comparison with entrance systems used in other countries they provide a remarkably fair and valid passport to higher education for your child. If your child actually can do passing or better work in traditional college studies of standard quality, entrance tests will almost certainly open his way to an extraordinary number and variety of college opportunities.

The tests can still help your child if the boy or girl cannot do passing work in some colleges, by flying warning flags of likely failure. Though such flags would obviously not help your child get into those colleges, they could serve two equally important purposes: At least they could signal possible anguish and waste ahead; at most, they could give him guideposts by which to steer into a kind of college program he could profit from.

What Your Child's Admissions Test Scores Would Really Mean

Much has been said in public in recent years about the meaning of admissions test scores, as we noted before. Most of it has condemned one or another aspect of the tests—the character of the multiple-choice questions which the tests mainly use, the anxiety which has developed around the tests, the fact that the tests give little or no indications of qualities like creativity, resolve or high purpose. The bulk of this denunciation has, however, ignored the main point. What must be reckoned with fundamentally is the evidence—the massive, experimental evidence, on which the use of admissions tests rests.

This evidence can be seen most lucidly in a device called an "expectancy table." An appropriate expectancy table tells the whole truth, and nothing but the truth, about what the scores of your child on an admissions test would really mean.

If your child were to come upon flags warning of danger of possible failure at a particular college, they would fly conclusions drawn from the facts of an expectancy table. Were your child to be welcomed into a much sought-after college largely because of his test scores, the red carpet would rest on probabilities like those of an expectancy table. In a highly practical way, an expectancy table shows the combined effect of key ·qualities of a test—the qualities of validity, reliability and error of measurement which were explained in an earlier chapter. Yet such a table can be understood, completely, by anyone who can read numbers.

Most often, one of these tables will sum up the connection between the scores which students at one college earned on an admissions test and the average of the freshman-year marks or grades they later obtained. An expectancy table gives the odds with which you can expect a student with certain test scores, like your own child, to earn average freshman-year grades of certain levels. As an example, the accompanying table is an actual expectancy table prepared for a large Midwestern university by the American College Testing Program. The ACT program makes up a complete set of expectancy tables like the accompanying one for each of the several hundred colleges which take part in its annual Research Service. (This table, reproduced by permission of the American College Testing Program, was used in 1962, and does not show refinements in form and content subsequently introduced into such ACT Research Service expectancy tables.)

Expectancy Table for a Large Midwestern University—Average Freshman-year English Marks as Predicted on the Basis of ACT Test Scores, and as Actually Earned in Freshman English Courses

Freshman English average as predicted on the basis of ACT test scores *	*Percentage of students in each prediction range who earned actual freshman English averages indicated:*				*Number of students in each prediction range*
	D & up	C & up	B & up	A	
A	0	0	0	0	0
A-minus to B-plus	0	0	0	0	0
B	100%	96%	63%	17%	180
B-minus to C-plus	98%	87%	31%	3%	763
C	97%	69%	9%	0	626
C-minus to D-plus	92%	43%	1%	0	158
D	100%	26%	13%	0	15
Lower	0	0	0	0	0
Total					1,742 Students

* These predicted averages in the ACT program represent certain ACT test score levels—the levels of scores typically earned by students in this particular college who later earn the corresponding freshman-year English averages shown. ACT computes and reports the predicted averages to the individual colleges so that its admissions officers can most easily understand what the test scores generally mean for that college's own students.

This table is not so complicated as it may seem to you at first. You could use it, very easily, for your own child. Suppose that your child had gotten ACT test scores which the college would know corresponded to a freshman English average in the "B-minus to C-plus" range. By reading along that line in the table, you could see that, for a large group of students at the college who earned test scores much like those of your child, 98 per cent of these students actually earned freshman English averages of D and up, 87 per cent earned averages of C and up, 31 per cent earned averages of B and up and 3 per cent earned A averages.

How Well Your Own Child's College Marks Might Be Predicted

Now, what would this have to do with your child? First, you have to decide for reasons outside the facts shown in the table whether or not your child was similar to the students going to the college—in things like age, high school education, home and cultural background and health and personal development. Suppose that he or she is, which is quite likely. Then you would know that, for every 100 comparable students who earned test scores like his, 98 averaged D and up, 87 averaged C and up, 31 averaged B and up and 3 averaged A. These numbers indicate the chances with which you could expect your child to earn similar grades, so far as his test scores are concerned. With scores falling in this "B-minus to C-plus" prediction range, your child is almost certain to do passing work in freshman English at this college; only 2 of every 100 students with similar scores averaged below D. On the other hand, it is very unlikely that your child would earn a freshman English average of A in the college; only 3 students of 100 with scores like his do. In the same way, his chances of earning an average of B or better can be said to be about 1 in 3 (31 in 100, to be precise); his chances of averaging C or better seem quite large—87 in 100. As his prediction range indicates, your child would be most likely to average about B-minus to C-plus in freshman English.

Two things about the table may surprise you. First, it shows again that there are *no certainties* for an individual like your child so far as test scores indicate—there are only *probabilities*. The vital consequences of this will be taken up shortly. Second, notice what happened to the very few students—15 of the 1,742 for whom a D average was predicted. All averaged at least D in freshman English, though 12 of them (100 per cent minus 26 per cent, or 74 per cent) averaged below C. But 4 of them (26 per cent) averaged C or better, and of these 4, 2 students (13 per cent of the 15) made averages of B or better, but not A.

Though few in number, these low-scoring students did better than you might at first imagine in view of the performance of the higher-scoring groups; none of these 15 lowest-scoring ones failed, for example. These lowest-scoring young people seem to be students who find studies hard but who enter and get through college because of unusually strong determination and hard work. Other students who scored equally low would probably not have had the determination or interest to continue at studying because they find it unusually difficult.

Over the years, testing psychologists have found that the marks students earn in high school predict future marks in college with as good or slightly better approximate accuracy than test scores. Psychologists have also found that still more nearly accurate predictions result when both test scores and high school marks are combined. Many hundreds of colleges using admissions tests today would accordingly combine your child's test scores with his high school marks to get an idea of the college marks he is most likely to get.

The ACT Research Service uses both ACT test scores and high school course marks in this way to make up further expectancy tables for individual colleges. These tables look just like the ACT expectancy table in form, but in most cases they show higher percentages of students actually earning the college freshman-year averages that ACT predicts for them. That is, these tables show the college graphically that predicted college averages based on both test scores and high school marks prove correct with more students than do predictions based on either test scores or high school marks alone.

A predicted college average of this kind for your child would still be uncertain, for three main reasons, Psych Corp President George K. Bennett points out: the inaccuracies of test scores and high school grades as true indicators of your child's abilities; the possibility that he will work harder for high marks in college than he had on entrance tests and prep courses; and variations in difficulty levels of college courses and course marking standards.

Were your child to apply to one of the 540 or more colleges which require the College Board SAT instead of the ACT test, the college might accordingly use an expectancy table like the accompanying one in estimating the freshman-year marks the boy or girl might earn. It is based on both SAT scores and standing by high school marks. This table applies to the men's college at Tulane University; it gives most of the actual "index numbers" that admissions director Cliff W. Wing, Jr., and his colleagues considered in admitting the college's class of 1967.

Expectancy Table for Men Applicants at Tulane University's College of Arts and Sciences—Chances in 100 of Obtaining a C-plus or Better Average in Freshman-year Liberal Arts Work (Based on SAT Scores and Rank in High School Graduating Class; Used as "Index Numbers" in Selecting 1963 Entering Freshmen) *

DECILE RANK IN CLASS	SAT VERBAL 40							45							50							55							60							65							70						
	SAT MATH							SAT MATH							SAT MATH							SAT MATH							SAT MATH							SAT MATH							SAT MATH						
	40	45	50	55	60	65	70	40	45	50	55	60	65	70	40	45	50	55	60	65	70	40	45	50	55	60	65	70	40	45	50	55	60	65	70	40	45	50	55	60	65	70	40	45	50	55	60	65	70
1	42	47	52	56	61	65	69	48	53	57	62	66	70	74	53	58	62	67	71	75	78	59	63	68	72	75	79	82	64	68	72	76	80	83	85	69	73	77	80	83	86	88	74	77	81	84	86	89	91
2	35	39	44	48	53	58	62	40	45	49	54	58	63	67	45	50	55	59	64	68	72	51	56	60	65	69	73	76	56	61	65	70	73	77	80	62	66	70	74	78	81	84	67	71	75	78	82	85	87
3	28	32	36	41	45	50	54	33	37	41	46	51	55	60	38	42	47	52	56	61	65	43	48	52	57	61	66	70	49	53	58	62	67	71	75	54	59	63	67	71	75	79	59	64	68	72	76	79	83
4	22	25	29	33	37	42	47	26	30	34	38	43	47	52	31	35	39	44	48	53	57	36	40	45	49	54	58	63	41	45	50	55	59	64	68	46	51	55	60	64	69	73	52	56	61	65	69	73	77
5	16	19	23	26	30	34	39	20	23	27	31	35	40	44	24	28	32	36	40	45	50	29	33	37	41	46	51	55	33	38	42	47	51	56	61	38	43	48	52	57	61	66	44	48	53	58	62	66	71
6	12	14	17	20	24	28	32	15	18	21	24	28	32	37	18	22	25	29	33	37	42	22	26	30	34	38	43	47	27	30	35	39	44	48	53	31	35	40	44	49	54	58	36	41	45	50	54	59	63
7	8	10	13	15	18	21	25	11	13	16	19	22	26	29	14	16	19	23	26	30	34	17	20	23	27	31	35	40	20	24	28	32	36	40	45	25	28	32	37	41	46	50	29	33	38	42	47	51	56
8	6	7	9	11	13	16	19	8	9	11	14	17	20	23	10	12	14	17	20	24	27	12	15	18	21	24	28	32	15	18	21	25	29	33	37	19	22	26	30	34	38	43	23	26	30	34	39	43	48
9	4	5	6	8	10	12	14	5	6	8	10	12	15	17	7	8	10	13	15	18	21	9	11	13	16	19	22	25	11	31	16	19	22	26	30	14	17	20	23	27	31	35	17	20	24	28	32	36	40

* Reproduced with permission from the publication, *Admissions Information: A Report on some of the Characteristics of the Class of 1967*, Tulane University Office of Admissions.

To see how this table would work, suppose that your son was applying to Tulane and has a verbal score on the SAT of 584 and a mathematical score of 523. Also, assume that the average of his high school marks placed him in the second highest tenth—the second "decile"—of his graduating class. Tulane's prediction system follows the fairly widespread practice of taking rank in high school graduating class as an index of high school marks, rather than the overall average of high school marks. (Your child's rank in class would, of course, be where he stood among his classmates on the basis of average of the marks he had gotten in all or some of his high school courses. Methods of figuring class rank vary; some, for instance, use average of marks in only college prep courses.) Class rank may reflect the student's motivation for high academic achievement to a greater degree than overall average of marks, some authorities believe. Their belief cannot be proven since no one yet knows how to measure motivation validly and reliably.

To read the table for your son, then, you would first take your son's SAT verbal score of 584 and drop the third digit to make it 58;

you would next round it off to the nearest multiple of 5, or 60. You would also take the same steps with your son's SAT mathematical score, converting the 523 to 50. Then, in the section of the table headed with the large "60" under "SAT VERBAL," you would locate the narrow column headed "50" right under the small "SAT MATH" heading. You would run your finger down this "50" column two boxes, to locate the row identified at the far left by "2," which corresponds to your son's rank in the second decile or tenth of his class. Finally, you would read the number "65" in this box. The "65" means that 65 of every 100 men students with similar scores and class rank averaged C-plus or better at Tulane in their freshman-year liberal arts work.

Tulane calls the numbers like the "65" for your son a "scholastic index," and explains that men applicants with an index of 50 or better have been accepted about 95 per cent of the time. It seems very likely that your son would be admitted if he did have an index of 65. Applicants with an index of between 35 and 50 have had a reasonably good chance of being admitted, Tulane further explains. Those with an index between 25 and 35 are "in a borderline zone," in which "a decision may be turned in the favorable direction on the basis of the type of preparatory school background (i.e., schools where the senior class average SAT verbal is over 550) and strong recommendations." The odds are about 9 to 1 against admission of a student with an index below 25.

It should be pointed out that Tulane does not use these index numbers as the sole basis of admission. All the factors in the student's file are taken into consideration in arriving at a final admissions decision. While Tulane believes that index numbers such as these provide a better basis for describing the admissions process than either test scores or school records taken singly, it uses these indexes with caution, and the overall impression given by a candidate's file may well provide a basis for a decision which would not go strictly according to the numbers.

Dr. Wing of Tulane expresses a view widespread among admissions directors when he comments on his methods: "Though numbers are helpful, they can be misused when one attempts to make distinctions within their error ranges. Numbers can form a basis for a decision-making process, but once the number system fails to distinguish or you want something not reflected by the numbers, you have to rely on other types of judgment."

You may be struck by the very large effect which rank in high school class seems to have on getting high marks in Tulane's College of Arts and Sciences, compared with the apparently lesser effect of test scores. A student with the somewhat modest SAT scores of 450 verbal and 400 mathematical but who ranks in the second tenth or decile of his class has an index of 40. A student like this would be a fair bet for admission. However, a student with the very high scores of 700 verbal and 700 mathematical but who ranks in the ninth decile of his class also has an index of only 40. The striking contrast in scores and class rank in these two instances clearly illustrates that neither test scores nor an index of high school marks alone give as useful information as both together.

The meaning of class rank naturally varies from one kind of school to another. In view of this, Tulane uses "more refined procedures" than those reflected in the table for applicants from "preparatory schools with selective admissions standards and where approximately 99% of the class is college bound." For other schools "where under 50% of the graduates attend college," Tulane also notes, "the index numbers in the table tend to be slightly higher than those actually assigned here if the student is in the lower half of his graduating class."

Many other CEEB member institutions have similarly prepared predictive indices and expectancy tables of their own. In addition, the Board is also experimenting with making up such research data for individual colleges through a central "prediction service," as in its current "Indiana Prediction Study."

Both CEEB and ACT colleges would base advice to your child about admission on such expectancy data were he or she to visit as an applicant. Also, they are giving more and more data like these to counselors in your child's school who have the further experience needed to interpret it wisely.

Colleges Require Your Child to Take Admissions Tests So That They Can Forecast Most Accurately—and, Therefore, Most Fairly—for All

From these tables, you can see why colleges have found it essential to use admissions tests with applicants like your child. Whatever else colleges must do, they must first try to provide as effective education as they can. And the basic yardstick of the effectiveness of their education has to be the judgments of their own professors—grades or marks in college courses—despite all the shortcomings of grades given by professors. David Riesman, the sociologist, recently remarked that the grades given by himself and his Harvard colleagues provided a way of comparing "often incommensurable performances" that could still not be dispensed with. "But we should be clear to ourselves and others," he added, "that it is a short cut, not a substitute for more qualitative and more differentiated judgments."

Necessarily, then, colleges must take their professors' grades as their basic standard, and must take into account the best indicators of future college grades they can get in considering applicants. And the best indicators available, though far from perfect, are the combinations of test scores and high school marks on which expectancy tables like the ones we have seen are based.

You may think, "Oh, a college will use these mechanical things like average of high school marks and test scores just to save time, with all the hundreds of young people applying. But the college could certainly do a better job of finding out how well a student could do there academically if some understanding person just sat down and talked with the boy or girl."

If you did think something like this, though, you would be wrong. Colleges do like to have their admissions officers and professors talk with applicants, and they would be glad to interview your child. But a number of studies have shown that they should interview your child in order to exchange information and clear up possible misunderstandings of his about the college, rather than to get an impression of the marks he might earn. These studies have found that interview impressions make the mathematical predictions *less* accurate, not more.

One such study, for example, concerned interview judgments of applicants to the Harvard Graduate School of Business. It was made by Lewis B. Ward, a research professor at the School, and S. A. Kendrick, now the CEEB staff member in charge of the Board's research program. One year, as an experiment, forty men were admitted to the school's entering class because a favorable interview impression had tipped the balance in favor of admitting each of the forty. Another forty men were admitted because other qualifications (like college marks) indicated that each man would do well in spite of relatively *unfavorable* interview impressions which would otherwise have kept them out.

During the school's two-year program, ten of the forty men for whom the favorable interview impression had been decisive flunked out. But only three of the forty men who had made unfavorable interview impressions flunked out, and these forty also earned consistently higher marks than the first forty. On top of that, faculty members overwhelmingly rated the men who had initially made unfavorable interview impressions as the students with higher "executive potential," while classmates also rated them preferable as future bosses, fellow workers or employees. Both the faculty members' and the classmates' high opinions of this forty closely agreed with the high marks the forty had earned—that is, in general, the higher the opinions held about one of the forty, the higher the marks he had earned. Accordingly, the Harvard Business School stopped including interview results with the information it used in making admissions decisions.

A question much larger than one of only academic ability was the major point in this study—the question of whether interviews added anything of value to an overall appraisal of the applicant, not only in intellect, but in character. As the reactions of professors and classmates indicated, interview assessments seemed actually misleading in picking the best all-around men.

However, the larger question still remains open. According to Mr. Kendrick, colleges today are "quite divided" about whether to use interviews to evaluate applicants, or merely to be cordial and informative with applicants; some colleges evaluate in interviews, while many merely inform. And no conclusive evidence of the value of the admissions interview for either academic or personal prediction has yet been produced.

By using only combinations of test scores and high school marks, then, colleges can most surely predict the kinds of marks in college which an entering class as a whole will earn. From any one year to the next, the averages which groups of freshmen actually earn differ very little from the averages which can be calculated for them in advance on the basis of expectancy tables. This results because the character of a college's student body, and of a college's course work and grading practices, change quite slowly—and all that an expectancy table does is to sum up how students with various levels of scores and school marks have performed in the college in the past. With expectancy tables based on scores and school marks, then, a college can predict how *groups* of prospective students which might include your own child would do in academic work at the college with near certainty. One college which makes extensive use of pure mathematical prediction in its admissions decisions declares, for example, "The percentage of students who flunk out is negligible."

For your child, this greater accuracy in prediction with tests insures greater fairness in being considered for admission along with all others applying. Forecasts without tests would be less accurate and would therefore give greater scope for the exercise of unfair hunches and impressions in judging your child's academic ability—which is his basic qualification—as compared with the academic ability of all other children applying with him.

But the Final Truth—Both Shocking and Reassuring—About Your Child's Admissions Test Scores Is Their Ultimate Uncertainty

For your own child—for any *individual* student—what do admissions test scores mean in the light of expectancy tables? The ultimate answer is shocking from one point of view, yet reassuring from another. As we saw before in connection with other tests, your child's scores on college admissions tests mean *nothing certain at all in his individual case.*

Some writers believe that this is disturbing only if the probabilities applying to your child's test scores and school marks indicate that he is only slightly more likely to get average marks in a college than he is to get either failing or superior marks. But the meaning of your child's admissions test scores is still uncertain even if he has very high probabilities of doing superior work or failing work in the college. For no one has yet found any way of telling which individual children will be the exceptions—which children will be the 5 in every 100 for whom A is predicted but who nevertheless flunk out, or which ones will be the 3 in every 100 for whom D is predicted yet who eventually get A.

Admissions officers see these exceptions in their own personal experience. As an example, scores on the College Board SAT range from a low of 200 to a high of 800, as we saw. And the admissions director at an Ivy League college has remarked, "The SAT is a measure of ability, but I have seen boys with test scores in the 700s flunk out, and I have seen boys with test scores in the 300s graduate." However, very low SAT scores, he pointed out, were "almost conclusive" for his college, at which "verbal aptitude at the bottom of the pack makes a boy a poor risk for any degree program, no matter what his other credentials show, and very low mathematical aptitude makes a boy a poor risk for a bachelor of science program." He could recall only "one exception in thirteen years—a boy with consistently low Scholastic Aptitude Test scores who had an excellent record in high school and in college." But he added that, "I never saw anyone who could succeed in a bachelor of science program with low mathematical aptitude."

Still, the uncertainty in the case of your own child is there, and it is bottomless. There is no way to tell if he or she would be one of the exceptions—the 1 in 100, or even the 1 in 100,000. This may shock you, for it has shocked many people—this fact that colleges base admissions decisions which seem terribly important to them, personally, at least in part on indications which might be far wrong in the case of their own individual children.

Colleges are not complacent about this; they know they commit an injustice when the indications on which they rejected a student later prove false, and they have long been pressing research specialists to develop more accurate individual predictions. However, more accuracy has proven extremely difficult to achieve. And in the meantime, hundreds of studies and years of experience with many hundreds of thousands of students all show massively that the colleges would commit *more* injustices—not fewer—by giving up their standardized admissions tests. You can be sure that the colleges try to be as fair with your child and all other children as scientific research and seasoned judgment now make it possible for them to be.

The conscientious care of the college admissions officer was well expressed by Frank Bowles, then head of the College Board, in a talk ten years ago. As quoted in the College Board volume, *College Admissions 1*, he said:

> ...it is this significance [of each application] which can make the job of the admissions officer so difficult and so rewarding. He must deal not only with the facts that are on the record, but with the mind and spirit behind the facts. He is entrusted with some part, perhaps small, perhaps large, of the life of each candidate. Dealing with this trust is as inescapable a part of the admissions responsibility as is the obligation to select carefully in choosing a freshman class.

Viewed in a different light, however, the inevitable uncertainty of your child's test scores is reassuring. It has, first, a great practical value. A strong indication that the odds are against your child's doing passing work in a college could be just the thing that fires him to do passing or even superior work there—if he gets the chance to try. Small but genuine odds that your child might fail, even though his test scores indicate an A average in college, could keep him from feeling that he will get his As without any effort. Predictive odds can thus be a potent factor in your child's determination, in the resolve with which he faces up to his tasks.

Even more important, the basic uncertainty of your child's test scores has a deep personal significance. It means that science has no way of making an absolutely certain determination of your child's mental caliber. By being unambitious and lazy, your child can betray the highest expectations of future brilliance. Or by effort and good luck, your child might eventually turn out to be a genius despite lack of any early indications. Whatever his test scores, your child still ultimately controls his own destiny. This is not just pious sentiment. The expectancy tables prove it.

Your Child Could Get Jarring Evidence of Uncertainty Should His Test Scores Drop

No more alarming proof of the uncertainty of your child's test scores could appear than if the test scores on which he is depending to get into college took a large, sickening drop. He could experience such a drop in this way: Your child might well take the SAT in both the junior and senior high school year were the boy or girl trying for admission to one of the highly selective colleges. More than a million students a year do take the SAT (or the largely equivalent PSAT, the Preliminary Scholastic Aptitude Test) as high school juniors before taking the SAT as seniors. Taking the SAT or PSAT in the junior year, many high schools believe, provides students with useful practice and with advance scores for college guidance, before they are examined on the SAT as seniors for admission itself.

Ordinarily, your child's SAT scores would go up from his junior to his senior year. His increase in verbal SAT score would be some 35 points if his case were just like the average of all students—10 points more through the effect of practice, and another 25 points as a result of normal growth of capacities measured by the verbal parts of the

SAT over the seven or eight months which usually intervene between testings.

But the ultimate uncertainty of your child's SAT scores would be dramatically driven home if he should happen to be in the minority of students whose SAT scores *drop* from their junior to their senior year. In a few cases, this drop can be an alarmingly big one for no apparent reason—as big a difference as 100 or more points on the 800-point SAT score scale. A 100-point difference could keep your child out of a preferred college under certain rare circumstances. The chances your child would run of having his SAT verbal score drop have been calculated by the CEEB and made public so that colleges and high schools would be forewarned. Were several thousand young people to take alternate forms of the SAT verbal sections two days in a row, 42 in every 100 should find that their SAT verbal scores had dropped by the following amounts:

Score Drop of:	Experienced by This Many Students in Every 100:
90 points or more	2
Between 60 and 90 points	6
Between 30 and 60 points	13
Up to 30 points	21
Total	42 Students

Spectacular or smaller *jumps* in their SAT verbal scores would be gotten by the other 58 children in every 100, as follows:

Score Jumps of:	Experienced by This Many Students in Every 100:
90 points or more	5
Between 60 and 90 points	11
Between 30 and 60 points	18
Up to 30 points	24
Total	58 Students

(This table, and the similar one above, are reprinted with permission from *College Board Score Reports: A Guide for Counselors*, published in 1962 by the College Entrance Examination Board. This publication is revised annually and distributed to counselors.)

Your child would run only a small chance of suffering a score drop as large as 100 points—less than 2 chances in 100. However, of every million young people a year who take the SAT or PSAT in their high school junior year, the SAT verbal scores gotten by some 20,000 in their senior year show, in effect, drops of 90 or more points. Just by chance, and as a stunning illustration of the uncertainty of his test scores, your child might be one of the 20,000.

A drop of this order could occur from the nature of testing itself, and could happen on *any* test. It would not result because of any failings of the SAT as a test. Technically and educationally, the SAT is as sound a test of general aptitude for college studies as can now be made, most test specialists and educators familiar with assessing college potential would tell you.

Counselors and colleges would also assure you that even a 100-point drop in your child's SAT verbal score from junior to senior year would not decisively change his prospects for admission at a particular college in most cases, however. For, if the second score seemed totally inconsistent with your child's high school marks, colleges would use the first, higher one as an index of his academic potential. If not, they would average the scores and subtract 10 points or less from the average to allow for the effect of practice. Doing this would give an adjusted SAT verbal score within 60 points of the highest score your child had earned. And a difference of 60 points in verbal score seldom acts as the sole, decisive factor in a child's admission or rejection by a college.

It does not, mainly, because colleges know that the standard error of measurement for the SAT verbal sections is about 32 points. They would therefore realize that the odds are about 2 to 1 that any actual score for your child lies within 32 points of his theoretical "true" score, and about 19 to 1 that any actual score lies within 64 points of his true score.

Stay Open-minded About Colleges for Your Child Because Test Scores— and Other Indicators—Are Uncertain

Because the admissions test scores of any individual child like your own are unavoidably uncertain, critics have atacked admissions tests in recent years. Behind their attacks has stood the unspoken idea that the tests ought to be much better predictors, or even perfect ones, if colleges are to use them at all. But most of these critics have failed to point out that any other indicators which colleges could use are also uncertain. As we saw earlier, marks in high school courses used alone do not predict college academic performance with as high a degree of accuracy as marks and test scores together. Impressions obtained in an interview, or in a student's recommendation by his school principal or guidance counselor, forecast academic work still less reliably, though they are helpful to colleges and students for other obvious reasons involving character, health and emotional stability.

In the face of this uncertainty, you could be most helpful to your child by taking a broad rather than a narrow view of the colleges to which your child might go. To set your heart and your child's hopes only on one or more colleges which are very demanding academically today would risk bitter and totally needless disappointment. It may be that your child actually could keep up with the rapid pace of studies at a Yale or a Stanford despite high school marks and admissions test scores that indicate probable failure. But you would have to agree that the college would be fair in taking another applicant instead for whom passing or better work were indicated.

Moreover, colleges like these have several times as many fully qualified applicants as they have room for. And at colleges that have to be highly selective, some students who are rejected seem to be better qualified on academic indications alone than other students whom the college accepts on the basis of academic ability plus other qualities—among them, musical talent, residence in a distant part of the country, overcoming handicaps as a Negro, athletic ability and leadership in school or community affairs. In other words, you could not count on your child's admission to a particular highly selective college even if the boy or girl should have very high marks and admissions test scores.

Your wisest course today would accordingly be one that many families follow with the help of school guidance counselors. They have their bright children apply to at least three colleges—one or more of the highly selective variety, one moderately selective to which the student would probably be admitted and one—perhaps a little-known college or the local community college—where admission is practically certain. It would of course make you feel proud, and it might help your child somewhat in later life, if he does go to one of the most famed and rigorous colleges in the land. However, the kind of record your child makes in college counts far more in his future success than which college he goes to, in and of itself. An honors graduate of Ohio State or Oklahoma (universities which still accept almost any high school graduates of their states) would command considerably more respect for his powers than the man who barely makes it through Princeton.

How Colleges Would Use Your Child's Test Scores in Deciding His Admission

No two colleges would consider your child's test scores in exactly the same way in weighing his application, for no two colleges are exactly alike in their views of qualifications or in the kinds of applicants and students they have. However, these four basic points would be true of the effect of test scores on your child's admission at any and all colleges:

1. Your child's test scores would be considered as only one of several different and about equally important kinds of qualifications.

2. Your child's test scores would be looked at to see if he might be able to do at least passing work in his studies at the individual college, or to see about what level of work—like average, above average or terrific—he might do there.

3. Your child's test scores could not be so low that he would not get into any college. Test scores alone cannot keep your child out of college altogether.

4. Your child's test scores could be quite low and he could still be admitted to any of some 700 colleges in the country which accept all or almost all high school graduates. Low scores would be 300 or less on the College Board SAT (on which the score scale is 200–800), or 8 or lower in composite score on the ACT test (which has a 1–36 score scale).

Out of what appears to be almost morbid fascination, national magazines and popular books have explained how admissions selection works today at only a few of the most highly selective colleges in the country—at Yale in *The New Yorker*, for example, and at Princeton in *Life*. Accounts at colleges like these have been about as helpful to most parents in the country as stories about raising penguins for fun and profit would be. To say the least, the most highly selective colleges represent a rare extreme in the national admissions picture. Besides, most popular accounts of such extreme selection at work have played up the thrills and chills in the process.

One explanation of admission to a highly selective college was given without thrills and chills by Emery R. Walker, Jr., then dean of admission at Brown University and now admission dean at three of the

Claremont Colleges in California—Claremont Men's, Harvey Mudd and Pitzer. Speaking at a College Board admissions colloquium several years ago, he gave examples of actual decisions from his work at Brown in highly abbreviated but fully authentic form. These were not typical examples, he said, "since there is really no such thing. Every kind of variation is possible." The examples appear in the College Board volume, *College Admissions 3*, and are reprinted here by permission.

"Here is Case A," Dean Walker began, taking up an applicant in his condensed account of the way in which the boy had been considered by the university's board of admissions.

> I start on the outside of the folder, which bears a form summarizing key data and steps in our processing:
> "David A., Suburbia, Massachusetts, Suburbia High, A.B. program applicant." Then I open the folder. "SAT 651, 676. [These are the SAT verbal and mathematical scores; College Board Achievement Test scores, also reported on a 200-to-800-point scale, follow.] Social Studies 607, Spanish 691, Advanced Math 592. With recommendation grade of B [the grade required by the boy's high school for its college recommendation], he has nearly all As. No gaps." That is, requirements complete. "Number 1 in a class of 265. IQ 154. Superior in everything." That means, in all nine personal qualities on the character check list. "Exceptionally." The principal checked him as exceptionally ready and willing to do the work at Brown. "Mature, able, conscientious and gifted." This is the principal's statement about the boy.
> The point of decision has been reached, but we go on quickly, "A interview." We grade interviews A, B, C, D, and almost no one gets an A. "One of the very best; he's got everything," reports the interviewer. "Father, life insurance; both parents college graduates. Two hundred pounds, 6 foot 5. Football 3, 4; basketball 1, 2, 3, 4; track 1, 2, 3, 4 [the numbers refer to high school years in varsity sports competition]; honor society president, student council, dramatic society president, and so on." Now we're just reveling. We could stop, but they don't come like this very often. One reference—a teacher—checks him superior in everything. The other checks him average in emotional stability, superior in everything else, and says, "Inclined to be moody in defeat, too sensitive. Shows improvement." Small fault, and just about the only one he has. Obviously, we take him.

In contrast to this clear-cut acceptance, the dean gave the following example:

> Robert B. of Pin Point, South Dakota, High School. Engineer [the boy's college program preference]. "SAT 310, 332. Grades half Cs and Ds, no

language [foreign language, a subject requirement]." The point of decision is reached. We will not take him, but we flip it through. "Forty-first in a class of forty-six. 'Probably' ready. (This, again, is the principal's recommendation.) C interview. Choir. Average references." The action is obvious.

How personality can offset high marks and scores was illustrated in a third example described by the dean, one concerning a boy he called Dennis F.

Big City High School, Big City, Ohio. Wants arts [liberal arts program]. College Board SAT scores 620, 640. Sixty-five is recommended [college recommendation grade average of the boy's high school]. Grades—85 average. First fifth of class. IQ 145. "Clearly" ready. School says, "This boy is clearly superior material with a clear goal ahead. He has considerable drive and vigor and should do very well in science. He has courtesy and tact, as well as integrity." Interview—D; interviewer says, "This boy said, 'But of course I realize that Brown's engineering and physics courses don't rate very well.' A very blase and most unattractive young man." Father lawyer. Normal activities [extracurricular activities in high school]. Good reference from business associate of father's. We turned down this soul of tact and courtesy. An interview can be important.

In another case, the Brown admissions board deliberately discounted low test scores.

Peter E. Milltown, Massachusetts, High School. Chemist. SAT 341, 501. Eighty is recommended; he has all 90s and 95s. Eighth in a class of 410. California IQ 118. Superior qualities. "Excellent pianist." "Clearly" ready. Born in Milltown, but both parents born in Syria. Both references teachers; one says, "unusual boy ... good mind ... great capacity for works ... hours of practice on the piano ... fine musician." We hesitate a moment over his low SAT. However, foreign language background probably accounts for this; his true aptitudes are lower than they should be, but not so low as those scores indicate. With so many assets, we take him.

A California boy, Larry D., hovered on the borderline in Dean Walker's account.

Waltersville, California, High School. Chemist. SAT 471, 395. English 399, Chemistry 486, Intermediate Math 416. B is recommendation grade and he's half As and half Bs. No gaps. Eighth in a class of 147. Stanford-Binet IQ 131. Superior in everything. "Clearly" ready. They say, "Larry has done an outstanding job as our student body president. He has maintained a good scholarship rating while engaging in outside activities. His ability to endure frustration and continue to discharge his responsibilities is of high caliber. He will be a success." Father Army officer, college graduate. Student body president, Spanish club president, member of the California Scholarship Federation, math club, Hi-Y. Both references check him tops but one, the teacher, says his weakness is "his ability to express himself in writing." Here we go all the way through without reaching the point of decision. There is good and bad here—fine record, but in a school we don't know. IQ good, but College Board test scores weak. Finally, we decide to take him. We certainly want him from the personality and character point of view, and there seems to be enough academic quality to indicate that he will get by; he might even be a pretty good student. However, we accept him for an A.B., not for our B.S. program, since his mathematical aptitude is low.

Today, the College Board test scores of corresponding applicants might be slightly higher, for larger numbers of students applying have resulted in more students with higher scores trying for highly selective colleges like Brown. Also, many of these colleges more systematically combine test scores and high school marks or class rank into a predictive index, as we saw in the case of Tulane. For a number of years Yale has used an "adjusted school grade," and Princeton a "predicted rank list"—both of them systems for producing more accurate predictions from school marks and test scores. One highly selective college admits half of its class today strictly by prediction formula, and uses preferences for other qualities decided by the college along with academic ability to fill the rest of the class.

However, the basic elements entering into an admissions decision—the academic indicators (school marks, rank in class, preparatory courses and test scores) and personal qualifications (as evidenced in the applicant's activities, family background, past history and recommendations)—are judged at most highly selective colleges much as in these cases at Brown. At all such colleges, the applicants divide quite readily into three categories—the clearly in, the clearly out and the difficult and fairly large number of borderline cases.

Admissions officers at highly selective colleges say that their predictions for *individual* students prove roughly correct with about 80 per cent of their students. Albert I. Dickerson of Dartmouth, for example, has made this observation of his days as admissions director there. An entering class as a group, however, does freshman-year work very much as expected; almost exactly the percentages of students for whom work at about A, B, C, D and failing averages can be predicted are actually realized. But the admissions officers now know of no way to single out the 20 per cent who do not perform as individually predicted in the freshman year. They wish they did.

How hard it is for even experienced admissions officers and guidance counselors to guess what individual students will do in college was brought home with a set of case histories belying the usual predictors that were considered at another College Board admissions colloquium. The cases, assembled by Henry S. Dyer of Educational Testing Service, were all absolutely authentic. One that Dr. Dyer posed for admissions judging by the eighty educators at the meeting concerned a girl whose father was an engineer and whose mother had gone to the college at which the daughter had applied. An interviewer at the college noted that the girl "likes chemistry, hates French. Mother says high school against having her come here. Mother and father both determined that she come here. I can find no spark of enthusiasm in the girl herself for coming here. Girl said she would 'stick it out' if she came. She is not a good risk for this place. Much pressure from father to get her in here." The girl said on her application that she preferred another college but her mother wanted this one for her.

In high school, the girl had been a cheerleader, hockey team captain and member of the music club and several committees. About a B-average student, she had averaged A-minus as a high school freshman and B-minus as a senior; she ranked 117th in a class of 386. Her father said that her recent grades were low because she had been an officer in two community charities, and in one had had to handle large funds. Her school's recommendation said that, though intelligent, the girl was not intellectually mature, lacked intellectual curiosity and was more interested in cheerleading, sports and social life than in abstract ideas; it did describe her as wholesome, attractive, a good citizen, well poised, and well adjusted socially. The girl's SAT verbal and mathematical scores were 494 and 505; on the College Board Achievement Tests, she had scored 578 in English, 570 in French and 444 in Social Studies. The average SAT verbal score of students at the college was 575.

Of the eighty admissions officers and counselors, forty-three guessed that this girl would do inferior work at the college and twenty-four that she would flunk out. Only thirteen guessed average college work for her, and none guessed superior work. In the college, the girl had actually moved up from an average of C as a freshman to B-minus as a senior—which represented about average academic work for all four years. Her freshman dean had noted that, "She is delighted she chose this college rather than the other one." The girl majored in political science, and was considered very loyal, popular and co-operative, yet independent. She was vice president of her dormitory, co-chairman of a music festival program and head of the student scholarship fund. The college's dean concluded, "an outstanding girl."

Your Child's Admissions Chances at All Colleges in the Country— And Especially the Selective and Highly Selective Colleges

In thinking about possible colleges for your child, you may find it helpful to know how practically all colleges in the country can be grouped according to levels of entrance test scores and related high school marks that would mean fairly good chances of admission.

At many colleges your child would not need very high test scores in order to have fairly good admissions chances. It is at a minority of selective and highly selective colleges that rather high scores might be important to getting in—and even these colleges admit some low-scoring students who have other strong qualifications.

America's 2,000 colleges today divide roughly into the following five groups, according to how selective they are in admission. Here are the groups, together with some idea of the extent to which they are selective and the very approximate numbers of colleges in each group:

> *Highly selective*—some 70 or more colleges;
> *Selective to highly selective*—some 235 colleges;
> *Moderately selective to selective*—about 500 colleges;
> *Somewhat selective*—about 400 or more colleges;
> *Hardly selective at all*—some 700 to 900 colleges.

These groups are based on the data given by the country's colleges about their admissions policies in another work of the author's, *The New American Guide to Colleges* (second edition, 1962).

It is only in the last twenty years that these groups have developed.

By long tradition, almost all American colleges had had admissions policies represented by just the "somewhat selective" and "hardly selective" categories, requiring but a minimum competence in specified college prep subjects, until the deluge of World War II veterans backed by the GI Bill in the late 1940s. The public did not generally grasp what had happened until the country's first admissions panic gripped parents, particularly in the crowded Northeastern states, in the early 1950s. Moreover, the picture continues changing rather rapidly, with more and more colleges moving from the less selective to the more selective categories every year.

Between these groups there are large differences in the levels of entrance test scores which would normally mean good chances of admission for your child. For the colleges that are "hardly selective at all," your child's scores on entrance tests would be less decisive than his high school record. He would be admitted if his record showed passing work in high school, and if he were of ordinarily good health and character. This group of colleges is especially numerous because it includes many very small private colleges, as well as most of the country's several hundred public two-year colleges which serve mainly their local communities.

Colleges "somewhat selective" in admissions would expect your child to have test scores above only very low levels so long as his high school record showed about a C average, preferably with college prep studies. Most of the "moderately selective to selective" colleges would look for a high school average of, say, C to B, and test scores above about the bottom quarter on national norms for high school seniors, in order to consider your child a fairly well qualified applicant. Some of the colleges in this group, though, would similarly expect about a B average and scores in the top half nationally.

Two things about colleges in the three less selective groups are especially important for you to keep in mind. One is that a number of very bright and able students go to these colleges, even ones in the "hardly selective at all" group. This means that a bright child of yours could get a good education in at least some colleges that are not hard to get into. It also means that students at these colleges often represent a very wide range of ability. The other point to remember is that some of these colleges wait until after admission to do their real selecting;

they admit on indulgent standards, but instruct on standards rigorous enough to lead perhaps a fourth or more of their freshmen to flunk or drop out. Colleges like this often use admissions test scores in advising applicants who seem weak of possible failure if they do enter.

The majority of the country's state universities still carry on in the tradition of "somewhat selective" or "hardly selective" admissions with required subject preparation, and are in these categories today. However, some stand in the two more selective categories, and more state universities are being forced into the more selective groups each year. This raises serious questions for your children and for the country, as we shall see later. But as noted above, state universities and other colleges in the two least selective categories often have students who represent a wide range of ability. Because of this, they use entrance test scores most extensively for placement—placing students in freshman class sections or courses appropriate to their ability and preparation—rather than in admission.

You and your child might be especially interested in selective or highly selective colleges, though, for these colleges attract several times as many applicants as they can admit. It is this special popularity of theirs which of course enables and even forces them to be selective.

At the same time, it is important for you to know which colleges they are and what would insure fairly good chances of admission to them. On the one hand, knowing this could save you needless disappointment. On the other, it might acquaint you with the opportunities open to your child at these colleges if he or she seems possibly qualified for them.

First, let us look at the nation's highly selective colleges—the ones hardest to get into. Sixty-eight of these colleges are in the following list. These are the colleges which reported having "highly competitive" admissions policies in giving information for *The New American Guide* (for which "highly competitive" was defined as, "rejects many applicants who have earned B or even A averages in college preparatory programs"). The sixty-eight in the list include most of the country's highly selective colleges today. Not all are included because some did not give admissions data in the survey, and also because at least a few colleges have become highly selective since the survey was made. However, those which have since become highly selective would be included in a second list which identifies some 235 "selective colleges."

Highly Selective Colleges

New England (Conn., Me., Mass., N.H., R.I., Vt.)
Amherst College
Bennington College
Brandeis University
Bowdoin College
Brown University
Dartmouth College
Endicott Junior College
Harvard College (of Harvard University)
Jackson College for Women (of Tufts University)
Massachusetts College of Art
Massachusetts Institute of Technology
Middlebury College
Mount Holyoke College
Pembroke College (of Brown University)
Radcliffe College (of Harvard University)
Simmons College
Smith College
Trinity College
Tufts College (of Tufts University)
United States Coast Guard Academy
Wellesley College
Wesleyan University
Wheaton College
Williams College
Yale College (of Yale Uiversity)

Middle Atlantic (N.J., N.Y., Pa.)
Barnard College (of Columbia University)
Bryn Mawr College
Colgate University
Columbia College (of Columbia University)
Columbia University School of Engineering and Applied Science
Cooper Union

Cornell University—College of Arts and Sciences, School of Hotel Administration, State College of Home Economics
Dickinson College
Hamilton College
Harpur College (of the State University of New York)
Haverford College
Princeton University

Pennsylvania, University of—College of Arts and Sciences, College of Liberal Arts for Women, School of Allied Medical Professions
Rensselaer Polytechnic Institute
Rochester, University of—College of Arts and Science
Sarah Lawrence College
Swarthmore College
Union College (of Union University)
United States Merchant Marine Academy
United States Military Academy
Vassar College
Webb Institute of Naval Architecture

South Atlantic (Del., Md., D.C., Va., W.Va., N.C., S.C., Fla., Ga.)
Duke University—Trinity College, The Woman's College
Hollins College
Trinity Collegé (D.C.)
United States Naval Academy
William and Mary, College of

North Central (Ill., Ind., Iowa, Kan., Mich., Mo., Minn., Neb., N.D., S.D., O., Wis.)
Carleton College
Grinnell College
Oberlin College

Highly Selective Colleges

South Central (Ala., Ark., Ky., La., Miss., Okla., Tenn., Tex.)
Rice University
South, University of the

Mountain (Ariz., Col., Idaho, Mont., Nev., N.M., Utah, Wyo.)
United States Air Force Academy

Pacific (Alas., Cal., Hawaii, Ore., Wash.)
California Institute of Technology
California Maritime Academy
Pomona College
Reed College
Stanford University

What would insure fairly good admissions chances for your child at most of these highly selective colleges? The explanation here will give you a general idea as essential background information. However, you should consult an experienced counselor in your child's school, or the college itself, before making even any tentative decisions about applying or not applying to one of them. Each of these colleges has a unique and complex admissions policy which would have special bearing on the equally unique case of your child.

Almost all sixty-eight of these highly selective colleges would require your child to take the College Board SAT, usually in December of his senior year in high school, if he intends to apply. The following general accounts of what SAT scores indicate for your child at most selective and highly selective colleges are based on the College Board's *Manual of Freshman Class Profiles*, a technical publication designed for professional use by guidance counselors.

At least a quarter of all applicants who had SAT verbal scores of about 600 in recent years have been accepted by each of these highly selective colleges, with the exception of only a few colleges. Most of these colleges, in fact, have been accepting from one-half to three-quarters or more of all applicants with verbal scores of 600 or higher. For some of the several colleges that are exceptions, your child would need an SAT verbal score of 650 or 700 in order to have a fairly good chance of admission. For others that are exceptions, verbal scores in the 500s would mean a fairly good chance, but high selectivity on the basis of other (and usually obvious) qualifications. Most of these colleges have, of course, accepted still higher proportions of applicants with SAT verbal scores higher than 600—and the higher the scores, the higher the proportions accepted.

You can conclude, then, that if your child had an SAT verbal score of about 600 or more and met certain other conditions, he or she would have a fairly good chance of being admitted to one of these colleges in all but a few instances. The "certain other conditions" for most of these colleges are: that your child's SAT mathematical score and scores on two or three College Board Achievement Tests were similarly high; that your child ranked in the top fifth or quarter of his high school class (unless all his schoolmates were of unusually high ability); that your child wrote clearly and correctly; that your child held leading positions in one or more school or community activities (or showed marked accomplishment in a hobby, art or sport); and that your child had a mature, upright and stable character. In addition, to have fairly good admissions chances at a technological college among these sixty-eight, your child should have an SAT mathematical score of 650 or more, and strong preparation in the sciences and math.

You should not take this to mean that your child must have an SAT verbal score of at least 600 in order to be admitted to one of these sixty-eight highly selective colleges. As we saw in the case of Brown's acceptance of the boy whose parents had come from Syria, these colleges accept some students with verbal scores ranging as low as the 300s, in a few special cases. Most of these colleges are extremely anxious to have students with unusual qualifications, but not very high test scores continue to apply. Despite possibly modest test scores, your child should apply to one of them if he is particularly interested in the college and thinks some unusual qualifications of his might interest the college. His (and your) only precaution should be not to count on being accepted there.

Your child should feel no disgrace whatever if he applied and were not accepted by one of these colleges. Some students with very high test scores, scores of the maximum 800 or in the very high 700s, are rejected by each of these colleges every year. And Arthur Howe, Jr., admissions dean at Yale, has remarked that, as an admissions officer, "you so often know you have turned down boys who are just as promising as the ones you've taken."

Some of these highly selective colleges have been admitting a few more students with comparatively low SAT scores in the last few years than they had before—a fact which might prove useful to your child. Brown and Williams have foundation grants with which to admit small percentages of students who appear to be academic risks on the basis of high school record and test scores but who seem strongly qualified on other grounds, and to see how these students do in college.

Henry S. Coleman, Columbia College admissions director, has followed the performance of seventy-two students with SAT verbal scores below 550 who were admitted in 1961, largely because they "showed other indications of great promise." Sixty-three of the seventy-two finished the sophomore year, he recently reported, and as sophomores earned academic standings as follows: 5 per cent in the top quarter of the class, 17 per cent in the second quarter, 37 per cent in the third quarter, and 41 per cent in the bottom quarter. No conclusions have been drawn, he said, but the college is "reasonably pleased with the results so far" and will follow the students "with keen interest."

At Harvard College 9 per cent of the students admitted in 1963 had SAT verbal scores below 500, compared with only 3 per cent admitted in 1961. "Personal ratings" have most often offset relatively low scores in the decision to admit these students; the ratings are not "narrowly defined," according to Fred L. Glimp, admissions dean, but are assessed on a scale ranging from 1 to 6 and represent "a combination, though certainly not an 'average,'" of such qualities as effectiveness, energy, judgment, integrity, generosity of spirit, and "cussedness"—as well as "the touch of greatness" when it seems to appear.

A second and larger group of 235 or more colleges and universities make up the "selective" category. These colleges, listed below, are the ones that reported having "competitive" admissions policies in the survey for *The New American Guide* (for which "competitive" was defined as, "rejects some applicants who have earned B or even A averages in college preparatory programs").

At most of these "selective" colleges, your child would have a fairly good chance of admission if he or she had a SAT verbal score of some 525 or 550—subject to all the same kinds of qualifications as in the case of the highly selective colleges. That is, your child should be a similarly strong applicant in other respects, and should feel free to apply to a selective college if he cares to try, even though his scores may range around 300.

Selective Colleges

New England

American International College
Bates College
Boston College
Boston University (all divisions except School of Education and College of Basic Studies)
Bouvé-Boston School (affiliated with Tufts University)
Bridgeport, University of
Castleton Teachers College
Clark University
Colby College
Colby Junior College
Connecticut College
Dean Junior College
Eliot-Pearson School (affiliated with Tufts University)
Fairfield University
Forsyth School of Dental Hygienists (affiliated with Tufts University)
Goddard College
Hartford Art School (of the University of Hartford)
Holy Cross, College of the
Lasell Junior College
Lesley College
Maine Maritime Academy
Maine, University of
Marlboro College
Nichols College of Business Administration
Northeastern University
Norwich University
Plymouth Teachers College
Regis College
Rhode Island College
Rhode Island School of Design
St. Anselm's College
Southern Connecticut State College
State Colleges of Massachusetts—at Bridgewater, Lowell, Salem, Worcester

Vermont, University of
Worcester Polytechnic Institute

Middle Atlantic

Albright College
Alfred University
Allegheny College
Beaver College
Bennett College
Bloomsburg (Pa.) State College
Briarcliff College
Bucknell University
Business Training College
Cedar Crest College
Centenary College for Women
Chestnut Hill College
Chatham College
Colleges of Education (of the State University of New York) at Albany, Brockport, Cortland, Fredonia, Plattsburgh
Cornell University—College of Engineering, College of Architecture, State College of Agriculture, State School of Industrial and Labor Relations
Columbia University School of General Studies
East Stroudsburg (Pa.) State College
Elmira College
Drew University
Drexel Institute of Technology
Erie County (N.Y.) Technical Institute
Fordham University
Franklin and Marshall College
Georgian Court College
Gettysburg College
Glassboro (N.J.) State College
Grove City College
Hobart College
Hudson Valley (N.Y.) Community College

Selective Colleges

Hunter College (of the City University of New York)
Jersey City (N.J.) State College
Juniata College
Keystone Junior College
Kutztown (Pa.) State College
Lafayette College
La Salle College
Lebanon Valley College
Lehigh University
Lock Haven (Pa.) State College
Lycoming College
Manhattan College
Manhattanville College of the Sacred Heart
Margaret Morrison Carnegie College (of Carnegie Institute of Technology)
Marymount College
Muhlenberg College
Millersville (Pa.) State College
Montclair (N.J.) State College
Notre Dame College of Staten Island
New Rochelle, College of
New York University—Washington Square College of Arts and Sciences, University College of Arts and Sciences, College of Engineering
Newark (N.J.) State College
Pennsylvania Military College
Pennsylvania, University of—Wharton School of Finance and Commerce, The Engineering Schools, School of Education, School of Fine Arts, School of Nursing
Pittsburgh, University of—School of Engineering and Mines
Queens College (of the City University of New York)
Russell Sage College
Rochester, University of—Eastman School of Music

Rosemont College
Rutgers, The State University of New Jersey—Rutgers College, Douglass College, College of Nursing, College of Pharmacy
Seton Hill College
St. Bernadine of Siena College
St. Bonaventure University
Saint Peter's College
St. Lawrence University
Skidmore College
Slippery Rock (Pa.) State College
State University of New York Long Island Center
Stevens Institute of Technology
Syracuse University (all divisions except State College of Forestry)
Temple University
Thiel College
Trenton (N.J.) State College
Upsala College
Ursinus College
Villanova College
Washington & Jefferson College
Wells College
William Smith College
Wilkes College
Wilson College

South Atlantic
Agnes Scott College
Belmont Abbey College
Bethany College
Catholic University of America
Citadel, The
Clemson Agricultural College
Converse College
Davidson College
District of Columbia Teachers College
Duke University—School of Engineering, School of Nursing
Dunbarton College of Holy Cross

Selective Colleges

East Carolina College
Emory University
George Washington University
Georgetown University
Georgia Institute of Technology
Hampden-Sydney College
Goucher College
Greensboro College
Guilford College
Hood College
Johns Hopkins University
Mary Baldwin College
Medical College of Virginia School of Nursing
North Carolina, Woman's College of the University of
Notre Dame of Maryland, College of
Queens College
Radford College
Randolph-Macon College
Randolph-Macon Woman's College
Rollins College
Salem College
St. John's College
Stetson University School of Business
Sweet Briar College
Virginia, University of
Wake Forest College
Washington College
Washington & Lee University

North Central
Albion College
Antioch College
Ashland College
Augustana College
Beloit College
Bethel College and Seminary

Blackburn College
Carroll College
Chicago, The College of the University of
Concordia Teachers College
Cornell College
De Pauw University
Drake University
Earlham College
General Motors Institute
Hanover College
Illinois Institute of Technology
Illinois, University of (at Chicago)—College of Pharmacy, College of Nursing
Iowa, State University of—College of Engineering, College of Nursing
Kalamazoo College
Kenyon College
Knox College
Lake Erie College
Lake Forest College
Lawrence College
Marietta College
Milwaukee-Downer College
Michigan, University of (all divisions except School of Nursing)
Muskingum College
Northwestern University
Ohio Wesleyan University
Ripon College
St. Benedict's College
St. Mary's College (Minn.)
St. Teresa, College of
Saint Xavier College
Wabash College
Washington University
Wheaton College (Ill.)
Wittenberg University
Wooster, College of

Selective Colleges

South Central
Auburn University—School of Architecture and the Arts
Berea College
Centre College of Kentucky
Judson College
King College
Loyola University
Southwestern at Memphis
Vanderbilt University—College of Arts and Sciences, School of Engineering

Mountain
Colorado College
Colorado School of Mines

Pacific
Chaminade College of Honolulu
Claremont Men's College
Harvey Mudd College
Los Angeles Conservatory of Music
Mills College
Occidental College
Redlands, University of
Scripps College
Westmont College
Whitman College

Many students capable enough to qualify for highly selective colleges, of course, go to these selective colleges. Also, these selective colleges range evenly right up into the highly selective ones and down into the moderately selective ones. This means that at some of these selective colleges your child would need a SAT verbal score of perhaps 575 or 600 for fairly good admissions chances; at others, a verbal score even in the 400s would insure fairly good chances.

Some of these selective colleges require the ACT test—the test of the American College Testing Program—instead of the College Board SAT. For these colleges, ACT test scores at about the 50th percentile on ACT norms for college-bound students would correspond to fairly good chances of admission, subject again to the same qualifications described above. You or your child could learn the percentile ranks on college-bound norms to which your child's ACT test scores correspond from his high school, to which the percentile ranks are reported. Ranks at the 50th percentile on these norms would fall, very approximately, at standard scores of around 15 or 20 on the 36-point score scale of the ACT test.

Again, you should not base any decisions about these colleges on what is said here if you can possibly consult an experienced guidance counselor in your child's school instead. Counselors have detailed information about test score distributions and many other matters bearing on admission at most of these colleges in the current edition of the College Board's *Manual of Freshman Class Profiles*, which was mentioned before. Many counselors would show you the manual's data for a college in which your child was interested, and would explain its meaning to you in detail. In addition, a counselor in your child's high school can provide information on how other students from the school have fared in admission and in their studies at many colleges, as well as information acquired from years of acquaintance with colleges and their admissions officers.

Still another reason to work closely with a capable guidance counselor is that more colleges are becoming selective and highly selective as time passes. The numbers of such colleges will increase especially rapidly with the sudden sharp increases in the numbers of young people expected to apply for college in 1964 and 1965.

A concrete picture of typical colleges in the five groups explained here may help you remember major things about them. Such a picture is shown in Figure 4.

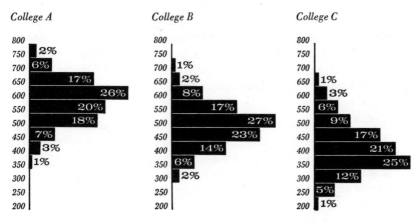

SAT *Verbal scores of freshmen at three colleges*

(Reproduced with permission from *College Board Score Reports; A Guide for Counselors*, published in 1958 by the College Entrance Examination Board. This publication is revised annually and distributed to counselors.)

The graphs show only one very limited thing about each of the three colleges: the percentages of freshmen at each college who have SAT verbal scores in each 50-point range of the score scale. The "College A" shown in the graph is typical of those called "highly selective" here. Similarly, "College B" is typical of this account's "selective" colleges, while "College C" is typical of "somewhat selective" colleges. No graphs are shown to illustrate colleges that would be "moderately selective," which would stand between the College B and College C profiles. Nor is a graph shown for a "hardly selective" college.

You can judge these typical colleges in comparison with American young people generally by knowing what SAT verbal scores mean for all high school seniors. The College Board recently estimated that the average verbal score for all high school seniors is about 350. It also estimated that only some 15 per cent of all seniors score above 500; that only some 3 per cent of the boys and 6 per cent of the girls among them score higher than 600; and that less than 1 per cent of the boys and about 1 per cent of the girls score higher than 700.

You should clearly understand that, again, if your child should have high college ability as indicated by high school marks and test scores, he would by no means have to go to a selective or highly selective college in order to get a good college education. High-scoring students enroll at many colleges and universities that are fairly open in admission. One indication of the quality of the education they receive is that, if they make outstanding records in college, graduate and professional schools accept them as readily as well-prepared graduates of selective and highly selective colleges.

Achievement Tests of the College Board—the admissions tests we have not yet looked at closely—would generally play a minor role in a college's decision to admit your child. However, if a college knew little about the quality of preparatory work in your child's high school and your child's scores on two or three Achievement Tests were far lower than his aptitude scores and record of courses and marks would indicate, the Achievement scores might mean his rejection. Also, for engineering programs at highly selective colleges, scores on the mathematics Achievement Tests count rather heavily in admissions decisions. More often, your child's Achievement Test scores would be used for placement rather than admission. That is, they would be used in placing or assigning the boy or girl to appropriate freshman courses and course sections instead of in deciding his admission.

Finally, though it is not a standardized test, the College Board's "Writing Sample" (or one-hour essay your child might be asked to write at a College Board test center) could possibly win or lose your child's admission to a selective or highly selective college on a very rare occasion. Some ninety colleges require the "Writing Sample" for applicants, most of them along with one or two Achievement Tests in addition to the SAT. The essays are simply duplicated and sent to colleges without being scored in any way by the Board. Colleges read them as direct evidence of a student's writing ability. Your child might not be accepted by a college in the very unlikely event that he would otherwise seem qualified but had done an atrociously poor "Writing Sample." Or, if he or she were a borderline applicant in other respects, an extremely brilliant and well-written essay might tip the scales in your child's favor.

You Might Make Tentative Long-range Forecasts of Your Child's Future College Ability—And Admissions Prospects

As you have already seen, you could be fairly confident that your child will have the ability for college when he reaches college age if his IQ test scores after about the fourth or fifth grade generally range above 105 or 110. Scholastic ability test scores above about the 65th percentile in large, nationally representative groups of children his own age would mean much the same thing. Higher IQ or scholastic ability test scores—scores ranging up from IQs of about 120 or from national percentile ranks of about 85—would augur possible future ability typical of students at selective and highly selective colleges.

However, the reverse would absolutely not be true. That is, if your child earned IQ scores below 100 (or scholastic ability test scores below a 50th percentile nationally) through the elementary grades, you would not be justified in thinking that your child might not develop average or higher college ability. If your child were just ordinarily bright and made normal progress through the early grades, the boy or girl could show a sudden spurt of scholastic growth as a teen-ager. Children sometimes develop in bursts, and occasionally take sharp turns in interest, and your child's scholastic bursts and turns might lie ahead. Such bursts might lie ahead for your child even if he had a certain amount of trouble in the early grades—provided that he or she did not fall far behind, in reading ability in particular, and did not come to hate school work deeply and permanently. Of course, college would still not be ruled out if your child should not happen to develop above-average academic ability in the 'teens—for, as we noted, college programs for young people of below-average ability are multiplying.

It would be particularly dangerous for you to assume that your child may not have college ability—or for his school to assume it—on the basis of test scores through the elementary grades. For example, during recent years, the manager of a large New York bookstore had become increasingly worried about whether his boy would have the ability for college. The boy wasn't at all bookish, and his indifference to studies produced mediocre marks all through school. His father gingerly brought up the question of college one night when the boy was not far along in high school. "Oh, I'm no good for college," the boy replied casually. "I've got an IQ of only 100, my guidance teacher says." The shocked parents had the boy take the Stanford-Binet at a private counseling bureau, and he earned an IQ score of 128 on it. He is now at the University of South Florida, and doing very well there.

Moreover, as pointed out in Chapter 2, the childhood IQ or scholastic ability test scores of whole generations of underprivileged children—Negroes especially—are depressed below the levels which their native abilities would reflect if they had grown up instead in comfortable homes with lively cultural interests. The great "Higher Horizons" experiment, started in the late 1950s in Junior High School 43 in Manhattan, proved that substantial numbers of such children who earned conventional verbal IQ scores in the 80s could be equipped through an enriched program and special guidance to succeed in highly selective colleges.

At one critical turning point in your child's schooling, you should be especially vigilant to be sure that test scores will not slam the door to a traditional college education for your child if you think the door should be kept open. This point comes in the eighth, ninth or tenth grade. It is the point at which your child would decide to take a college preparatory or non-college-prep program through high school. Deciding on a commercial, technical or general program at this point could close out the possibility of later college work toward regular four-year degrees in the liberal arts and sciences. It may be most helpful for your child to finish his education with high school, learning salable job skills there. However, all too many boys and girls whose parents and neighbors think of college as odd and unnecessary slip through this critical point of decision with no idea of what is being settled for the rest of the child's life. Often, the decision is made on the basis of average or lower IQ and scholastic standing for the child—plus especially what the child and his parents expect for him in life.

You should not let this decision be made for your child as a matter of unquestioned routine. Find out from your child's school when it will come, and consider it, carefully and sympathetically, with your child before it is made. Unless your child had consistently done very poor work in studies and on tests, your insistence on having your child at least try a college prep program, if you feel strongly, would probably get him into college prep work.

You Could Even Develop Your Child's College Potential From Infancy On

If you want to improve your child's eventual college prospects right from the start, you should concentrate on certain vitally important things in your child's early school years. Among these are his general sense of security and curiosity, plus his exposure to pictures, toys, games, letters, numbers, words, stories, trips, music, drawing, painting and conversation. His life should be safe and interesting, and he should receive much attention without suppression from you. Such guidance and cultivation, plus familiarity with the kinds of puzzles posed on IQ tests, make up the essential advice given in David Engler's book of a few years ago, *How to Raise Your Child's IQ*.

Your child's pre-school years may be especially vital, Henry Chauncey, president of Educational Testing Service, has observed in his *Annual Report* for 1963–1964. Citing an unpublished study by Benjamin Bloom, a University of Chicago psychologist, he suggests that a good half of the difference in lifelong intelligence which may result from a loving and cultured home as against an insecure and impoverished home develops before the age of *four*. Dr. Bloom estimates that favorable surroundings can increase a child's IQ up to some 20 points more than it would otherwise be by the time the child is seventeen years old—and that 10 points of the 20-point potential increase come in the child's first four years of life, or else are lost forever.

SCAT-V vs. SAT-V

Chances in 100 That Students with Various Scores on SCAT Verbal Will Earn
Selected Scores on SAT Verbal

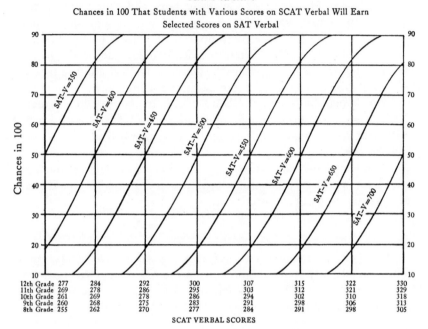

	12th Grade	11th Grade	10th Grade	9th Grade	8th Grade
	277	269	261	260	255
	284	278	269	268	262
	292	286	278	275	270
	300	295	286	283	277
	307	303	294	291	284
	315	312	302	298	291
	322	321	310	306	298
	330	329	318	313	305

SCAT VERBAL SCORES

A counselor could use this graph to estimate what future verbal score your child is likely to earn on the Scholastic Aptitude Test of the College Board—and, therefore, estimate one important factor bearing on your child's possible admission to a highly selective or selective college—as early as the eighth grade. The estimate would be based on your child's verbal score on the School and College Ability Test of ETS. How to use the graph is explained in the accompanying pages. (Reproduced by permission of Educational Testing Service.)

When your child is in his high school years or just before, some tests might give you a very approximate idea of how your child is likely to score on the College Board SAT. ETS has studied the connections between scores on its School and College Ability Tests and later scores on the SAT for several hundred students in each grade from 8 through 12. The results have been plotted in "expectancy charts" like the accompanying one, which can be used to see about how many chances a student has in 100 for earning future SAT scores of given levels on the basis of his present SCAT test scores.

For example, suppose that your child were in the eighth grade and made a SCAT verbal score of 277. To see what his future SAT score is likely to be, you would find his 277 SCAT verbal score in the line of numbers labeled "8th grade" at the bottom left of the chart. Then you would look up along the vertical line directly above this 277, and read off your child's chances in 100 of later getting various SAT verbal scores opposite each point where this vertical line cuts through a curving line, as follows: about 18 chances in 100 of getting an SAT verbal score as high as 550; 50 chances in 100 of getting an SAT verbal as high as 500; and 82 chances in 100 of getting an SAT verbal as high as 450. Similarly, if your child were to get a SCAT score of 305 in the eighth grade, he would have about 50 chances in 100 of getting an SAT verbal score as high as 700 when applying for college, and 80 chances in 100 of getting an SAT verbal as high as 650. You should remember that these expectancies are based on the actual experience of several hundred children per grade level, and that the degree to which the expectancies would apply to your own child would depend on how similar his experience were to the experience of the children studied.

In a similar study, The Psychological Corporation looked into the relations between scores on its widely used Differential Aptitude Tests earned in tenth grade by 145 boys and girls, and the SAT scores the students earned two years later when they were applying to college as seniors. Prediction equations were developed to give the combinations of scores on the DAT which yielded the closest predictions of the students' SAT verbal and mathematical scores. (For SAT verbal scores, the equation was: seven times the DAT Verbal Reasoning Test "raw" score, plus the raw scores on the DAT Spelling and Sentence tests, plus 169. Raw scores on the DAT are simply the number of questions answered correctly.) Of those students for whom a SAT verbal score of 600 or more was predicted with the equation using their tenth-grade DAT scores, 65 per cent actually earned verbal scores of 600 or more two years later, while 31 per cent earned scores between 500 and 600 and 3 per cent earned scores in the 450–499 range.

When your child starts the eleventh grade, he might get a direct indication of his future SAT performance on the Preliminary SAT. As we saw, the PSAT is now given to about a million high school juniors in October of each year by their schools. It is a two-hour version of the SAT, with two-digit scores ranging from 20 to 80 to parallel the SAT's 200-to-800 scale. You and your child would get a report of his PSAT scores with an explanation of them if he does take the test. From the report you could gauge his likely SAT scores as a college applicant.

What Will Best Prepare Your Child for Admissions Tests—And What Will Not

If you look under "Tutoring" in the classified phone books of the country's largest cities, you will often find listings for commercial services and schools which offer "Preparation for College Boards." Were you to call or visit one, you would probably be assured that your child should score 50 or 100 points higher on the College Board SAT with special tutoring than without. You might even be shown lists of boys and girls who actually did score 100 or more points higher when they took the SAT a second time, after they had been coached. And you would find, if you could question any of these young people, that indeed they did. By this time, you would probably feel that your child would be at a terrible disadvantage in applying to a selective or highly selective college unless the boy or girl had this expensive "proven" coaching.

Despite such plausible stories, however, coaching for the SAT would almost certainly waste your money and your child's time. Teachers, colleges and the College Board have, of course, been concerned that special drill might give the children who get it an unfair advantage over children who could not. They have accordingly made studies of the effect of coaching—at least seven in the last eleven years, with different children and coaching methods. The results are summed up in an official College Board statement. It says:

> The evidence collected leads us to conclude that intensive drill for the SAT, either on its verbal or mathematical part, is at best likely to yield insignificant increases in scores.

On the average, you could expect increases "of less than 10 points on a 600-point scale," the statement reports. "It is not reasonable to believe that admissions decisions can be affected by such small changes in scores"—a conclusion that seems "especially true since the tests are merely supplementary to the school record and other evidence taken into account by admissions officers."

It is "the imperfect nature of the testing process" rather than coaching which causes the scores of individual students to jump by as much as 100 points or more, the statement argues. "About one student in 15 will find that his scores increase by 100 points or more between junior and senior years in high school, *and this is true whether he is coached or not*. It is not surprising, then," the statement continues, "that tutors are often able to point to particular students who have made large increases in their scores." As we saw in an earlier section, there are small chances (some 2 in 100) that your child's verbal SAT score could suddenly drop 100 or more points for no apparent reason. There are somewhat larger probabilities (1 chance in 15, or about 7 in 100) for your child's score to jump by 100 or more points in the same natural course of events over a span of some months.

Two of the latest coaching studies analyzed what kind of results actual coaching programs realized for all students in representative groups enrolled for coaching—not only of those students being coached whose scores accidentally increased. In one study, made by Dean K. Whitla, associate admissions director at Harvard College, fifty-two students who were enrolled in a coaching school were compared with fifty-two students who were otherwise similar but had no coaching. The ten hours of class work plus homework put in by the coached students resulted in their gaining only 10.2 points more in SAT verbal score, on the average, than the uncoached students. And the SAT mathematical score averaged by the coached students on the second testing was 7 points *lower* than the corresponding average score of the uncoached students. The other study was made by Edward Frankel, then a teacher at the Bronx High School of Science. Half of the ninety students in his school who took part in the study got an average of thirty hours of coaching in a variety of regular commercial coaching schools. The other half had no coaching. The average scores of the coached students showed gains only 8.37 points higher in verbal score and 9.07 points higher in mathematical score compared with the average score gains of the uncoached students.

Coaching does not work, the College Board believes, because "this particular Scholastic Aptitude Test is a measure of abilities that seem to grow slowly and stubbornly, profoundly influenced by conditions at home and at school over the years, but not responding to hasty attempts to relive a young lifetime."

Coaching, then, will not help your child prepare for the SAT. But what will? And how about the Achievement Tests? And the ACT test?

No one has yet discovered any tricks to the process. Good schooling and active cultural interests in a comfortable and secure home are the factors most likely to develop capable college students. These are also the factors which most often develop students who score highest on tests of general capability in college studies. Nothing would be more important than good schooling and a good home in preparing your child both for college and for these tests.

To a minor extent, it would be helpful for your child to be generally familiar with taking standardized tests. However, even if your child had not been taking tests regularly all through school, he would get all the practice and pointers he needed for these tests in booklets provided by the CEEB and ACT without charge through his high school.

Getting high scores on the ACT test, the American College Testing program examination, has not been felt so crucially important by as many families as in the case of the SAT. It has not because, in part, many colleges using the ACT test receive indices for applicants in which school marks are combined with test scores. Little effort has been made to coach students for it, and no studies of the effects of ACT test coaching have been made. However, the ACT test functions in much the same way as the SAT, and it seems very likely that intensive drill for the ACT test would not increase your child's scores to any significant extent. The ACT test measures how well your child has learned to think in broad subject areas, and these thinking abilities also require many years to develop. They can be increased only very little by a few weeks or months of drill work.

By contrast, College Board Achievement Tests examine your child on how skillfully he can use what he has learned in specific subjects, and they hence seem coachable to a limited extent. Your child's school would carry the main responsibility to see that he had been taught what he needed to know for these tests. This should not be difficult for the school, for the content of the tests is set by committees of professors and high school teachers who try to have the tests cover evenly what the schools across the country actually teach. General descriptions of the tests, with illustrative questions, are also published by the Board, so that schools can see what the tests do cover. In addition, these descriptions and questions would be among the material given without charge to your child by the Board through his school. He could therefore compare for himself what the tests cover and what he had learned. If your child wanted to, he could also get these descriptions and sample questions through his high school two or three years before he took the Achievement Tests or the SAT.

Your child apparently could be coached with some effectiveness for the Achievement Tests—to the extent that the coaching represented teaching of the respective subjects. However, it should be far more useful for your child to concentrate on his course work in those subjects all through high school than to drill over innumerable sample questions and try to cram in masses of facts in the last few weeks or months before being tested. The College Board has not made studies of the effectiveness of coaching for the Achievement Tests, the Board's statement declares, and adds: "We suspect that the question of coaching for these tests is a matter of choosing a method of teaching the subject. We cannot believe that drill on sample questions is the most productive method available."

Just before taking any of these tests, your child is advised by the College Board to go through quite specific preparation: forget studying, relax and get a full night's sleep. Most psychologists and educators agree that the relaxation part of this advice would be the best preparation—for both you and your child—through the whole intricate process of college admissions testing and admission itself.

What to Do If Your Child Panics or Has an "Off Day" on Admissions Tests

Your child could take admissions tests on only the few specified Saturdays a year when they are offered. It is possible that, on the particular Saturday for which he had registered, he will feel ill or upset or nervous. Something quite accidental, like a misfortune in your family or a bitter quarrel, could lead your boy or girl to do far worse on admissions tests than his actual ability warrants.

You need not feel that all is lost for your son or daughter if something like this should happen—if the boy or girl gets panicky and confused while taking the tests, or has an "off day" in working them for a combination of minor but distressing reasons. You or your child should do one or both of two things if this does occur.

First, be sure to explain to your child's principal or guidance counselor, as soon as you receive scores that evidence below-normal performance, why the scores seem unduly low, as well as what was bothering your child during the tests. In explanations like this, you will have to be both firm in arguing for your child and reasonable in discussing other evidence (and not just your own opinions) of your child's abilities. Genuine reasons for your child's atypical work on the tests can then be pointed out by the school in its comments recommending him to colleges or in special letters. You or your child could instead write to the colleges receiving the scores to explain the disrupting circumstances, but an explanation coming from the school would generally be more effective.

Second, if it were the SAT or the ACT test on which your child had done far less well than seemed right, he may have time left in his high school senior year to take the test again. (He could do this in one of the next few months, if he had first taken the ACT test in November or the SAT in December—the months in which they are taken by the largest numbers of students.) One very bright girl who is a professor's daughter did just this, for example. When she first took the SAT as a high school senior, her verbal score came out at a far too low 408. On the second try, her verbal score was 683—and appropriately, for she graduated only last year from a highly selective college with a four-year average of A-minus.

Achievement Tests of the College Board on which your child had done below-normal work could also be taken over again so that better scores might arrive at selective and highly selective colleges before they made their admissions decisions.

In Case of Admissions Test or Other Trouble, an "Admissions Center" Might Help

Should your child run into difficulty in getting into college because of abnormally low test scores or for any other reason, the boy or girl might very well still gain admission through one of the three non-profit "admissions centers" run by groups of colleges. He would register at a center by sending information, much as if he were applying to a college, and paying a nominal fee. Many colleges using the center to locate applicants would look through his records, and those interested would invite him to apply. The oldest and largest of the centers is operated by the Association of College Admissions Counselors and used by regionally accredited colleges throughout the country. Students have found it helpful not only for uncovering opportunities for admission as freshmen entering in the fall, but for mid-year freshman admission, searching for scholarship offers from colleges and seeking admission as transfer students upon completing studies at two-year colleges. Information about the Association's center may be obtained by writing: College Admissions Center, 610 Church Street, Evanston, Illinois.

The two more recently founded centers are: College Admissions Assistance Center, 41 East 65 Street, New York 21, N.Y.; and Catholic College Admissions and Information Center, 3805 McKinley Street, Washington 15, D.C.

How to Gauge Your Child's Chances of Winning a Scholarship

American families today pay an average of about $10,000 to educate *one child* for four years at a private college, as we noted before, and a corresponding $6,000 at a public college. Tuition costs have doubled since 1950 for the nation as a whole, and they are certain to continue going up.

Hard facts like these about the cost of sending your child to college have probably led you to hope that, when he is ready for college, he might also be ready to win a scholarship. Could he?

His chances would be fairly substantial of getting at least some sort of scholarship aid if he were fairly good in his studies. About one in every five or six students in college today holds a scholarship—in all, an enormously increased number compared with scholarship students of only a generation ago. More than $175,000,000 worth of undergraduate scholarships are awarded in the U.S. every year. Another $275,-000,000 a year are provided in loans and jobs to help pay for college expenses, but it is of course the millions in scholarships that are most helpful to students and their families.

You can judge how helpful from the fact that the *average* four-year value of a scholarship today is some $1,200. Moreover, an award in the large National Merit Scholarship Program can be worth as much as $6,000 for the four college years, while some scholarships—as in the program for part-time employees as well as children of employees of the W. T. Grant Co., the five-and-ten-cent-store chain—can range up to a four-year value of $10,000.

For your child, winning a scholarship would be much like winning admission, with tests counting as much or more in the outcome. In fact, the tests your child takes for admission would often be the ones he would take at the same time for scholarships. The main reason for this is that some $100,000,000 of the $175,000,000 annually given in scholarships is provided by the colleges themselves—and awarded to their admissions applicants who are also applying for financial aid. Another $40,000,000 annually is provided by companies and other private organizations—such as unions, lodges, civic groups, American Legion posts and small foundations—which most often have committees of college admissions officers select winners in their programs. The remaining $35,000,000 or more is given by individual states like Illinois, California, Rhode Island, New Jersey and especially New York (which gives more money for scholarships than all other states combined; New York's grants to undergraduate and graduate students in 1964–1965 total $50.5 million). These state programs also use methods for selecting students of high academic potential which are very similar to the colleges' own methods.

Only a few scholarships, though well-known ones, are awarded by special selection methods. These include the scholarship awards in the Westinghouse Science Talent Search; in the competition of the Fisher Body Craftsmen's Guild of the Fisher Body Division of General Motors, in which boys submit beautifully made model auto bodies; in another competition involving bodily beauty, the Miss America contest; and in the annual Betty Crocker "Search for the Homemaker of Tomorrow" of General Mills Corporation.

Your child would be most likely to take the College Board SAT in trying for a scholarship award. Colleges which require the SAT are also the ones which give the most scholarships. The SAT is used as well in some state scholarship programs, like California's, and in about 250 scholarship programs sponsored by corporations and other private groups.

Your child would take the ACT test in trying for one of the substantial numbers of scholarships offered by colleges using the test, by some foundations and other private scholarship sponsors and by the Illinois State Scholarship Commission.

And for what are probably the country's most famous awards—the National Merit Scholarships—your child would take the National Merit Scholarship Qualifying Test, as we saw in the first chapter.

What test scores and other qualifications would your child need to win a scholarship? This would depend basically on the competition he would have to meet for one or another kind of award. In gauging his chances for an award from a college, you should remember that colleges give their scholarships to young people whom they especially want as students. You might also keep in mind the facts that selective and highly selective colleges generally award the largest numbers of scholarships, and have more awards for boys than for girls.

Suppose, first, that your child's strongest point was his academic ability, and that he or she had won some distinction in extracurricular activities. Your child would then be a possible prospect for a scholarship at a selective or highly selective college if it seemed he would rank in the upper half of his college class—and his scholarship prospects would become stronger the higher in the upper half he gave promise of standing. Insofar as test scores alone were concerned, he would have perhaps a 1-in-3 chance of winning a scholarship at a highly selective college if he had a SAT verbal score of 600 or higher with other qualifications to match. His chances for a scholarship would rise to about 2-in-3 if his verbal score was in the 700s and his other qualifications were comparably outstanding. An SAT verbal score of about 525 or higher would often put your child in the running for a scholarship from a selective college, with his chances rising to some 2-in-3 if his verbal score was over some 625 or 650—again, in each instance, if he had other qualifications to match.

Colleges take many other kinds of qualifications besides academic ability into account in making scholarship awards, however. Your child could, therefore, have a somewhat lower SAT verbal score than indicated above and still win a scholarship from a selective or highly selective college for other reasons. One reason might, of course, be outstanding ability in an intercollegiate sport—football, most notably. Others could include residence in a part of the country or the world distant from the college, good ability in playing an unusual band or orchestral instrument and unusual distinction for a teen-ager of almost any other conceivable kind—having a one-man art show, or starting a successful business, or having writings published in general magazines, or heading the state Boy's Fair or winning a state or national debate contest.

One set of fairly certain qualifications for getting a scholarship from a college may be especially encouraging to you. Scholarships go by tradition to the very promising and the very deserving. Your child would be very deserving if he or she had struggled against unusual handicaps to do very good work in school and to aspire to further education. Colleges are especially anxious to help capable students from families who have continued to strive for a better life despite poverty, social discrimination, political persecution and such natural catastrophes as the severe illness or death of a parent or the physical handicap of a child. If your child seemed capable of average or better work in a college and were so handicapped—were poor, or a Negro, or partially orphaned, or a political refugee or physically handicapped—the boy or girl probably could get at least a substantial partial scholarship from the college. Other agencies might provide the remaining help needed for your boy or girl to go to college if you could not or if the child could not earn it.

One particularly notable agency of this kind is the National Scholarship Service and Fund for Negro Students, with offices in New York City. NSSFNS gives only supplementary scholarships—scholarships worth only several hundred dollars a year—to students who have already been given scholarships worth as much as $2,000 a year or more by colleges. These Negro students—often ones from segregated high schools in the South—are young people who have already received the maximum aid from the Northern colleges they attend but whose need is so great that they still could not go to these colleges without the modest additional aid of NSSFNS. Equally helpful to the students are the counseling services of NSSFNS, which often enable the students to win their primary scholarships.

Your child's chances of getting a scholarship could, of course, be quite good at a college which was open in admissions policy although his chances were quite slim at a selective or highly selective college. For example, one college which accepts all applicants who rank in the top three-quarters of their high school graduating classes awards aid to a few girls with SAT verbal scores in the low 250-to-300-point range of the SAT score scale—though the college aids no students who ranked in the bottom quarter of their high school classes. A third of the college's applicants for aid who have SAT verbal scores ranging from 350 to 400 receive aid, as do about two-thirds or more of its aid applicants with verbal scores from 400 to 500. This college, incidentally, is also attended by a few students who have SAT scores in the high 600s and low 700s. The college clearly illustrates how much your child's chances of winning a scholarship would be affected by the kind of competition for an award he chooses to enter.

For much of the $40,000,000 offered annually in scholarships by corporations, foundations, labor unions, churches, clubs and other private agencies outside colleges, your child would meet less demanding competition than he would in trying for a scholarship at highly selective colleges. These scholarships are often offered locally—to the children of a company's employees, of a union's members or of a county's or town's residents—and such limitations would generally pit your child against others of about an average range of college ability rather than ones of fairly high ability. Avon, Inc., a cosmetics manufacturer, for instance, offers several community scholarships, for each of which students in only one or two high schools near Avon plants are eligible. In the program for children of Ford Motor Company employees, one in about every fifteen of its current applicants wins an award which can be worth as much as $2,000 or more a year for four years. To increase your child's chances of scholarship aid, he should certainly search for all such privately sponsored local programs for which he or she may be eligible. He can do this by asking about them in his school, watching for word of them in local newspapers and looking through scholarship directories.

In the large National Merit Program, however, your child would enter a competition about as stiff as the scholarship competition typical of highly selective colleges. Your child would be about as likely to win a Merit Scholarship as he would to win a scholarship awarded to him directly by Yale, Vassar or Stanford, in other words. Moreover, in the Merit Program, your child could be disqualified by his test scores alone in the first stage of the competition, as he would not in trying for a college-awarded scholarship. Still, the stakes in the program are attractive enough to encourage some 800,000 high school juniors a year to try for one of the 1,600 or more new Merit Scholarships offered annually. The 1,600 awards can each range up to $1,500 or more a year, and in all total more than $6 million for the four college years. These awards were made possible by grants from the Ford Foundation totaling $34.5 million and by the additional support of some 220 corporations, unions, other private agencies and forty or more colleges and universities which provide Sponsored Merit Scholarships. Like the recipients of National Merit Scholarships awarded out of NMSC's own funds, winners of all sponsored Merit Scholarships are selected from the finalist group in the competition. Most of the sponsored awards go to finalists who meet additional criteria, such as place of residence, choice of field of study or career, plans to attend a particular college, or relation to an employee or member of a sponsoring organization.

Your child's first hurdle in the National Merit Program would be the National Merit Scholarship Qualifying Test, which would be given him on a set day in March of his high school junior year. He would be considered further in the program only if he were among the few students in his state who earned a very high NMSQT score—a score which placed him among less than 1 per cent of the highest-scoring students in his state, and thereby qualified him as a Merit semi-finalist. Scores on this level would be roughly on the order of SAT scores in the 700s.

Your child might be likely to score at such a level if he or she had previously scored above the 90th or 95th percentile nationally on other standardized tests of ability in high school. How he had done earlier on the Iowa Tests of Educational Development should provide a particularly close parallel, for the NMSQT embodies questions similar in construction to those of the widely used ITED.

Chance would be the largest factor in deciding whether your child qualified as a Merit semi-finalist if he had consistently stood among the top 5 per cent or 10 per cent on ability tests among students in his state. As we have seen, how well a boy or girl does on tests varies rather widely from one testing to another. For example, according to the College Board, there would need to be a difference in the SAT scores of two students amounting to some 60 points before you could say with reasonable assurance that there is likely to be an actual difference in college ability between the two students. But the Merit Program necessarily sets specific cut-off scores for each state by ranking the students according to test scores and running down the state list until the state's complement of semi-finalists is filled. Each state's semi-finalist complement is a uniform small percentage (under 1 per cent) of the state's high school graduates. As an example of the state cut-off score, students who happened to get a "qualifying score" of 142 or higher in Michigan on the March 1962 NMSQT became semi-finalists; those scoring 141 or lower did not, even though the 1-point score difference has no reliable significance whatever. Qualifying scores for the states that year ranged from 135 to 149.

John M. Stalnaker, president of the National Merit Scholarship Corporation, clearly recognizes the major part played by chance in qualifying as a semi-finalist. It is natural that he should, for Dr. Stalnaker is a measurement psychologist who worked with Carl C. Brigham in creating the College Board SAT in the 1930s. Dr. Stalnaker recently commented on the chance effects of NMSQT testing by remarking, "The people just below our cut-off point may be better than the people just above. All we can say is that on a certain day we ran a race."

Even if your child had run fast enough to become a semi-finalist, he would still have only about one chance in eight of eventually winning a Merit award. Winning one would again be much like winning a scholarship at a highly selective college. For, in further competition he would take the SAT to "confirm" his high NMSQT scores and be considered on the basis of his high school record and recommendations by a Merit selection committee of college admission and school guidance officers. About 97 per cent of the 14,000 or more semi-finalists a year have consistently qualified as finalists. Merit considers all finalists it selects as fully qualified for scholarships, but has funds to give awards to only some 1,600 of them. In a variety of ways, the program helps the others—plus its "commended" students, who are the 37,000 who scored highest nationally on the NMSQT after the semi-finalists—to get scholarships from other sources.

Your child's basic time schedule in the Merit Program, should he win, would be: NMSQT testing in March of his high school junior year, semi-finalist notification in September of his senior year, and award notification in April of his senior year.

Competition for scholarships offered in state programs is generally less demanding than in the Merit Program. The overall odds in the Merit Program from testing to winning would be several hundred to one against your child. But the 1,280 tuition scholarships offered annually in the California state program represent one award for about every 150 high school graduates. New York State offers more than 16,000 Regents College Scholarships a year worth as much as $700 a year—enough awards for 1 in about every 10 graduating high school seniors. In addition, more than 135,000 "scholar incentive awards" worth as much as $300 a year are offered by New York State to undergraduates who meet the sole requirement of maintaining good academic standing at colleges in the state. The Illinois program makes more than 1,500 awards worth as much as $600 or more a year—about one award for every twenty students applying. In most state programs awards can be used only at colleges in the state.

For a California state scholarship your child would be required to take the College Board SAT. For a New York Regents scholarship he would take the six-hour Regents Scholarship Examination in his high school, and he would qualify or not for an award solely on the basis of his scores on the test. The examination includes objective tests of scholastic aptitude and achievement in school subjects, plus a short written composition in which your child would have to show minimum competence to win an award no matter how well he might do on the multiple-choice questions. The exam serves also as the admissions test for the forty-five or more colleges of the State University of New York, which are located throughout the state rather than on a central campus. For the Illinois state scholarships the ACT test is required, and winners are chosen on the basis of their ACT scores and their high school class rank combined.

One last key factor in your child's chances of winning scholarship money has nothing to do with his ability, tested or not. This is financial need. If your family did not need scholarship aid to send your child to his chosen college, he would almost invariably receive no money or only a minimum amount, ranging from about $100 to $250 a year, should he win an award. Scholarships are awarded on the basis of ability, but in almost all programs today the amount of money given is adjusted according to financial need. If a winner's family has no need, his scholarship is often an "honorary" one carrying the minimum cash award or no money at all.

State programs would often estimate your need on the basis of your state income tax payments. Colleges and most private scholarship program sponsors would estimate need by having you fill out a form giving a detailed picture of your financial situation. Your statement would be held in complete confidence, and from it an estimate would be made of how much you could afford to spend toward your child's college education (plus what your child should be able to earn in the four summers before each college year). This sum would be compared with your child's expected costs at his college, and financial aid would be offered to make up part or all of the difference if your child had qualified for aid by ability. The aid might often be in the combined form of a scholarship, a low-interest loan and a part-time campus job for your child if he won aid from a college. All sums would be computed on an annual basis in adjusting an award according to need, with the aid usually subject to renewal for four years and the annual amount subject to revision up or down should your family financial circumstances change substantially.

You should not assume automatically that your child might not receive scholarship aid of a worth-while amount simply because your family's income seemed fairly high to you. The most widely used methods for estimating need take many elements besides income into account. (These are the systems, incidentally, of the College Scholarship Service of the College Board, in which more than 500 colleges participate, and of the National Merit Scholarship Program.) At some colleges, more than one-fourth of the applicants for aid whose families have incomes of $13,000 or more a year are offered aid by the college.

In case your child might not evidence enough ability to win a scholarship, the boy or girl should by no means give up plans for going to college. As noted earlier, loan and job aid available for college students exceeds scholarship aid by some $100,000,000 a year. In addition, night study, "co-operative" work-study programs, in which students spend alternate terms on a job and in college, and low-cost or free colleges also open many opportunities for higher education for young people of modest means—and determination.

Your Child's Personality Would Affect His Admissions Chances— But Not as Appraised by a Personality Inventory

As we saw in looking at how colleges would use your child's admissions test scores, his admissions chances would depend in part on his personality and interests. However, as you may have noticed, colleges use methods of long standing in these elusive matters. Almost no colleges your child could enter from high school now require psychological inventories of personal qualities or vocational interests for its applicants in order to use the results routinely in deciding to accept or reject your child. Instead, colleges depend on what your child has done, on what he writes in his application, on what others (chiefly in his high school) write about him and, perhaps, on how he acts in an interview, to indicate what kind of a person he is.

Colleges do not use psychological inventories with applicants like your child because they know a lot about these instruments, rather than a little. Almost all the authors of inventories have been college professors, and students have served as the guinea pigs in much of the research on which the instruments are based. Literally hundreds of studies have been made to see if such inventories or other systematic means of assessing personal qualities could help in admissions. None has yet made a convincing case.

Speaking for a membership which includes more than 500 colleges, the College Board recently issued another statement to explain why personality inventories should not be used in admitting young people to college—at least as things now stand.

Its first point holds that your child and his school could not tell clearly what the college was after from a personality inventory—that is, what personal qualities the college considered desirable in students and gave preference to in admissions. Even the college might have trouble deciding. Does the college want students who are highly original or highly diligent? Aggressive or unselfish? Active or reflective? Versatile or penetrating? Any test or statement required for admission is taken "as a highly significant communication of college policy and values by schools, students and parents," the statement declares. But at present, admissions officers themselves "may find measures of personality especially difficult to understand and explain."

The statement's second point holds that a required personality inventory would put your child in an acute ethical bind. As you recall, these inventories would depend on having your child answer what he really feels when he is asked, for example, if his friends think he is a hard worker, or whether he would prefer a concert of chamber music to a steak dinner. Almost any conceivable questions might strongly tempt him to lie in putting forward what he thinks to be his best foot. Moreover, an inventory that probed deep into his psychic nature might place information about him that is properly personal and private into the college's hands.

The statement's third point holds that inventories are vulnerable to faking and coaching. Aside from the problems of faking—which pose functional as well as ethical difficulties—coaching could strike at a fatal weakness in the use of inventories in admissions as the instruments can now be made. Practically equivalent forms of ability tests—tests of aptitude and achievement—can be produced readily and indefinitely; several new forms of the Board's SAT are made a year, and have been for many years. But equivalent forms of personality inventories are almost unheard of. As a result, if the single form of any present inventories were put into use for admissions, students and commercial coaches would eventually capture the key that insures admission, and the instrument would be not only worthless, but misleading.

Colleges nevertheless need to know more about the personal qualities of students than they do now. When their predictions of the academic performance of individual students prove wrong—when the boy predicted to make an A average flunks out, or the girl who was barely expected to scrape through catches hold and earns Bs—the reasons can almost always be traced to factors in personal development which went undetected before the young people entered college. The College Board has accordingly spent many thousands of dollars to support promising lines of research in personality measurement and the ways in which colleges influence young people personally rather than intellectually.

As the Board's statement observes, colleges faced with a large excess of well-qualified applicants "are increasingly concerned with measuring characteristics of applicants that will help identify those who will be most productive as adults, or who will find the particular college's environment most congenial and stimulating." Recently, it notes, "a number of independent efforts have each carried research in personality measurement to the point of development of instruments that give promise of providing a base from which effective practical programs eventually may come."

These developments underlie a prophecy of personality assessment which may be used with your child by the time he applies for college. The statement closes:

Everyone concerned with the future development of college admissions procedures should be aware that these new and very complicated tests may become a part of advisement, if not of selection, within a few years.

Your Child Could Earn College Credit Through Tests

Course credit is what you would buy in paying your child's college tuition—that is, if he passed the courses for which you paid when he registered after admission. The bachelor's degree so much sought after today usually represents 120 points (or "semester-hours") of credit—at a tuition charge approaching $60 a point in the country's most expensive colleges (or $1,800 for a year's 30 points, $7,200 for the full 120 points). Moreover, your child's living expenses and lost earnings would amount to at least several thousand dollars each year that he is in college.

From a financial viewpoint alone, then, it is of some moment that your child can earn college credit through tests today. At some colleges—among them, Harvard, Columbia, Princeton, Cornell, Michigan, Michigan State, Stanford and California at Berkeley—your child could enter with as much as a year's credit for which he had qualified on tests. Earning college credit on tests would be still more important to your child for educational reasons, as we shall see.

Your child could earn credit by tests at the colleges above, and several hundred more throughout the country, under the Advanced Placement Program of the College Board. Two other large-scale systems under which he might do so are now being developed—the College Proficiency Examination Program of New York State and the Comprehensive College Tests Program of ETS.

It would be possible but unlikely for your child to earn college credit by tests through the Advanced Placement Program unless his high school were one of the 1,700 or more which give Advanced Placement courses. These courses cover essentially the material dealt with on the Advanced Placement Examinations of the College Board. The dozen present examinations are in the subject areas of English, history, foreign languages, the sciences and mathematics. "Essay" questions—ones to which your child would give written answers—predominate on the exams, though some include multiple-choice questions typical of standardized tests. The exams are not standardized; standardized tests would undoubtedly function as well in telling what the students have learned, but the results of standardized tests would not be as readily acceptable to professors who use essay exams for such courses themselves and who must approve giving credit for performance on Advanced Placement Examinations.

Your child would have to be academically "able and ambitious," in the words of the program's first director, Charles R. Keller, in order to finish his regular high school studies early and start as a senior in Advanced Placement courses. During a week in mid-May of his senior year he would take any of the three-hour exams for which he felt prepared; if he earned a mark of 3 or better (as awarded by teachers serving as "readers," on a scale with a low of 1 and a high of 5), his college might give him credit exactly as if he had taken the course in college. Some colleges may not give credit, but instead give him only "advanced placement," waiving introductory courses in those subjects.

The educational advantages of Advanced Placement studies for your child are that he need not waste his time and energies in either high school or college on courses too easy for him, and that he can go further in his education with less time out of his young life. Each year, incidentally, a few of the 22,000 or more students taking Advanced Placement exams had prepared for them by studying on their own or under the informal tutoring of individual teachers. As you might expect, doing Advanced Placement work as a high school senior would increase your child's chances of admission and scholarship aid at most colleges, although his marks on the exams would not reach selective or highly selective colleges until practically all of their admissions and scholarship decisions had been made.

Should your child take New York State's College Proficiency Examinations for college credit in coming years, he would be more likely to do so as an adult or in college rather than in high school. "Soon it will be generally accepted that there can no longer be any fixed terminal point to education," James E. Allen, Jr., state commissioner of education, said in the fall of 1963, when the program was launched. "People will need access to opportunities throughout their lives. Some of these opportunities will be provided in the traditional manner, but with the demands on our formal system of education already greater than can be effectively met, much of this education will have to be done by new means." The program opened with seventeen three-hour exams, including six from the Advanced Placement Program. Its examinations can be used to meet teacher-licensing requirements. More than 140 colleges in the state have agreed in principle to grant credit for satisfactory exam performance. Credit is granted only by colleges, some of which will give up to half of the credits required toward a degree by examination. Your child might take these very useful examinations, then, to accelerate his progress through college, to continue college work whenever he cannot continue attending on campus (as with a boy who enters the armed forces, or a girl who marries and starts having a family), or to start college later in life if he had gone to a job right from high school.

Your child might encounter the Comprehensive College Tests being developed by ETS in trying to obtain credit for work in the first two college years, which the tests are designed to cover. These CCTs are standardized, multiple-choice tests, though optional essay examinations are being provided in some subjects. Some colleges have shown interest in having such exams with which to give credit for studying done either in college, through correspondence courses, with television or on one's own. The first tests in this extensive series were issued in the spring of 1964, and colleges have been waiting to get experience with the tests before making arrangements for granting credit through them.

How to Keep Your Head as Your Child Nears College

You are now in a good position to judge for yourself how fair or unfair the main admissions and scholarship tests of today would be for your child. Some writers in recent years have tried to stir parents to panic or outrage, or both, about these tests. It has been tempting for them to do so, for cries of alarm and charges of scandal attract readers, and these tests bear on pretty deep concerns for us all—how well our children may be prepared for their lives. But the plain, true story, though important, is not really alarming. It tells how reasoned and humane practices have developed in colleges and schools through long years of trial and experiment, and shows why many shortcomings require further improvement in these practices in the future. Only the main essentials of the present situation and solutions have been touched on here. But enough information has been given, hopefully, so that you will not fall prey to the panic which grips many parents today as their children approach college.

You need not succumb to panic or anger as long as you know the facts, keep a level head and consider your child's future with his or her best interests at heart. The main things to remember are:

1. Your child has an enormous range of college opportunities from which to choose. It is a range unparalleled in practically any other country, with the possible exception of the Soviet Union—and there, your child would go to college and study as the government permitted rather than as he might want. Admissions tests open the whole vast range of American college opportunity to your child, and free him to go to almost any college for which he can qualify—and qualify mainly on the basis of his demonstrated ability and individual attainments, without regard to his creed, color or social class. At the same time, if his abilities seem modest, he can still get higher education to fit him for a satisfying life and a career in which he can stand on his own feet. Or, also with apparently modest ability, he still has many chances to try his wings in programs which demand rather high ability.

2. Admissions and scholarship tests function fairly well as indicators of aptitude or general ability at college studies. One of the main advantages of the aptitude tests predominant among admissions tests is that they give a child from a high school unknown to the college a chance to qualify. Another advantage is that they give bright children who have had a weak, spotty or unorthodox high school education a chance to qualify.

3. There are many things which admissions and scholarship tests do *not* do and for which they are still roundly criticized, such as:

A. The tests do not directly examine students on their writing ability. This galls some college professors, for whom written examinations are largely a sacred cow—or bull, in the college students' term for much of their own exam writing. These professors remain ignorant of the evidence about written and standardized examinations as predictors of academic performance in college because they ignore the evidence.

As an example of this evidence, a former English professor at Yale who is now a College Board vice president, Edward S. Noyes, summarized a study last year as follows: The study "has proved conclusively that indirect measurement of writing ability by means of objective items has high validity," Dr. Noyes said. "It has proved that, on a small scale at least, a combination of direct and indirect measurement [with direct measurement being careful marking of written essays] slightly increases that validity." The question to decide, he concluded, is "whether slightly better measurement and possibly greater influence on the amount of writing done in secondary schools outweigh the increase in cost that would inevitably result from adding essay to objective questions."

B. The tests do not have enough sensitivity to measure differences of ability which are slight compared with the whole scholastic range. The tests are only our best present tools for identifying groups of students at various broad levels of ability: very able, more able than average, normally able and the like. They cannot tell, for example, which students among the very able will really catch fire in college literature courses, and which others will become great political science majors.

C. The tests do not yield fairly accurate measurements for all individuals. In fact, they are far off as predictors of academic accomplishment for rather small percentages of individual young people—but there is no sure way of telling for which individuals the test scores are far off. They are, therefore, ultimately and absolutely uncertain indicators for any particular individual.

D. The tests do not, of course, give any indication of originality or creativity. They may even penalize originality in bright students who are both original and inclined to kick up their heels on tests.

E. The tests do not indicate degrees of other important personal qualities, like motivation, honesty, integrity and sense of social responsibility.

4. Your child is playing the odds in competing for any scholarship—long for some, short for others, depending on the source. Chance will figure largely in the outcome in programs that select at any point by test scores alone—as in the National Merit Program or the New York State Regents Scholarship Program. However, in picking those who score highest on a test, a scholarship program picks the group of students most likely to get high marks in college so far as can now be determined on any large scale. That is, no other single index which can now be gotten (such as rank in high school class) will be both as fair and as accurate a predictor of grade-getting for the group as a whole as standardized test scores.

5. Children suffering from poverty or discrimination, or both, seem to earn lower scores on the tests than their later college work indicates they should. In analyzing the college work of 509 Negro scholarship students, for example, Kenneth B. Clark, a psychology professor at the City University of New York, recently said that SAT scores "and those from similar examinations, cannot be used as a basis for predicting the academic success of the Negro students in this sample—or probably Negro students in general—in the same way that they are used to predict college success for more privileged white students." There are "many intangibles—including motivational ones—which influence academic persistence and success of Negro students," he said. Dr. Clark's report strengthens the hand of the many admissions officers at selective and highly selective colleges who have long admitted Negroes if they seemed possibly capable of passing or better work, and who still could not find as many Negroes as they would like to enroll.

6. Selective admission on the part of a college always keeps out some students who would have done well in the college. Because of this your child should feel that it is no reflection on his ability at all if he should happen to be rejected by a selective or highly selective college.

Expectancy tables like those at the beginning of this chapter show that a few students for whom very low college marks are likely (on the basis of tests and high school marks) do get higher marks in college. But selective colleges find it necessary to accept students with higher test scores and school marks, because more of them are likely to get higher marks in college (and actually do get higher marks).

Still, it is very important to the country—and it may be very important to your child—that we continue to have enough good colleges, like some of our leading state universities, that accept any high school graduate who wants to try college. The University of Kansas has been especially effective in driving this point home. Earlier this year Chancellor W. Clarks Wescoe of Kansas stated some important truisms about tests and class rank in observing that, "Top-ranking high school graduates have scored at the bottom of the university's placement tests, and low-ranking graduates have scored high in the tests. Top-ranking students have flunked out, and students ranking near the bottom in high school have earned degrees and honors." He added, "The hidden premise in the statements about selective admission is that there is some effective way of determining upon admission those students who will succeed and those who will fail. Every study indicates this is not true." As we have seen, Chancellor Wescoe is perfectly right, with respect to *individual* students.

Moreover, in the mid-1950s Dean George B. Smith of the University of Kansas reported that about one-eighth of the students in each of five graduating classes, some 1,100 students, had scored below the 50th percentile on two placement tests—one a verbal and mathematical aptitude test much like the SAT, and the other an English achievement test. Had these students been rejected on the basis of their test scores, Dean Smith said, "The loss to the state and nation would have been 202 teachers, 176 engineers, 22 journalists, 32 lawyers, 25 doctors, 43 pharmacists and 482 graduates of the College of Liberal Arts and Sciences and the School of Business who majored in areas where the supply of trained manpower is in equally short supply."

Losses on this order would surely result if the colleges in any one state or even urban area all became selective in admission—and we cannot tolerate such losses either for the sake of our children or our general welfare. As citizens and parents, we *must* provide enough college places open to all high school graduates who want to try college studies—despite the fact that many weaker students will find that they cannot do passing work.

You should realize, though, that keeping open admission in some colleges does not discredit the justice and value of selective admission using tests and other evidence in other colleges. Dean Smith did not also point out in his report that if the students who had scored *above* the 50th percentile on the two tests had been rejected, the loss to the state and nation would have been *eight times* as great.

If you were at a selective college and could admit only half of your qualified applicants, what would you do in fairness to your applicants, your college and your country?

Chapter 7

Test Hurdles for
the Professions, for Jobs
and in the Armed Forces

Aside from the tests we have looked at so far, your child is likely to meet many others which could also affect the course of his life—in training or licensing for a profession beyond college, after his education, in getting jobs and in the armed forces. A few of these other standardized test series are used on as large a scale as some of the giant series in American education. However, many tests taken by tens of thousands of people a year, rather than some tests taken annually by half-millions and millions, are used in these areas. This chapter briefly sketches the use of these other tests and the heated controversy surrounding the personality inventories sometimes given with them, to round out your acquaintance with major test hurdles your child will probably find in his path.

Tests on Your Child's Way Into a Profession

Your son or daughter would be very likely to meet standardized tests in qualifying for a profession, especially in qualifying for a professional school after college. Here are the main professional school entrance tests used today, and how widely each is used:

Medical College Admission Test. All schools awarding the Doctor of Medicine degree in the U.S. and about a third of those in Canada require this four-part test, given in a "secure" testing program at centers throughout the U.S., Canada and Europe by The Psychological Corporation. The test examines students on verbal ability, quantitative ability, general information and science. "It is used largely as a screening instrument," according to Wimburn L. Wallace, director of The Psychological Corporation's professional examinations division, "rather than primarily to predict whether an applicant will be a good student or a great student." Harvard's medical school, he notes, has ten times as many applicants as first-year openings, enough to make up several classes which would be academically successful. It and similarly sought-after medical schools use the test to help judge between applicants in a general way on a uniform standard.

Law School Admission Test. This day-long test given by Educational Testing Service at centers throughout the U.S. is "now practically universal" in use, according to an ETS spokesman, being required by 95 of some 120 "recognized" American law schools. The questions on the part-tests given in the morning are designed to measure "capacity to read, to understand, and to reason logically with a variety of verbal, quantitative, and symbolic materials." The two afternoon part-tests examine students on their "writing ability" and their "general background" with multiple-choice questions. Scores on this test have been found to be a more valid predictor of marks in law studies than the average of undergraduate marks, for at least some law schools. For example, in one study of the performance of 4,138 students in twenty-five law schools, the correlation between standing on the basis of undergraduate marks and standing on first-year law school marks was .36. However, the correlation between standing on the LSAT and first-year law marks was .45. The best-weighted combination of LSAT scores and average of undergraduate marks gave a correlation with average of first-year law school marks of .54. The corresponding expectancy table for the .54 correlation is:

If a student's standing on weighted combination of LSAT scores and undergraduate marks is:	Then the chances in 100 that he will stand as indicated below according to his average first-year law school marks are as follows:		
	Bottom 20%	Middle 60%	Top 20%
Top 20 per cent	4	50	46
Middle 60 per cent	17	66	17
Bottom 20 per cent	46	50	4

Henry Chauncey, president of ETS, accordingly comments with

some satisfaction, "It's amazing that you can have an index based on only a few hours of testing which works better than four years of work on all kinds of courses in a college."

Graduate Record Examinations. Over 80,000 students a year take this extensive examination series in applying for admission as candidates for master's and doctorate degrees after finishing college. An additional 135,000 or more students enrolled in more than 700 colleges and universities are given GRE tests annually by their institutions for a variety of purposes, including graduate student admission. ETS offers the GRE tests. The series consists of a two-and-a-half hour morning test of verbal and quantitative aptitude, and over twenty three-hour afternoon achievement tests in as many college majors—including French and Spanish; individual sciences like biology, math and psychology; social sciences such as economics, government, history and sociology; and education, engineering, literature, philosophy and physical education. GRE tests are required for the National Science Foundation Fellowships—3,000 of which were offered for 1963–1964—and for many other fellowships offered by universities and corporations.

Miller Analogies Test. This "difficult test of information and verbal reasoning ability" is also "in widespread use" as a graduate student admissions requirement, according to its publisher, The Psychological Corporation. The fifty-minute test is protected with a degree of secrecy unusual even in secure testing programs; more than 400 centers in England, Canada and Australia as well as this country are "licensed" under stringent regulations to give it. All scores on the test are recorded at Psych Corp, and registrants who want to take it a second time must give a reason for wanting the re-test. With the Miller Analogies, centers give three comparably difficult exams—the Doppelt Mathematical Reasoning Test, the Minnesota Engineering Analogies Test and the Advanced Personnel Test. The latter, also a verbal reasoning ability test, is for "employment and upgrading of management and research personnel," and is part of the program because these tests are used in employee selection as well as graduate student admissions.

Admission Test for Graduate Study in Business. Some two-thirds of all students entering graduate business programs in the U.S. take this test. It is made and given by ETS. The test is a special three-and-a-half hour examination yielding verbal, quantitative and total scores.

Validity studies have indicated that "in general, the scores are somewhat better than undergraduate grade average for predicting average grades in the first year of graduate study," ETS states.

Other Professional School Entrance Tests. Other standardized tests required for entrance by at least some of the professional schools or programs in the respective fields include the Veterinary Aptitude Tests, Entrance Examination for Schools of Nursing, Practical Nurse Tests and Dental Hygiene Aptitude Tests, all made by The Psychological Corporation. In addition, the American Dental Association and the National League for Nursing are among a number of professional or professional school associations which have developed standardized entrance tests for their schools with the help of consulting or staff psychologists.

Entrance testing for professional education on the graduate level has spread widely in recent years and is continuing to expand. President Chauncey of ETS observes that each of these programs that it serves "is growing very rapidly."

For Professional Certification—Medical Boards and Others. Your child would also be quite likely to take standardized tests for professional certification, for standardized tests are steadily replacing the older essay and oral certifying examinations. For example, the extensive examinations of the National Board of Medical Examiners, which most states accept in officially approving physicians to 'treat people, were converted from essay to multiple-choice form with the help of ETS a decade ago. So highly respected have the standardized tests become that John T. Hubbard of the National Board recently stated:

> Following the change to multiple-choice testing, and as the reliability, validity and impartiality of these examinations gained recognition, medical school faculties began to see in these examinations a means of measuring their students class by class and subject by subject, and comparing the performance of their students in considerable detail with the performance of other medical school classes across the country. Thus, these examinations have come to be widely used as extramural evaluations of medical education throughout the United States.

Among other standardized tests which your child might take for professional certification are: ones for graduate nurses, dental assistants or neurologists and psychiatrists, prepared with the help of The Psychological Corporation; or the National Teacher Examinations, the

Modern Language Association Foreign Language Proficiency Tests for Teachers or parts of the certifying examinations required for chartered life underwriters, architects, surgeons, obstetricians, gynecologists or anesthesiologists prepared with the help of ETS.

Ability Testing for Jobs Faced by Your Child

For Jobs With Companies. Should your son or daughter look for a job through any of the state employment service offices in the country, he or she would probably take one of America's very widely used test series—the General Aptitude Test Battery, or GATB (pronounced "Gat-Bee"), developed by the U.S. Employment Service. More than one million persons a year take the GATB, including a number of high school juniors and seniors who are given the test in vocational guidance. Versions have also been made for try-outs or use in twenty-seven or more foreign countries.

As an aptitude battery the GATB is similar to the Differential Aptitude Tests of The Psychological Corporation, and to the rather widely used Army Classification Battery to be described shortly. The GATB includes a kind of general intelligence test, tests of verbal and numerical aptitude, a test of spatial perception aptitude, aptitude tests of "form perception" (with problems like matching jig-saw puzzle shapes) and "clerical perception" (recognizing identical names and addresses in lists, and marking discrepancies in style and spelling between otherwise identical pairs) and three tests of "motor skills." These three include speed tests of making pencil marks, moving pegs from holes in one board to another and back and assembling and putting back rivets and washers using both hands. Most tests in the GATB are far shorter than those in the Differential Aptitude Tests and hence give somewhat less reliable scores; the GATB is given in two and one-quarter hours.

Patterns of GATB scores typical of at least small groups of persons in each of many different occupations have been compiled, and state employment services would use these to advise your child about work for which he seems suited and to recommend him for jobs. For example, score patterns have been assembled for groups in such white-collar occupations as dentist, engineer, draftsman and tabulating machine operator, as well as groups in blue-collar occupations like machinist, radio tube mounter, upholsterer, poultry laborer and drill-press operator. Occupational score patterns and other data on the GATB have not been distributed outside the employment service offices. As a result, if your child had taken the GATB in school, counselors in the school would not have the information needed to advise your child on the meaning of his scores.

In going directly to companies for jobs your son or daughter would most often take tests of general verbal and numerical abilities, and tests of proficiency—if he or she was tested at all. People applying for jobs as salaried office workers or in retail sales with large companies are most often given tests. Most large companies—among them, Westinghouse, IBM, Sears Roebuck, Standard Oil of New Jersey, U.S. Rubber and Lever Brothers soap—give ability tests. Members of labor unions are seldom tested by employers, however, because the unions often control job qualifications within their spheres.

Young man works on the Bennett Hand Tool Dexterity Test of The Psychological Corporation, a test of manual ability sometimes given applicants for jobs as repair men and home fixtures service men. (Reproduced courtesy of The Psychological Corporation.)

Typically, your son or daughter would be given intelligence or general mental abilities tests much like those used in school, but usually far shorter and, hence, more likely to yield inaccurate results. These might include the Psychological Tests for Industry of The Psychological Corporation (three tests taking five, fifteen and twenty minutes each), the twenty-five-minute Thurstone Test of Mental Alertness of SRA or the older twelve-minute (or untimed) Wonderlic Personnel Test. Verbal ability subtests of longer batteries would often briefly examine vocabulary, spelling and grammatical correctness, while numerical ability subtests would often cover simple arithmetic operations and sometimes puzzles or word problems in numerical reasoning as well. Your child might frequently encounter these as parts of clerical aptitude tests, in which further sections would test speed and accuracy in alphabetizing, recognizing code numbers or letters and catching errors. Widely used clerical batteries include the Short Employment Tests and General Clerical Tests of Psych Corp, the SRA Short Tests of Clerical Ability and the Minnesota Clerical Tests. Girls might also be given standardized tests of typing and dictation skills, usually called tests of stenographic proficiency. For repair or manufacturing production jobs your child might take speed tests of manual dexterity like the tests of "motor skills" in the GATB—tests such as the Purdue Pegboard or the Hand Tool Dexterity Test. For technical jobs tests of mechanical reasoning ability are often given, as are tests of ability to grasp spatial relations in two or three dimensions (among them, the Test of Mechanical Comprehension of Psych Corp and the Minnesota Paper Form Board). Your son might be given tests of knowledge in one or more skilled trades, like electrician, machinist, carpenter and auto or factory mechanic (such as a popular omnibus one, the Purdue Mechanical Adaptability Test). Engineering applicants also often take the "MEAT"—the Minnesota Engineering Analogies Test given by The Psychological Corporation. Less often, a company would also give your son or daughter an inventory of personal qualities or vocational interests—a very dubious practice for the firm, as we shall see.

For Government Jobs. Were your child trying for a civil service post he might well take the Federal Service Entrance Examination or FSEE, a test much like the College Board's SAT. The FSEE is taken by more than 100,000 people a year, and more than 10,000 were hired in 1962 through it, for example. There are, of course, hundreds of other tests for federal, state and local government jobs. Most of these are not standardized, though many are written in multiple-choice form. Many are of poor technical quality, psychological test experts believe, though the rather plentiful information available on what they cover should give your child a good chance to do well on them if he gets the information and studies it.

Tests for Everyone Going Into the Armed Forces. On enlisting or being drafted into the Army, Navy, Air Force or Marine Corps your son would take the Armed Forces Qualification Test or AFQT, which measures verbal and mathematical abilities and perception of spatial relations. Some 18 per cent of the men currently called up in the draft are rejected because they do not score high enough on this test (and similar supplementary ones) to indicate sufficient "trainability" for service. These tests are the ones on which Cassius Clay, world's heavy-weight boxing champion, was disqualified from the Army in a celebrated incident in the spring of 1964. As in Mr. Clay's case, inquiries can be made to protect against deliberately low scores. Your daughter would take the similar Armed Forces Women's Selection Test in applying for the armed services—and would have to score higher than the 50th percentile on the AFWST to be accepted for enlistment. Some three million Americans are in service now, and these two tests are taken by several hundred thousand new recruits a year.

All new Army enlisted men also take a set of some eleven tests called the Army Classification Battery or ACB so that they may be assigned to duty according to an "aptitude areas" system. The eleven tests include ones of verbal ability, arithmetic reasoning, pattern analysis, mechanical aptitude, clerical speed, radio code aptitude, general information, shop mechanics and automotive or electronics information. Your son would be assigned within an aptitude area of Army service on the basis of his physical condition and prior experience as well as his ACB test scores. As an example, he would be a good possibility for the "electronic" aptitude area had he scored high on the mechanical aptitude and electronics information tests of the ACB. Or, if he had made high scores on the general information and automotive information tests, he might be assigned within the "armor, artillery and engineers—combat" aptitude area.

To become an Army officer your son or daughter would have to score above about the 60th percentile on one of several tests in which verbal and mathematical aptitudes would play at least a substantial part (as well as be recommended for Officers Candidate School by an evaluation board). These tests are the Officer Candidate Test, the WAC Officer Candidate Test, and—for young men in college ROTC units— the ROTC Qualifying Examination required for college sophomores who want to go on for advanced ROTC training and commissions. The Army standard score required to qualify on each of these tests is 115, which corresponds to about the 60th percentile level, but a candidate whose record indicates that he is an "outstanding leader" can qualify with a score between 110 and 114. On most intelligence tests the 60th percentile level on national norms is around scores of 110 IQ. However, in considering possibly equivalent score levels—like 115 on the Officer Candidate Test and 110 IQ—you should remember that even apparently similar tests measure things which can differ considerably, and that the score scales of tests are based or "normed" on sometimes very different "representative" groups of people.

Many other tests are used throughout the armed services. David A. Goslin, a sociologist engaged in a study of testing at which we shall look in the next chapter, has judged it "likely" that "tests play a considerably greater role in military personnel allocation than in other occupational areas."

What Justifies Having Your Child Take Ability Tests for Jobs

Requiring your son or daughter to take ability tests in applying for a job is justified when the company or other agency knows that there is some proven and significant connection between scores on the tests it gives and the kind of job for which your son or daughter is trying. Businesses find out about connections between ability test scores and job success in one of two ways. The first is by direct experience. For example, only secretaries who could type sixty-five words a minute or more may have been judged satisfactory in the past by the executives in the firm for whom they worked. Similarly, a company may have learned by experience that only file clerks who could put material in alphabetical order with an accuracy and speed indicated by an upper range of scores on a test of this skill had worked out well in its offices. Verification of this kind is usually used with tests of proficiency in skills bearing very directly on the job.

The second way in which businesses might find out about connections between ability test scores and job success is by conducting rigorous validity studies. These are essentially the same as the validity studies carried out in schools and colleges. To make them companies determine the correlations between indexes of successful performance in each kind of job under study and scores on tests they may want to use for typical groups of people they hire over a period of time—and, ideally, with scores on the tests *not* being used in hiring those people.

It is harder for companies to make validity studies than it is for schools and colleges because of the difficulty of getting a good index of successful job performance compared with the regular supply and professional quality of teachers' marks in education (not to mention the relatively uniform demands of schooling). Large companies can sometimes use rate of advancement in a department as an index in validity studies that cover a period of years. Amount and quality of work can also be used in some cases. More often, the index of job success (or the "criterion," as it is called) against which test scores are validated will be supervisors' ratings of people who work for them. Ratings like these are usually not as accurate or reliable a criterion as ones like average of high school course marks—even though industrial psychologists have worked on rating systems for many years.

Authorities who know a great deal about the complexities of tests strongly recommend that companies regularly make such validity studies in using ability tests with applicants who could include your son or daughter. For example, in their widely respected work on *Effective Personnel Selection Procedures*, C. Harold Stone and William E. Kendall point out that, "Test packages cannot simply be bought and applied and effective selection be the automatic result. Tests must be tested for the specific use for which they are to be applied. This can be done only through careful research. One must actually conduct an experiment."

Lee J. Cronbach emphatically observes:

The crucial step in prediction research is experimental trial of the instruments. One gives the test to typical *applicants* and observes the correspondence of test scores to success. In practical work there is much pressure to omit the experimental study; this pressure must be resisted. When the psychologist reports to his boss that he believes test X will eliminate poorer employees, the boss is far more anxious to install the test and benefit from it at once than to withhold judgment during weeks or even years of investigation. Full experimental trial is indispensable. No hypothesis can be trusted, because there have been many instances in which "likely" tests proved to be of no value in selection.

Saul W. Gellerman, personnel research director of IBM World Trade Corporation, stresses the importance of repeated experiments to insure current validity. "There is no such thing as general validity for any test," he says; "its usefulness has to be proven for every job in every company for which it is used, and periodically re-proven as well." He adds, "Too many companies have installed tests that had proved to be valid elsewhere without troubling to revalidate locally."

The report of a large-scale study of clerical testing made several years ago indicates why validity studies should fit actual conditions as closely as possible. The Psychological Corporation aided the American Bankers Association in making the study, in which 126 banks tried out selected tests in screening more than 30,000 applicants for clerical jobs. The Association's customer and personnel relations department noted in the report, "One cannot state that a particular test is the most valid for all situations. Even in a single department in a bank, validity co-efficients may change with changing supervision, standards, or functions." It urged that, "Every bank with a hundred or more clerical workers should endeavor to conduct research studies," recommending such large numbers because experimental samples even as big as thirty or forty persons can yield misleading results. However, the report went on to say, "Since smaller banks can rarely undertake research investigations, their use of tests must rest on the assumption that tests of demonstrated value in larger banks will also be helpful in smaller ones."

In sum, you have no reason to feel hostile toward ability tests in employment merely because they would put your son or daughter on his mettle—when they do put him on a mettle that has a proven connection with the job, that is. Tests are scientific instruments only when they are used scientifically. When they are not, they are no more scientific than, say, a chemistry beaker used as a beer stein. But many companies do use personnel tests scientifically, with adequate information on their current validities and full technical understanding of their limitations. Such companies also have a full technical understanding of the limitations inherent in all other kinds of evidence of capability for a specific job or future career—education, past experience, references, interviews and the like. Your son or daughter should welcome a chance to show his competence in taking ability tests for work at such a firm, for doing so would be open and businesslike on both his part and the company's. In taking valid tests he might show his ability and get the job even though he lacked some formal qualification for it. And if he did not show enough ability on the tests, he might be spared starting on a job in which he could not succeed in the work.

Your Child and the Heated Controversy Over Personality "Tests" in Employment

"Anyone who uses a personality inventory for selection, at least so far as the present evidence indicates, ought to be taken out and shot."

This is what one of the leading test publishers says in private conversation about giving personality inventories to job applicants—which are often misleadingly called personality "tests," as we saw. Nevertheless, your son or daughter might fairly often be required to answer one of these inventories in addition to ability tests when applying for a job.

The publisher's irate views are based on the same serious technical shortcomings that personality and interest inventories would have in being used with your child in school, as described in Chapter 5. As you will recall, the reliability of these inventories—the stability with which they measure—is comparatively low; this means that they may be measuring passing impulses or moods, rather than stable personal qualities. Also, the definition of what they measure is open to serious question, for they yield numerical scores on personal characteristics which are only vaguely identified but given such emotionally loaded names as "neurotic tendency," "passivity," "dominance" and "depressive." And even subtle uses of special "lie scales" and "forced-choice" response systems in them have not been able to eliminate successful cases of deliberate faking which defeat their whole purpose.

One large employer who gives many ability tests—the U.S. Civil Service Commission—accordingly declares of such personality measurement:

> The Commission recognizes that significant improvements in the prediction of job adjustment may result from the development of methods of this kind, and, therefore, supports some research and keeps in touch with promising developments in other organizations. However, it rec-

ognizes that at the present stage of development, these methods, as a group, are of little practical value in public personnel selection since not enough is known about those personnel characteristics necessary to success in specific positions, and available methods are difficult to score, to interpret, and to control against intentional distortion by applicants.

Nevertheless, personality inventories have become widely used for hiring in business and industry because plausible though unfounded validity statistics can be developed for them in limited studies with small numbers of people. In addition, many companies have adopted them without any validity studies on the advice of psychologists who are at best uninformed and at worst corrupt. As a result, it would not be very unusual for an applicant to have to work inventories like these along with ability tests in applying for jobs.

Recent popular attacks on the use of personality inventories make it somewhat less likely that persons looking for jobs would have to take them today, though, as compared with past years. Inventories used in corporate hiring were denounced several years ago by William H. Whyte in *The Organization Man*, and at length in Martin L. Gross' book of 1962, *The Brain Watchers*. Many similarly critical articles in general and professional magazines of the last few years have also helped move at least a few companies to suspend the devices. These attacks have made personality inventories a topic of heated controversy today, with the heat being brought to the argument by the attackers, but little said publicly in defense.

The attacks have also denounced the use of "projective techniques," like the famous Rorschach inkblot method or the Thematic Apperception "test" (and others discussed in Chapter 5), to appraise applicants for executive jobs. These techniques, which were developed mainly for use in clinical treatment of the mentally ill, are often very carelessly called "personality tests." Many authorities question their use in personnel selection even more strongly than the use of standardized inventories. The difficulty with projective techniques, according to one clinical psychologist, is that four or five clinicians will often come up with four or five different interpretations of what they reveal about a person.

As for the personality inventories, the critics contend that a company would be wronging a job applicant in two major ways if it nevertheless handed him an inventory to fill out. One wrong would stem from the fact that inventories do not work well for the technical reasons cited above, and they could inaccurately and therefore unfairly bar an applicant from a job for which he was really well fitted. The other wrong would result even if the inventories worked well; indeed, the better they worked, the greater the wrong. This kind of wrong would represent an invasion of the person's rights—first, his right of privacy. A company has no right to pry into things about an individual's inner nature which even he might not be aware of, or to use psychological deception to get him to reveal inner quirks, tensions and weaknesses without knowing what he is doing or how the findings might be used against him.

Second, an applicant's right to a job on the basis of his ability to do the work would be violated by an inventory, the critics also contend. The idea of this right goes deep in Americans. People can develop their abilities through education and effort, and one main driving incentive behind our whole system of great educational opportunity is that our people will want to develop their abilities in order to qualify for a good position in life. Americans accept the fairness of giving a job to the most capable person—"the best man for the job," as we say of candidates running for political office—but they will not accept awarding a job on the basis of such things as sexual adjustment, personal beliefs and successfully controlled complexes and phobias into which inventories try to probe. References and interviewing are the accepted ways by which a possible employer may satisfy his legitimate interest in finding out how co-operative, friendly, upright, sane, diligent and dependable an applicant may be. These are all qualities which anyone can strive to develop, and for which a young man or woman would openly provide direct evidence. But he or she is helpless in the face of some secret profile of interests or traits supposedly typical of acceptable candidates for a job.

He would be helpless, that is, if unwarned—and the books by Messrs. Whyte and Gross not only sound the alarm, but provide much ammunition for counterattack. They each give detailed tips on how to fake effectively on these inventories. Martin Gross explains with glee how he even coached a friend so effectively that the man won a well-paid executive post. In general, they say, the applicant should answer so as to appear conservative, sober, sociable, confident, hearty, outgoing and well-balanced. Self-doubt, artistic or intellectual interests and liberal economic and political views would heavily penalize him in being inventoried for an executive post, the writers contend. He might get around lie scales by keeping an eye out for fairly obvious traps (such as *never* taking a drink, or *always* going to church) and trying to avoid looking too rigidly consistent as well as impossibly high-minded.

Astute faking is even justified by some industrial psychologists. One, for example, remarks that faking on "many interest and personality tests that lend themselves rather easily to simulation by the testee" can show "whether the individual is sensible enough to portray himself in a reasonably acceptable manner, or whether he is so naive as to be overly candid, or (in the case of the test faker who gets carried away with his deception) clumsy enough to present an unbelievably sterling self-appraisal."

Does this advice about how an astute applicant should fake sicken you? If it also sickens an applicant, and if he has the moral stamina and financial independence to do so, he could instead tell the personnel director that he objects to personality inventories for reasons well known in the personnel field, and that he withdraws his application unless the inventory is skipped.

Another course he could take, at least to register an objection if he were kept in the dark about why he was being given an inventory and how the results would be used, is open to him under the current "Ethical Standards of Psychologists" regulations of the American Psychological Association, the APA. The regulations require psychologists to make full explanations as follows:

> The psychologist who asks that an individual reveal personal information in the course of interviewing, testing, or evaluation, or who allows such information to be divulged to him, does so only after making certain that the responsible person is fully aware of the purposes of the interview, testing, or evaluation and of the ways in which the information may be used.

If the applicant were handed an inventory, he would most certainly qualify as an individual asked to "reveal personal information" in the course of "evaluation." He is also the "responsible person" in the matter if he is in his right mind. This gives him the right to be made "fully aware of the purposes" of this "evaluation" and of "the ways in which the information may be used."

Now, the APA also requires that firms use personality inventories only under the supervision of qualified psychologists, who in almost all cases are APA members. If the applicant requested and was not given a satisfactory explanation, he should then ask for the name of the psychologist supervising the firm's use of the inventory.

He would have grounds for complaint of a breach of professional ethics whether he was given the name or not. If he was given it, he could report the psychologist for the ethical violation. If he was not, he could report the publisher of the inventory for an ethical violation—one of selling the inventory improperly. He should report either violation to the Secretary, Commission on Scientific and Professional Ethics and Conduct, American Psychological Association, 1333 16th Street, N.W., Washington 6, D.C. His complaint could lead to suspension of the psychologist's APA membership and loss of his professional status. It could also discourage the firm from making high-handed use of such inventories, or even close off its source of supply for them.

Using personality inventories in picking people to hire today, then, is both morally dubious and scientifically unsound. It is too bad that these present highly imperfect beginnings in personality measurement have been so abused, for they bear on urgent matters for research and they do have legitimate uses. It is, of course, legitimate for fully qualified counselors and therapists to use them to help individuals, as sources of clues subject to further verification in the experience of the persons being counseled.

Ability tests are worlds apart from inventories in their scientific grounding and the justice with which they apply to a job-seeker. This fact has been thoroughly confused by most of testing's current loudly indignant critics. Despite superficial resemblances, inventories are basically different in the way they function and in not having gotten beyond the stage of the research laboratory and the private counseling office.

The difference is simple and usually absolute as it applies to a person who is trying to get a job. Deliberate effort to succeed on ability tests leads most often toward truths. But deliberate effort to succeed on inventories leads most often toward lies.

Chapter 8

Testing in Store
for Tomorrow's
Children

Testing is a science which enters into many millions of lives today—with the widely used measuring instruments we have seen identified and described in this book, and for the major purposes we have explored.

But testing today is itself being examined and developed—as well as criticized—on a larger and more active scale than ever before. New ways of using tests for your children within the next few years are in the making. Certain basically different kinds of tests seem in store not too many years ahead. This chapter tells of what kinds of testing loom ahead for your children in the near and far future, and closes with a look at one crucial aspect of testing at its ultimate pitch of development.

Better Learning Through Testing

From the start testing has been closely connected with learning. Binet's original aim in measuring general intelligence was to sort out children learning, while the point of most testing today—even for jobs—is to try to see how well people can learn, and have learned. The extent to which testing has grown in this country directly reflects the growing importance we have had to attach to learning itself. Money spent for learning, years spent learning and public interest in learning have all reached peaks higher than any· behind, yet still lower than those urgently needed ahead. The enormous capacity to learn that marks mankind alone, and that has revolutionized existence time and again, is at last being recognized as a prime force behind any country's might, prosperity and well-being. Fast-multiplying machines which spring from acute minds do more and more of our drudgery better than we ever could without them—even the drudgery of routine thought. Organizations of all kinds grow increasingly complex as we capitalize more and more on our vastly enlarged material powers to enrich everyday life. We need still more and more people who can learn rapidly and well with each quickening step that we take in multiplying human capabilities and organizing human functions. Use of tests that above all test learning powers has naturally grown at a mounting rate.

It is not surprising, then, that much of the new work in testing centers around improved learning. Leaders of the country's major testing agencies most often mention work involved with learning when asked about imminent developments. Arthur E. Traxler, executive director of the Educational Records Bureau, says, "Now, the whole curriculum is in flux, with mathematics and science taking the lead." The administrative head of the agency through which most of the finest independent schools test their students extensively continues, "As we try to keep up with this, I think that the tests—like our new mathematics tests—are not going to be restrictive, but may go so far ahead that the schools won't be ready for them at first." He adds, "Test-builders are leading the curricular reforms, and hence probably overestimate the extent of actual curricular change in the schools."

Willis W. Clark, the psychologist who is a founder and chairman of the board of California Test Bureau, observes in his Monterey office that, among other new works, his company is introducing a series of "self-instructional materials" in basic school subjects and skills. He explains why by saying, "We have always had in mind that when the teacher sees a child in trouble, she should give him something to help him learn what he needs to know at that point."

Roger T. Lennon, head of the test department of Harcourt, Brace & World, says across the country in New York, "I believe the largest developments will come in better appraisals of learning outcomes, and in diagnostic appraisals of learning."

Lyle M. Spencer, president of Science Research Associates in Chicago, agrees. "I hope that the day is less than ten years away when no learning system will be put out that does not have an evalution system to go along with it," he says. The "learning systems" to which he refers contain material to accomplish the same ends as your child's regular textbooks, but provided in new content and forms—on printed pads, folders, booklets, filmstrips and cards—which are organized in classroom sets to give clearer focus on what the pupil should learn, and greater flexibility and effectiveness in use. SRA provides such systems with tests that children often take individually to gauge their own progress. The tests are not usually standardized, but they have multiple-choice questions which children can score themselves. SRA's Greater Cleveland program in "modern mathematics" for the elementary grades includes an evaluation system of special tests on each unit which are given by the teacher to the whole class. These "evaluation tests" in learning materials, Mr. Spencer says, "will largely supplant the final exam and the monthly exam prepared by individual teachers, rather than regular standardized achievement tests."

Educational Testing Service in New Jersey has begun supplying special short tests for teachers to use in similarly evaluating what students have learned in class, but without text materials to go along. Its first series of this kind contains eight "Topical Tests in American History" for high schools. Teachers give these to their students to supplement tests the teachers would make up themselves. Issued by the Cooperative Test Division of ETS, the topical tests offer such advantages as even coverage of the topic, ease of marking compared with written essays and interest-provoking novelty to stimulate thought and discussion. Topics covered in the American history series range from "Exploration, Colonization and Independence" through "The Second World War and Beyond." Topical test series in other subjects are projected by ETS. These tests are not standardized; the norm or standard on the American history tests is "a perfect score for all of the items you [as the teacher] consider relevant to your teaching objectives."

The Psychological Corporation in New York is also developing tests of what a person has learned which will not be standardized in the usual way on representative groups of people, but instead will measure on simple quantitative scales. These tests, which should find use in business and industry as well as in education, would determine such things as how many numerical operations a person can perform in a standard length of time, or how many words the person evidences having in his or her vocabulary. How findings like these compare with people in general would not be reported; rather, the findings would be compared with requirements for a particular job in which, say, a vocabulary of 8,000 or more words had been found to be necessary, or with similarly set goals of an educational or training program.

Recent critics have charged that at least some aspects of testing interfere with learning, however. Multiplication of testing programs offered to high schools by "external" agencies through the 1950s led to an indignant report called *Testing, Testing, Testing* in 1962. It was sponsored by three very influential organizations: the National Association of Secondary School Principals, the American Association of School Administrators and the Council of Chief State School Officers. Its basic complaint was that too many programs for college entrance and scholarships were being run. The report argued that these programs put pressure on the students, had to be given during school hours in some cases and duplicated one another. It granted the importance of testing within bounds, for this was the report that stated, "To teach without testing is unthinkable," as we saw in the opening chapter. But it demanded that excesses be curbed.

Actually, whether or not to take part in an external testing program is up to the individual school principal or superintendent. The report probably did stiffen heads of schools to forego some outside testing, though the numbers of students taking tests in the largest programs—such as National Merit, the College Board and ACT—continued to rise at about the same rate as in prior years. The basic difficulty in the situation appears to be that testing which served the needs of learning on one level of education—the college level—had pressed too hard on the needs of learning in a neighboring level, high school. Moreover, the pressure of admissions and scholarship programs grew very fast through the 1950s. Many steps have been taken to ease the difficulties, though vigilance on the part of school officers continues. Such vigilance should help protect your child from indiscriminate testing in the future.

Reiterating its stand last year, the National Association of Secondary School Principals singled out these four of the report's eighteen recommendations as "particularly helpful" guides to schools and school systems "in examining the impact of external testing on students":

5. That school officials, administrators, and teachers refrain from using

the scores made by their students on a single national test as the measure of the quality of their educational program.

9. That school teachers, administrators, and other professional personnel become more knowledgeable in the field of measurement and evaluation; that they learn what tests can do and what tests cannot do.

11. That all individuals or organizations having access to test scores refrain from publicly using them to compare students, schools, or states; and that the use of test scores for publicity purposes by test makers, test publishers, school administrators, or others be regarded as unprofessional practice.

12. That all external tests be given outside of regular class time. School administrators should have freedom to schedule external tests at a time convenient for the students and faculty involved. Further, local school systems should refuse to participate in nationally sponsored tests unless those tests can be demonstrated to have value commensurate with the effort, money, time, and emotional strain involved.

Critics within testing have long deplored another aspect of different test series which bear on your child's learning. As we have seen a number of times, widely used test series have been standardized with different nationally representative samples of young people. In consequence, an IQ score of 115 or a standing at the 85th percentile on two series of tests does not represent the same general level of ability on both series; most persons who score at the 85th percentile on the first series, for example, might score at the 95th percentile or the 75th percentile on the second. Your child could thus not be told by a teacher or counselor that his standing on the second test series was higher probably because his ability had actually increased between the first and second series he had taken.

Test publishers are taking steps to clear up this confusion at the urging primarily of Roger T. Lennon of Harcourt, Brace & World. Dr. Lennon is seeking agreement on a joint "anchor test" project sponsored by the major publishers. In it, a special general mental abilities test would be made to yield scores for verbal ability, numerical ability and the total or composite of the two. Five levels of the thirty-minute test would be written to cover the grades from first through the college sophomore year (with levels on grades 1-3, 4-6, 7-9, 10-12 and 13-14). The test would then be given to a sample of young people carefully picked to be representative nationally. Other test series would next be "anchored" to the first, essentially by using some of the questions from the anchor test in standardizing each other series. It would then be justified to say that equal standings on "anchored" test series did represent performances by groups of people of about equal levels of ability insofar as the standardizing of the tests were concerned.

However, you should also realize that equal standings on different "anchored" series by your child would not mean that his performance on one series corresponded exactly to his performance on another series. Different tests—even different IQ tests—measure sometimes very different abilities. But different standings on two different anchored series by your child would mean that the differences were due to the differences in what the tests measured and how your child had actually performed on the tests, rather than to accidental differences in ways of setting standards on the tests. Anchoring would help most with tests of general mental abilities or intelligence, according to Dr. Lennon; for a number of technical reasons, it would not result in as closely comparable scores between achievement test series.

Other technical reforms of a less extensive order are being made in many sectors of the testing field. These steps are small and widely scattered, but they are many and their combined effect on the use of tests with your child is large. They are leading to a steady improvement in the quality of the tests as measuring instruments used with your child and in the interpretation of your child's test scores. On the one hand, some test publishers in the past have tended to abuse the unusually demanding professional responsibility they bear in three ways: by not revising older series of theirs which continued in demand in order to keep them fully up to date; by not providing all the research data and interpretive material about their series that leading authorities believe to be important; and by making claims in advertising and manuals about what their tests can show that went beyond the support of research evidence. On the other hand, teachers and administrators who used tests extensively in schools and colleges have often been seriously uninformed about how tests work and what test scores mean. In recent years, however, the number of school officers who understand the meaning and use of tests very well has increased greatly for a variety of reasons. At the same time, errant publishers have increasingly stepped up their research and toned down their claims. Not all abuses by either publishers or educators have ended, but the trend toward better-grounded tests more intelligently used with your child is very strong and continues to grow. All along, of course, a substantial amount of testing has been both technically rigorous and educationally enlightened.

Your children stand to benefit handsomely in coming years from the many new experiments being made in education today—experiments with new curricula or things to learn, with teaching machines, educational TV or other new ways to learn, or with "team" teaching, "ungraded" systems (ones without the conventional year-long grade levels) or other new ways of organizing teachers and learners. If your boy or girl is taking part in one of the many experiments, the child may have mentioned taking "a lot of tests" to see how the experiment seems to work.

Tests provide one important way of seeing whether a new method of educating produces better results than the old. They are not the only way, and even remarkable improvement in learning indicated by tests may not be conclusive—often largely because of the so-called "Hawthorne effect," which leads people involved in any new way of working to do better through the stimulation of novelty, enthusiasm and attention to a greater extent than through any actual changes tried under the experiment. This effect can be offset, however. There is no question that tests have been a powerful aid to educators in developing better education for your children, because they can help prove that one way actually does produce results considered better or more desirable.

As an example, The Psychological Corporation conducted the elaborate testing and attitude polling used to evaluate one of the major new high school curriculum series in a recent year. These were the books and methods of the "blue," "green" and "yellow" programs of the Biological Sciences Curriculum Study. One of Psych Corp's many findings was that above-average students in the ninth grade did just as well in the new programs as typical students in the tenth grade. The finding could help your child by making it possible for him to take the new course a year earlier than he might otherwise be allowed to.

Better Use of All Information About Your Children With Computers

Electronic computers and other data-processing machines are

widely used to score tests and make analyses of test data. Conspicuous use of computers in testing has led some critics to denounce the field as inhuman, as one in which fascination with technical apparatus has led to the neglect of human concerns. However, test results are useful to the extent that they are in human affairs largely because of their relative impersonality; they tend to protect your children against errors of human judgment that might be made through unconscious bias, limited knowledge and chance personal impression. Moreover, as Paul L. Trump, president of the ACT program has observed, the use of computers to analyze test results and other data frees human judgment to concentrate on the supremely human questions involved in a decision—and frees judgment from coping intuitively with complex data which can be more validly summarized by machines.

Computers make it possible to carry protection for your children against snap judgments one step further than it would otherwise reach —and will do so increasingly in the future. People often tend to reach decisions about other people on the basis of just one thing. It is hard to keep all relevant factors about someone else in mind, in correct balance and proportion. Discovering what factors are relevant, and to what extent alone and in combination, is also a very difficult problem. Some mathematical ways of balancing factors in simple cases have been developed—for example, as in using the three factors (two test scores and rank in high school graduating class) which we saw combined in the "expectancy table" for Tulane University. Applying such math to data for students is very laborious, and computers are used increasingly to do it.

Perhaps the most extensive use of computers for this purpose in education today is made in the predictions of college freshman averages produced for individual students at individual colleges in the American College Testing Program. Eight factors are combined in each of these predicted averages, as we saw—the four subject-area scores on the ACT test, and the most recent high school course marks in the four corresponding areas. In the system "optimum" weightings which yield the most accurate predictions for recent entering students at the college are used in making the combinations.

E. F. Lindquist, a man of astoundingly varied works of genius in testing, sees such combinations of factors as a way of "reading between the lines" of the usual student record. Dr. Lindquist is the originator of the two very influential Iowa series of tests, as we saw. He also developed the country's first high-speed machines in 1952 for scoring test answer sheets, ones which score at rates up to 6,000 sheets per hour. And he developed the ACT test and the program's Research Service in which colleges receive masses of advanced research data about their own institutions and students as well as the predicted freshman-year averages of their applicants. These predictions or "grade expectancies," made for each college using the ACT Research Service, indicate the chances in 100 for each applicant to earn average grades of less than C and B or more in his freshman-year studies at that college.

Dr. Lindquist foresees increasing use of computers in testing your children, but to make the information that is now available about them "more useful and functional" rather than to generate new kinds of information. "For example," he observes, "there is a great deal of information on the high school transcript, but it hasn't been used, especially the information 'between the lines.' We have used single items of information, but we have not put together combined indices, with weights." Dr. Lindquist's indices of predicted college averages in the ACT program are produced on a very large computer, an IBM 1401-7090 installation at the State University of Iowa in Iowa City, where the main offices of the ACT program are located.

Henry Chauncey, president of Educational Testing Service, sees the schools making more use of data processed and analyzed by computers. "With computers, schools in the future may be presenting much more information, better organized and more regularly reported, than they are now," Dr. Chauncey declares. ETS now conducts a "Cooperative Plan for Guidance and Admission" in which electronic equipment is used to prepare the school's cumulative record cards and transcripts of high school students. In the plan, the school enters the basic information for a student by blackening spaces on computer "input" sheets sent to ETS. Schools receive printed reports which carry all the regular school information on the student plus many special computed indices—several kinds of rank in class and adjusted rank in class; averages of marks by year, by subject area (such as language arts) and by general field (such as courses calling mainly on verbal skills); and various combinations of test scores and course marks. Space is left on the sheet for personal appraisals and recommendations of the students by school officials, and copies can be used as transcripts for college and job applications. The plan was developed in Georgia, and seven additional pilot projects were run, with the help of a Ford Foundation grant, in Arizona, Florida, Indiana, Michigan, Minnesota, Vermont and the Catholic Diocese of Pittsburgh. Some 200 schools in twenty states now use the plan.

In addition, all school systems of the country's largest cities have computer equipment of their own which they use for such purposes as bookkeeping, budget control, making up payrolls, scheduling classes and analyzing enrollments. Many school systems of smaller cities and larger suburban districts, as well as most large universities, also use computers for these purposes. This widespread computer capacity in education is increasingly applied to local recording and analysis of the performance of young people on tests and in regular classroom work, in addition to central services provided by agencies like ACT and ETS.

More and more, then, schools are using computers to assemble and organize all information about your children for ready access and, hopefully, fuller understanding at times of important decision. Decisions which are sounder, because better informed, should result.

Another result seen by some testing experts is better information for teachers about what their students have learned and could learn, which in turn could often make teaching far more effective than it is today. This is what Roger T. Lennon has in mind when he sees larger developments ahead in using tests "in better appraisals of learning outcomes, and in diagnostic appraisals of learning." He adds, "I believe that the use of computers will lead to far more extensive use of tests, with teachers having much more information about their pupils than they do now."

More Profound Understanding Through Research

What kinds of new tests may be among America's "giant series" twenty-five years from now—peers at that time of the twenty-five test series identified in this book as the most widely used present ones? The answer is not at all clear. Few if any experts hazard guesses today on the question. However, current research in psychology strongly suggests that at least some basically different kinds of tests will have come into wide prominence by then. Only a very few of the most interesting lines of research, picked out at random, can be sketched here.

One large body of research is looking into the possibility of greatly increased learning ability. Some of it has exploded established ideas of what young people appear capable of learning at various ages. At Yale University, O. K. Moore recently succeeded in teaching three-year-olds who were even average and below average in ability to read and write with a method using a specially outfitted electric typewriter. In part, the many changes in course content of today—the many new curricula—often move material from a higher grade to a lower one. In the "new mathematics" being widely introduced, for example, some topics have been plucked from the advanced high school level or even the college math major level and placed in modified form into the first three grades—"inequalities" and "set theory" in algebra, among them. The prophet of this movement is Jerome S. Bruner, the Harvard psychologist mentioned earlier. In phrasing his most exciting thesis, he has said that "considerable evidence is being amassed" to support "the hypothesis that any subject can be taught effectively in some intellectually honest form to any child at any stage of development."

This can be done, he explains in his book on *The Process of Education*, by making the basic ideas and structure of a subject clear to the child in ways he can understand. "The task of teaching a subject to a child at any particular age," Dr. Bruner explains, "is one of representing the structure of that subject in terms of the child's way of viewing things." It is his "considered judgment that any idea can be represented honestly and usefully in the thought forms of children of school age, and that these first representations can later be made more powerful and precise by virtue of this early learning."

Studies since the Second World War, Dr. Bruner believes, have caused some psychologists to revise their ideas about whether skills learned in one discipline or subject "transfer" to another. It is the sense of "structure" developed in one subject, he suggests, that not only helps children to learn other subjects, but enables them to learn some essentials of any subject at any early school age. As you recall, Edward L. Thorndike largely exploded the old idea of using hard subjects taught with great emphasis on drill work to cultivate general "mental discipline" in children. But the new notion of how "transfer" may work is quite different. Dr. Bruner declares, "Virtually all of the evidence of the last two decades on the nature of learning and transfer has indicated that, while the original theory of formal discipline was poorly stated in terms of the training of faculties, it is indeed a fact that massive general transfer can be achieved by appropriate learning, even to the degree that learning properly under optimum conditions leads one to 'learn how to learn.'" Among psychologists, he adds, "These studies have stimulated a renewed interest in complex learning of a kind that one finds in schools, learning designed to produce general understanding of the structure of a subject matter."

How children develop has been studied by many psychologists in recent years, and the inquiries of a Swiss psychologist, the late Jean Piaget, have won the excited interest and respect of many others. Dr. Bruner accepts the view of three major stages in the child's intellectual development framed by Piaget and his school in sketching how the structure of any subject can be introduced at any school age. In the child's first stage, the "pre-operational" one which extends up to the age of five or six, the child learns to represent things in the world by symbols—words, pictures and toys. At this stage he lacks mainly the "concept of reversibility." The child cannot understand, for instance, that a clay ball can be flattened into a plate, then back again into a ball.

Next comes "the stage of concrete operations," which lasts to some age between ten and fourteen. In it he can carry out trial-and-error operations in his head, and does not have to do them physically. "The child tips a balance scale too far with a weight and then searches systematically for a lighter weight or for something with which to get the scale rebalanced," Dr. Bruner notes. Symbolic structures develop in the child's mind to represent things in the world—in the case of the balance scale, he says, "the structure is a serial order of weights that the child has in his mind." These internal structures are the key to learning in this stage. "It is into the language of these internal structures that one must translate ideas if the child is to grasp them,"

Dr. Bruner says. At this stage, the child "is capable of grasping intuitively and concretely a great many of the basic ideas of mathematics, the sciences, the humanities, and the social sciences." However, the child finds it difficult to deal with "possibilities not directly before him or not already experienced." In the third stage, however, entered some time between the ages of ten to fourteen, a child's "intellectual operations now appear to be predicated upon the same kinds of logical operations that are the stock in trade of the logician, the scientist or the abstract thinker."

Development in the early years can be speeded or hindered by the extent to which children under six are introduced to such ideas as "time sequence" and "conditional causation" in their daily lives, the psychologist observed in a recent address. Such ordinary dialogues as "I want cake," "After you eat your eggs," "I ate cake" are very important for early intellectual development. To raise your child's IQ, he suggested, take your child at about the age of five and show him two water glasses—one tall and thin, and the other short and fat, with water in the tall one. Then screen the glasses from him with a card, pour the water all into the short glass, pull the screen away and ask your child if there is more or less water than before. At first he is likely to say, "Less," because the level is lower. But when he understands that the amount is the same, he will have begun to pass earlier than usual into the stage of "concrete operations" by starting to develop the "concept of reversibility."

Dr. Bruner is much interested in using tests to improve learning, but he would like to see what would happen in an experiment if, rather than being tested under "neutral conditions," children were tested under "optimum conditions, with a real 'take-home' test, a 'maximum-hint' test," to test the "outer limits" of the child's capacity. Also, he says, "I would like to see a full year given to teaching and testing, teaching and testing, all through the day, to see how well our educational system is using the child's capacities when they are operating fully."

As you can see, theories like these raise certain fundamental questions about all kinds of ability testing today, as well as about our entire system of schooling. Were these theories further confirmed, tests of intelligence or general mental ability should be altered to examine development explicitly within each of the three main stages of the child's mental development, and to examine for evidence of transition between the stages. Similarly, achievement tests ought to focus more closely than they now do on the basic structure of a subject, and achievement test standings might be measured according to development within each of the three stages rather than along a base line of age or school grade level as at present.

Another revolutionary line of investigation has long been pursued by J. P. Guilford, head of the Aptitudes Research Laboratory at the University of Southern California. Dr. Guilford's work is one of the main supports behind the present widespread but as yet inconclusive efforts to test for creativity or creative thinking ability. As you will recall, "factor analysis" is an elaborate mathematical method for identifying the extent to which different parts of a test measure parts or factors in an ability independently. Dr. Guilford has carried factor analysis of general mental abilities tests to extreme lengths, devising many new types of ability tests and identifying dozens of new factors in mental ability through them. In addition, he has developed a theoretical model which provides for a total of 120 "differentiated abilities," all of which he believes could be effectively identified by tests, though not all of which would have practical significance. Some 50 of his 120 ability factors have been matched with tests, according to Lee J. Cronbach. One type of mental operation indicating creativity in Dr. Guilford's work is "divergent thinking," as opposed to what he also named "convergent thinking." Convergent thinking is what is often required on ability tests today—finding a unique right answer from given information. By contrast, in a problem in divergent thinking you would be asked to find as many good solutions as possible, such as lines to rhyme with another or titles for a story. After recent factor analyses of his own, another eminent psychologist, Robert L. Thorndike, concluded that the analyses "suggest that there is some reality to a broad domain, distinct from the conventional intelligence test, to which the designation 'divergent thinking' or 'creative thinking' might legitimately be applied."

Creativity tests have not been used to any great extent for two main reasons. First, it is hard to develop criteria against which to validate their results; people recognize creative individuals fairly well, but they find it hard to identify degrees of creativity to the extent that they can identify degrees of, say, scholastic performance. In one interesting study The Psychological Corporation is trying to develop criteria of creativity by having persons who serve as raters indicate just such relative degrees of creativity. An attempt is being made in the inquiry to have the raters base their assessments on elements in the typical behavior of each creative person, such as whether he prefers to work alone or with someone else, or whether his ideas come suddenly or after long study. Creativity in three main areas is being examined—in the liberal and fine arts, in which literary productivity, for example, is taken as one sign of creativity; in business, in which money-making serves as a sign; and in science, in which discoveries would be a sign. George K. Bennett, The Psychological Corporation president, says that, in the study, "We're trying to find out about the nature of creativity."

Perhaps an even more decisive restraint to wider development and use of tests of creativity is that the quality is honored more in the breach than in the observance today. Creative young people usually disrupt the smooth routine of schooling, and antagonize some teachers for not doing what is expected. In one rare instance of recognition a small number of special National Merit Scholarships are awarded to finalists judged unusually creative. These scholarships are awarded for past performance rather than test results, however. As John M. Stalnaker, National Merit president, explains: "What we have done is to find youngsters who have gotten recognition for work outside the school—won third prize in an art show, or been runner-up in the state oratorical contest, or had a short story published in the local paper, or built an amateur radio station. We assume such students are creative." Problems would airse if Merit had to judge degrees of creativity, as between an art show prize on one student's part and short story publication on another's. "We haven't gotten to evaluations like these," Dr. Stalnaker notes, "but we will have to."

In coming years, then, your children might be given mental ability tests representing more of Dr. Guilford's factors than the relatively few included in present tests—if practical criteria to correspond to more factors can be developed.

Many promising research studies suggesting other new kinds of psychological measuring instruments are being made. In one, Donald E. Super of Teachers College, Columbia University, may be getting close to discoveries which would lead directly to new instruments for your children to take for help in vocational guidance in not too many more years. "If this notion of 'vocational maturity' we're investigating works out," Dr. Super declares, "we may soon be able to develop ways of measuring it." A child's 'vocational maturity' in Dr. Super's theories represents the extent to which he has developed toward readiness for his life work. One key to such maturity, Dr. Super suggests, is the individual's "self-concept," the way in which he sees himself. An idea into which he and his associates are looking, he says, is that, "if a person has developed a clear self-concept, it's easy to make an occupational choice."

Such fundamentally new approaches in measurement for vocational guidance seem especially important to Roger T. Lennon of Harcourt, Brace & World. "The fact that perhaps as many as a fourth or more of the young people now in high school will at some time work in occupations which do not even exist today dictates quite different kinds of appraisal for vocational guidance than our present ones," he observes. "It is significant as well that many young people will go into not one but several different occupations in the course of their working years. We have to seek other dimensions of a person's make-up for effective guidance into this kind of rapidly changing occupational future." Generally, Dr. Lennon sees "increasingly great need for better knowledge of human potentials" because of many major "social forces" of our time, among them "the problem of the culturally deprived, the knowledge explosion, the population explosion and growing urbanization, as well as fast-changing occupational patterns."

One of the major current attempts to find more effective ways of locating talented young people among the culturally deprived on a large scale is being made in the new National Achievement Scholarships effort of the National Merit Scholarship Corporation. With a recent seven-million-dollar grant from the Ford Foundation, Merit will award 200 such Achievement Scholarships a year to outstanding Negro high school students starting in the spring of 1965. It plans to devise new means of selection for them, which could lead to original types or uses of tests for the culturally deprived.

In still another measurement area, personality, a wide variety of complex studies are under way. S. A. Kendrick, the College Board staff member in charge of its research program, sees an increasingly urgent need for some systematic means of personality assessment by selective colleges. Virtually every college, he says, will first explain its academic criteria in discussing its admissions policy, then go on to state that it "of course 'takes the individual into account.'" But this "indirectly gets into serious questions of reliability and relevance," he points out. If personality measuring methods were to be added in the College Board program, Mr. Kendrick indicates, you and your children would be fully informed about what they are, how they are used and what they signify. "I'm for having people report all scores on all tests that are good enough for them to give in the first place," he declares, "and especially for making those giving the tests responsible for interpreting the results."

Current research, then, suggests many different kinds of tests or other measuring instruments, and has also developed a large number for which widely practical uses have not been found. But the research most likely to bring new kinds of tests into your children's lives is research which first brings more profound understanding of your children, and which can help them realize greater individual fulfillment.

Two last, large research studies now in progress may lead, not so much to new kinds of tests, as to better ways of using tests with your children. The first is Project Talent, which in the spring of 1960 gave a battery of seventeen special aptitude tests and three special inventories to 440,000 boys and girls in grades 9 through 12 across the country. Much other information was obtained about their schooling from their superintendents, principals, teachers and counselors. Supported by U.S. Office of Education grants, Project Talent is designed as a national census of "the aptitudes and abilities of high school students" concurrent with the population census of 1960. It is run by John C. Flanagan and the American Institute for Research, which he heads at the University of Pittsburgh. A test author and authority himself, Dr. Flanagan led Air Force testing for personnel assignment in World War II. Project Talent will follow up its nationally representative sample of young people for a number of years, seeking to analyze many facets of their background, schooling and career choice in relation to how well the children realize their potential for themselves and the nation. Its findings should contribute to improved education, guidance and test use with your children.

The other large research effort portending better ways of using tests with your children is a study of "the social consequences of ability testing" being made by the Russell Sage Foundation with grants of more than $400,000. Under the direction of Orville G. Brim, Jr., the study is examining in great breadth and detail the effects of testing for ability on individuals and families, schools and colleges, and employees and businesses. A volume by David A. Goslin reporting on the use of ability tests in America and the issues their use raises has already been published by the Foundation under the title, *The Search for Ability; Standardized Testing in Social Perspective.* Two three-year studies are now being made, one a national survey of opinions concerning ability tests and individual differences in intelligence, the other an inquiry into the effects of testing programs in elementary schools on the attitudes and beliefs concerning individual differences held by children, parents and teachers.

No conclusions have been reached, but some of the serious concerns on which the study's final recommendations will bear have been described by Dr. Goslin:

As tests are improved technically "and are accepted as valid indices of an individual's abilities," will the reporting of test scores to the individual "have potentially greater consequences for his self-esteem, level of aspiration, and frustration level than at present"?

Noting that "the childrearing practices of the family" have been of considerable importance in developing "high motivation," he asks, "Does information that one's child is of only average ability change socialization practices by the parents away from those that would normally produce high achievement motivation on the part of the child?"

From the standpoint of the society as a whole, will the "cumulative effect of testing" result in "a raising or lowering of the level of productivity, depending on whether more people feel that the increasing use of test scores tends to reduce their chances of advancement and therefore causes a decrease in their motivation to strive for success"?

Will Tests Eventually Imperil Human Freedom?

Continued research seems certain to make tests increasingly dependable as measuring instruments, as well as certain to produce instruments that measure many more characteristics and qualities than can now validly be appraised. As these instruments improve and multiply, is there a danger that they might ultimately become so valid and comprehensive that they would leave little or no room for free choice of direction in life?

There are two reasons and a canon of faith to indicate that this shall never come to pass. The first reason is grounded in the logic of testing. By its very nature testing is a statistical process. Any test, however long, involves only a statistical sample of all the kinds of behavior being appraised. Criteria against which to validate test scores must also be developed statistically. As statistical instruments, therefore, tests can never give more than probable indications, however high the degree of probability may become. For your child, or for any other individual, test results can never be certain; it can never be certain that any particular earned score is the person's theoretically true score, or that any earned score signifies some inevitable later consequence. There is just as much chance that test results for an individual human being will eventually become certainties as there is for the life expectancy tables of an insurance actuary to become certain for a specified human being—and for much the same reasons: the complexity of human life and the probably endless variables acting within it.

Tests can infringe freedom only when the person making decisions on the basis of test scores—including oneself—forgets that tests are *necessarily* uncertain instruments. The future danger is that, as probabilities increase, they will be mistakenly taken as certainties. But then or now, to read any more validity into test scores than specific findings justify is to commit one of the most monstrous mistakes of the modern age: scientism, or using scientific techniques in an ignorance and arrogance that corrupts them into rank superstition.

Our freedom has been violated in any number of ways without standardized tests, through many centuries, by taking the warrant of human worth as tribe, church, hereditary privilege, wealth, viciousness in fighting or trading, race, accent, dress, manner—the list stretches on and on. Heavy pressures are now being brought to bear on psychological research to develop tests that will literally demonstrate human worth, and demonstrate it conclusively. Colleges feel enormous need to be just in their admissions decisions, and press psychologists to give them instruments to determine who the most worthy of their applicants are, positively and without doubt. Corporations feel an acute competitive need to hire the most worthy future executives, and press industrial psychologists to identify such persons with certainty.

The hopes of colleges and corporations, their quests for certainty, however, are vain. Tests work for certain limited human characteristics, and work fairly well for assembling groups of people with those characteristics, especially when used with other ways of judging people. Tests will be able to do this to an increasingly better degree, we may be sure. But we may also be sure that they will never, ever, do it to perfection. Some people will always erupt as stunning individual surprises. The lesson for us is always to keep the doors of opportunity open to the utmost we can manage so that talent has a chance to develop even where we may least expect it.

The second reason why tests will never stifle freedom takes medical science as an historical parallel. We have largely forgotten today how medicine was bitterly fought for generations because it interfered with the "freedom" people enjoyed in the natural course of events. Today physicians advise us on scientific findings or probabilities about ourselves which can concern questions of life and death—matters far more momentous for us than almost any on which psychological tests would bear. Yet any fair-minded person would say that medical knowledge about ourselves has enlarged rather than reduced our freedom. Perhaps even more important, knowledge of our physical functioning has enabled us to attain levels of radiant health far beyond the wildest dreams of a few generations ago. Knowledge of our psychological functioning likewise gives us the only power we can use deliberately to improve it.

The final canon of faith is—like freedom itself—essentially political. It is a faith that free peoples have shared from the early beginnings of popular freedom. This canon holds simply that ignorance enslaves, while knowledge liberates. Knowledge about ourselves to which tests can add may be useful to other people. Whether or not others should have it is a separate question, and a crucial one, which must be given far more attention than it has in the past. But knowledge about ourselves which testing does reveal is vital for each of us to have if we are to operate as self-knowing and, therefore, free agents. We should know the truth about ourselves, insofar as we can. And that truth can help make us free.

Getting & Recording
Your Child's I Q
and Other Test Scores

Having read this book, you are now fairly well-equipped to understand the test scores that your child will very probably earn throughout his education—to understand both what they mean and what they do not mean. Accordingly, you are urged to find out what test scores he earns, and to understand what light these may shed on his schooling and his future with the help of his teachers and counselors. You are also urged to record his scores, with important comments about them, on the record pages at the end of this appendix.

Some of the scores which he earns, particularly in high school, will almost surely be given to him and to you, with explanatory folders, through his school. These would include scores on the major college admissions and college scholarship tests considered earlier: the National Merit Scholarship Qualifying Test, the ACT test, and the College Board tests (among them, the PSAT, the SAT and the Achievement Tests). Scores and an explanation of them may also be given to you for a few other tests he takes earlier in his schooling; for example, all parents in Iowa are regularly given reports of their children's performance on the Iowa Tests of Basic Skills. If you accumulate such folders, you may find it convenient to keep them inside the back cover of this book.

For scores on the many other ability tests your child will probably take, you are urged to ask for reports and explanations of them from his school. Many schools will tell you about your child's scores on achievement, IQ and other ability tests at your request. In New York State and New Jersey, for example, all schools will do so, and many schools in most states explain achievement test results at the parent's request. You can see what the practice is on reporting scores to interested parents among schools in your state in the following section.

It seems most important for you to know and understand your child's test scores because these can figure in important decisions bearing on his education and career—on a whole future course of his life. Test scores convey important (though, as we have seen, by no means conclusive) findings about your child. Knowing what these findings are should enable you to be more helpful in furthering your child's growth and education in co-operation with his schools. Still other reasons are that some tentative idea about your child's future college prospects may be given by his early test scores. Assignment to the right grade or ability group in a new school district to which you are very likely to move, at one or more points in his schooling, might also be made easier if you have a careful and complete record of your child's test scores.

Test scores are not as important as the report cards and discussions through which your child's teachers and counselors regularly advise

Numbers of states with policies and practices for telling parents about the ability test scores of their children as indicated below

How many school districts in the state report scores at parents' requests	For achievement tests		For IQ and other tests of general mental abilities	
	Number	%	Number	%
All	6	10%	5	8%
Many	30	60%	13	26%
Some	10	20%	14	28%
Few	3	5%	12	24%
Few to none	—	—	3	5%
None	—	—	2	4%
No answer	2	5%	2	5%
Total	51	100%	51	100%

Notes: Figures include the District of Columbia as well as the 50 states. For full details, see the state-by-state report and explanation.

you about his progress. But they do come next in importance. And in special ways, they can help you develop a realistic understanding of his abilities and how they bear on his whole life.

Can You Learn about Your Child's IQ and Other Ability Test Scores from His School?

So that you might obtain and record your child's ability test scores from his school—if the schools in your state release scores to parents—a special survey was made for this book. The survey explored the policies and prevailing practices regarding reports of test results to parents in each state. The Commissioner or Superintendent of Education in each state, directly or through a specialist on his staff, generously provided the answers below. Their replies are also summarized in the accompanying table.

Key to the State Replies

The reply for each state answers the question, first for achievement tests and then for IQ or other general mental ability tests: "*May a child's test scores be reported to his parents at their request, by appropriate school personnel?*"

In most of the states, each school district sets its own policy on this question. Accordingly, in the replies below, this is the case in any one state unless noted to the contrary. If each school district in the state does set its own policy, the state was asked to estimate how many of its school districts—"Many," "Some," "Few," or "None"—actually release scores to parents on request. How many school districts do tell parents about scores *for achievement tests* is indicated in the state reply after the abbreviation "Ach." How many school districts tell parents scores for *IQ or other general mental ability tests* is indicated after the abbreviation "IQ." Any comments made in the state reply follow, noted "(for Ach.)" for achievement tests or "(for IQ)" for IQ or other general mental ability tests as appropriate.

As an example of these devices for reporting replies, consider the first state reply given below, the one for Alabama. First, since nothing is stated to the contrary, each school district in Alabama sets its own policy regarding score reporting to parents. Next, the word "Many" after the abbreviation "Ach." means that many school districts in Alabama do tell parents about their children's scores for achievement tests, on request. Then, the word "Many" after the abbreviation "IQ" means that many school districts in Alabama also tell parents, on request, their children's scores for IQ or other general mental ability tests. Last, the parenthetic note, "(for both Ach. and IQ)," after the word "Comments," means that the Alabama official replying made the following comments regarding scores for both achievement and IQ or other general mental ability tests: "Scores are usually released or discussed with parents in general rather than specific terms."

The State Replies: Do the School Districts in Your State Tell Parents about Scores?

Alabama. Ach.: "Many." IQ: "Many." Comments (for both Ach. and IQ): "Scores are usually released or discussed with parents in general rather than specific terms."

Alaska. Ach.: "Some." IQ: "Few or none." Comments (for IQ): "I know of no school where GMA [general mental ability] test scores or IQ scores are released to parents; but parents are informed by school personnel as to expectations of what an individual should achieve based on his ability."

Arizona. Ach.: "Few." IQ: "Few."

Arkansas. (Reply not received.)

California. Ach.: "Many." IQ: "Many." Comments (for both Ach. and IQ): "Many elementary schools use parent conferences as part of their pupil progress reporting. Junior high and high school counselors generally welcome parent conferences." (In addition, for IQ): "There is general reluctance to give parents actual IQs. Mental age, percentiles or other converted scores, and descriptive terms, are preferred. Although the term, 'IQ,' is a household word, the concept is not generally understood. A parent's reaction is apt to be limited to, 'Oh, that's good,' or, 'Oh, that's bad,' and the numbers persist like the combination of the safe that contains the family jewels."

Colorado. State policy favors, but does not require, telling parents about test scores at their request; each school district sets its own policy. Ach.: "Many." IQ: "Many."

Connecticut. Ach.: "Many." IQ: "Few." Comments (for Ach.): "Emphasis would be placed on interpretation and significance of pupil performance rather than on specific scores." (For IQ): "Few schools would wish to give a specific IQ score, preferring to use other types of derived scores and to take into account the S.E. meas. (standard error of measurement). Many schools are eager to discuss performance on such tests. We believe parents are entitled to and need information on their children's test performance, but try to give it in a way that will lead to a minimum of misunderstanding."

Delaware. (Reply not received.)

District of Columbia. "Yes," Ach. and IQ [are reported by schools upon the parents' requests]. Comments (for Ach.): "Not in terms of raw or converted scores but in terms of percentile, grade equivalent or stanine standing." (For IQ): "Only in terms of deciles or stanines, or percentile bands or descriptive IQ classification." (For Ach. and IQ): "Interpretation carried through by principal, counselor, or member of Pupil Personnel Staff."

Florida. Ach.: "Many." IQ: "Many." Comments (for Ach.): "We recommend that qualified people give and interpret test results. In the two state-wide tests the scores are sent to all."

Georgia. Ach.: "Many." IQ: "Some."

Hawaii. "Yes," Ach. and IQ [are reported by schools upon the parents' requests]. Comments (for IQ): "We report categories of 'high,' 'average,' 'low,' 'extremely high,' etc., and percentile ranges. The specific IQ score is not given in general."

Idaho. Ach.: "Many." IQ: "Some."

Illinois. Ach.: "Many." IQ: "Many." Comments (for Ach. and IQ): "If explained by qualified personnel."

Indiana. Ach.: "Many." IQ: "Many." Comments (for Ach.): "This information is usually given in counselor-parent interviews. In some cases it is mailed to parents." (For IQ): "Usually given in counselor-parent conferences. In a few cases percentile scores on so-called scholastic aptitude tests are sent home. I know of no school that sends an IQ score."

Iowa. Ach.: "100%," by state-wide administrative regulation. IQ: "Many." Comments (for IQ): "Generally, the person who interprets mental ability scores is the guidance counselor or the school psychologist."

Kansas. Ach.: "Many" secondary schools, "some" elementary schools. IQ: "Many" secondary schools, "some" elementary schools. Comments (for Ach. and IQ): "Our [state education] department encourages school authorities to make scores available, but suggests that proper orientation of parents be [conducted] prior to releasing scores to them."

Kentucky. Ach.: The state education department permits reporting scores to parents, but each "district may decide against this policy." IQ: No, as a matter of state policy.

Louisiana. Ach.: "Some." IQ: "Some." Comments (for both Ach. and IQ): "Will depend on parents' ability to understand, and philosophy of school. Generally, it is a prevalent practice."

Maine. Ach.: "Many." IQ: "Few." Comments (for Ach.): "Usually explained in detail by counselor or principal in terms of causal factors, weaknesses of sampling." (For IQ): "Always explained in terms of percentiles, weaknesses of such scores, possible causal factors."

Maryland. Ach. and IQ: "Yes," by state-wide administrative regulation.

Massachusetts. Ach.: "Many." IQ: "Many."

Michigan. Ach.: "Many." IQ: "Few."

Minnesota. Ach.: "Some." IQ: "Some." From *Guide for Formulation of Local School Board Policy:* "The 'Standardized Test Record' . . . should be released only with interpretation by appropriate professional personnel. . . . [It] may be released by the Superintendent, Principal or Guidance Counselor . . . upon the request of parent or guardian."

Mississippi. Ach.: "Many." IQ: "Few." Comments (for Ach. and IQ): "Mississippi H.B. No. 15, Legislative Session 1953, Section 2, prohibits release of such information 'to the general public.'"

Missouri. Ach.: "Some." IQ: "Some."

Montana. Ach.: "Many." IQ: "Some." Comments (for Ach.): "I feel most schools emphasize the following, regarding parents: 1) that the person interpreting test scores is competent; 2) generally speaking, I doubt if students are compared against their own group [of classmates]." (For IQ): "When IQ scores are reported, I feel most counselors interpret the score in the following manner: 95—your score is similar to scores made by persons who find school work rather difficult, but with application many graduate from high school."

Nebraska. Ach.: "Few." IQ: "Few."

Nevada. Ach.: "Yes [school districts are permitted to release scores to parents]. IQ: "Some."

New Hampshire. Ach.: "Some." IQ: "Some."

New Jersey. Ach. and IQ: "Yes," by state-wide administrative regulation. Comments (for Ach. and IQ): "Items of information contained in the records of a given pupil shall be made available, upon request, for inspection by a parent [or] guardian."

New Mexico. Ach. and IQ: Each school district sets its own policy. Comments (for Ach. and IQ): "I feel such scores should be released, but only in a conference situation with parents."

New York. Ach. and IQ: "Yes," by state-wide administrative regulation and court decision. From the Commissioner's decision, upheld by the courts: "The parent, as a matter of law, is entitled to such information."

North Carolina. Ach.: "Many." IQ: "Few." Comments (for Ach.): "Generally the case." (For IQ): "Many release this information, but in *general terms*, not as IQ scores."

North Dakota. Ach.: "Many." IQ: "Few." Comments (for Ach.): "We try to encourage this as much as possible." (For IQ): "We discourage the release of a specific IQ score to students and parents."

Ohio. Ach.: "Many." IQ: "Many." Comments (for Ach.): "According to a 1962 survey of 336 school systems in Ohio, test interpretation to parents is done by 53.6% on a regular, planned basis, 41.7% on an incidental basis, and 4.7% not at all." (For IQ): "Usually by descriptive terms rather than IQ."

Oklahoma. Ach.: "Many." IQ: "Many." Comments (for Ach. and IQ): "Depends on school policy."

Oregon. Ach.: "Many." IQ: "Few." Comments (for Ach.): "We know of no school district that would not reveal achievement test results of individual pupils to parents." (For IQ): "Very few release scores. Many indicate in terms of 'about average,' 'above average,' etc., verbally."

Pennsylvania. Ach.: "Many." IQ: "Many." Comments (for Ach. and IQ): "It should be understood that in many cases these test results are given in the form of ratings or ranges rather than as specific scores."

Rhode Island. Ach.: "Many." IQ: "Many."

South Carolina. Ach.: "Many." IQ: "Some." Comments (for Ach.): "We recommend that counselors and others use broad terms and not specific scores." (For IQ): "Schools adopt their own policies; most schools use 'below average,' 'average,' 'above average' and 'superior' when discussing ability test results."

South Dakota. Ach.: "Many." IQ: "Few to none."

Tennessee. Ach.: "Few." IQ: "Released [only] under special conditions."

Texas. Ach.: "Many." IQ: "Many."

Utah. Ach.: "Many." IQ: "Few."

Vermont. Ach.: "Many." IQ: "Some." Comments (for Ach.): "Usually through the school counselor or administrative personnel." (For IQ): "Usually the child's performance is discussed in descriptive terms with parents. Some schools use percentiles and/or stanines for this purpose; rarely is IQ itself given to parents."

Virginia. Ach.: "Many." IQ: "Few." Comments (for Ach.): "[We suggest] the release of achievement test scores to parents and pupils provided the scores are carefully interpreted." (For IQ): "[We do] not encourage the release of such scores to parents and pupils. If such information is released, our staff advises much caution and careful interpretation and the use of such terms as 'high,' 'low,' or 'medium' instead of actual scores."

Washington. Ach.: "Many." IQ: "Some." Comments (for Ach. and IQ): "Districts are perhaps a bit more wary of releasing IQ scores than they are of releasing achievement scores. In general, I would say that if the aptitude scores are available to be reported in percentiles or stanines, there is more reporting to parents than when IQ scores are used."

West Virginia. Ach.: "Many." IQ: Each school district sets its own policy. Comments (for Ach.): "With an interpretation of their meaning." (For IQ): "Usually, actual IQs are not reported. Rather, they are described to be within a range, 'high' to 'low.' "

Wisconsin. Ach.: "Some." IQ: "Some."

Wyoming. Ach.: "Many." IQ: Each school district sets its own policy. Comments (for IQ): "Ability scores are generally interpreted in terms of percentiles, and in conjunction with achievement test results."

Forms for Recording Your Child's Test Scores

Testing record for (name)_____

Date (month and year) test taken_____

Full name of test_____

Type of test_____

Scores and/or standings earned_____

_____

Interpretation and Comments

_____

_____

_____

Forms for Recording Your Child's Test Scores

Testing record for (name)_____

Date (month and year) test taken_____

Full name of test_____

Type of test_____

Scores and/or standings earned_____

_____

Interpretation and Comments

_____

_____

Forms for Recording Your Child's Test Scores

Testing record for (name)_____

Date (month and year) test taken_____

Full name of test_____

Type of test_____

Scores and/or standings earned_____

_____

Interpretation and Comments

_____

_____

Forms for Recording Your Child's Test Scores

Testing record for (name)_____

Date (month and year) test taken_____

Full name of test_____

Type of test_____

Scores and/or standings earned_____

_____

Interpretation and Comments

_____

_____

Forms for Recording Your Child's Test Scores

Testing record for (name)_____

Date (month and year) test taken_____

Full name of test_____

Type of test_____

Scores and/or standings earned_____

_____

Interpretation and Comments

_____

_____

Forms for Recording Your Child's Test Scores

Testing record for (name)_____

Date (month and year) test taken_____

Full name of test_____

Type of test_____

Scores and/or standings earned_____

_____

Interpretation and Comments

_____

_____

Forms for Recording Your Child's Test Scores

Testing record for (name)_____

Date (month and year) test taken_____

Full name of test_____

Type of test_____

Scores and/or standings earned_____

_____

Interpretation and Comments

_____

_____

Forms for Recording Your Child's Test Scores

Testing record for (name)_____

Date (month and year) test taken_____

Full name of test_____

Type of test_____

Scores and/or standings earned_____

_____

Interpretation and Comments

_____

_____

Forms for Recording Your Child's Test Scores

Testing record for (name)_____

Date (month and year) test taken_____

Full name of test_____

Type of test_____

Scores and/or standings earned_____

_____

Interpretation and Comments

_____

_____

Index

About the Author

Gene R. Hawes has worked for two of the country's largest testing organizations, serving as editor with the College Entrance Examination Board and as director of information for Science Research Associates, Inc. Articles of his have appeared in such magazines as *This Week*, the *Saturday Review* and *Esquire*, and he is also author of *The New American Guide to Colleges*, a directory of all U.S. colleges, for students, families and counselors. Mr. Hawes is a free-lance consultant, editor and writer who lives in Chappaqua, N.Y. He has a son and two daughters.